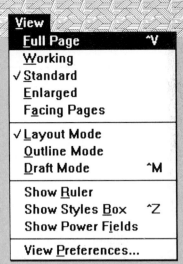

View
Full Page	^V
Working	
✓ Standard	
Enlarged	
Facing Pages	
✓ Layout Mode	
Outline Mode	
Draft Mode	^M
Show Ruler	
Show Styles Box	^Z
Show Power Fields	
View Preferences...	

MW01121343

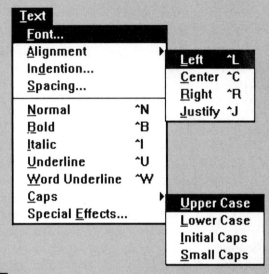

Text
Font...	
Alignment	▶
Indention...	
Spacing...	
Normal	^N
Bold	^B
Italic	^I
Underline	^U
Word Underline	^W
Caps	▶
Special Effects...	

Alignment
Left	^L
Center	^C
Right	^R
Justify	^J

Caps
Upper Case
Lower Case
Initial Caps
Small Caps

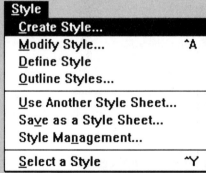

Style
Create Style...	
Modify Style...	^A
Define Style	
Outline Styles...	
Use Another Style Sheet...	
Save as a Style Sheet...	
Style Management...	
Select a Style	^Y

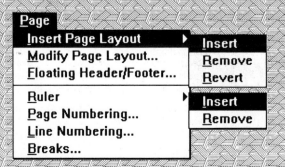

Page
Insert Page Layout	▶
Modify Page Layout...	
Floating Header/Footer...	
Ruler	▶
Page Numbering...	
Line Numbering...	
Breaks...	

Insert Page Layout
Insert
Remove
Revert

Ruler
Insert
Remove

Computer users are not all alike.
Neither are SYBEX books.

We know our customers have a variety of needs. They've told us so. And because we've listened, we've developed several distinct types of books to meet the needs of each of our customers. What are you looking for in computer help?

If you're looking for the basics, try the **ABC's** series. You'll find short, unintimidating tutorials and helpful illustrations. For a more visual approach, select **Teach Yourself**, featuring screen-by-screen illustrations of how to use your latest software purchase.

Mastering and **Understanding** titles offer you a step-by-step introduction, plus an in-depth examination of intermediate-level features, to use as you progress.

Our **Up & Running** series is designed for computer-literate consumers who want a no-nonsense overview of new programs. Just 20 basic lessons, and you're on your way.

We also publish two types of reference books. Our **Instant References** provide quick access to each of a program's commands and functions. SYBEX **Encyclopedias** and **Desktop References** provide a *comprehensive reference* and explanation of all of the commands, features and functions of the subject software.

Sometimes a subject requires a special treatment that our standard series don't provide. So you'll find we have titles like **Advanced Techniques, Handbooks, Tips & Tricks,** and others that are specifically tailored to satisfy a unique need.

We carefully select our authors for their in-depth understanding of the software they're writing about, as well as their ability to write clearly and communicate effectively. Each manuscript is thoroughly reviewed by our technical staff to ensure its complete accuracy. Our production department makes sure it's easy to use. All of this adds up to the highest quality books available, consistently appearing on best-seller charts worldwide.

You'll find SYBEX publishes a variety of books on every popular software package. Looking for computer help? Help Yourself to SYBEX.

For a complete catalog of our publications:

SYBEX Inc.
2021 Challenger Drive, Alameda, CA 94501
Tel: (510) 523-8233/(800) 227-2346 Telex: 336311
Fax: (510) 523-2373

MASTERING

AMI PRO 2

M A S T E R I N G
AMI PRO™ 2

Robert Bixby

SYBEX®

San Francisco   Paris   Düsseldorf   Soest

Acquisitions Editor: Dianne King
Developmental Editor: Marilyn Smith
Copy Editor: Marilyn Smith
Project Editor: Janna Hecker Clark
Technical Editor: Jon Britton
Word Processors: Ann Dunn and Susan Trybull
Book Designer: Julie Bilski
Chapter Art: Suzanne Albertson
Screen Graphics: Cuong Le and Thomas Goudie
Production Assistance: Aldo Bermudez
Typesetter: Stephanie Hollier
Proofreader/Production Assistant: Elizabeth G. Chuan
Indexer: Ted Laux
Cover Designer: Ingalls + Associates
Cover Photographer: Michael Lamotte

Library of Congress Card Number: 91-66628
ISBN: 0-89588-896-3

Manufactured in the United States of America
10 9 8 7 6 5 4 3 2 1

For Kathy

ACKNOWLEDGMENTS

I offer my thanks to the following people and companies who supported this project either in spirit or materially:

Star Micronics for the use of a LaserPrinter 8-II with LincPage (a PostScript emulator), an extremely rugged printer that has generated literally thousands of pages of text and graphics, including camera-ready graphics for this and many other books, without a single moment of downtime.

Lotus Development for its cooperation in providing technical assistance and access to Ami Pro 2 from the early betas through the completed product.

Inner Media, for permission to use Collage Plus 3.2, the best screen-capture program I have been able to find that will work with Windows, which was used to create the figures in this book.

Matt Wagner, my agent at Waterside Productions.

Marilyn Smith, my editor at SYBEX.

Janna Clark, my project editor at SYBEX.

COMPUTE Publications and its parent company, General Media, Inc.

My wife, Kathleen, and my children, Jennifer and Steven.

CONTENTS AT A GLANCE

CONTENTS

APPENDICES

INTRODUCTION

Mastering Ami Pro 2 is a guide to using Ami Pro version 2, a powerful word processor offered by Lotus Corporation. Windows word processing was a neglected area before Ami came along. When users saw what could be done with a Windows word processor, the demand became so great that virtually every major software publisher now offers or is developing a Windows word processor.

THE EVOLUTION OF A WORD PROCESSOR

When Samna Corporation of Atlanta, Georgia, introduced Ami (in those days there was an accent above the i and no Professional or Pro designation), many of us wondered why we needed yet another word processor. The DOS world is flooded with word processors—WordPerfect, Word, XyWrite, to name just a few—that cover virtually every niche in the field and cater to every taste.

And here was Ami, in its unassuming blue box. Time passed. Samna released Ami Professional, which was a word processor with graphics and desktop publishing features—fully as powerful as any word processor and rivaling high-end page design products in graphic features. The early Ami code was obtained by Software Publishing Corporation, and the product was released as Professional Write for Windows—the company's low-end word processor created for managers and other professionals who are too busy to learn a lot of features and just want to get their thoughts down on paper.

Lotus Corporation, looking for Windows expertise and a good word processor to promote, purchased Samna Corporation and released Ami Professional as Ami Pro, without the accent. Then something wonderful happened. Ami Pro 2, released in the summer of 1991, takes full advantage of the Windows environment for more powerful and friendly word processing.

WHO SHOULD READ THIS BOOK

This book is intended for the newcomer to Windows word processing, the intermediate-level user who may have some Windows word processing experience, and the experienced user who wants to make the transition from a previous version of Ami Pro to the new version.

To use this book, you need an 80286 PC and a hard disk, with Windows 3.0 or a later version and Ami Pro 2. See Appendix A for specific requirements. It is assumed you have a certain amount of computer expertise. You won't be told what a floppy disk is or which end of it to insert into the drive first, nor how to start up your computer.

You do not need experience with Ami Pro in its earlier versions or with Windows. However, if you have never used Windows before, you can turn to Appendix B for some basic instructions.

WHAT THIS BOOK CONTAINS

This book is divided into four parts, which build upon each other to guide you from the fundamentals of word processing with Ami Pro to the use of advanced techniques:

- Part 1, Ami Pro Basics, covers the information you need to begin word processing with the program. You will learn how to create, edit, and print documents.

- Part 2, Working with Your Documents, explains how to use the powerful word processing features to make your documents look professional. You will learn how to manage long documents, format your text, and import and export files.

- Part 3, Working with Graphics, contains two chapters about Ami Pro's graphic capabilities. The first chapter in this part describes how to use frames for separate blocks of text, charts, and pictures. The other chapter describes how to use the wide array of graphics tools to draw with Ami Pro.

- Part 4, Working with Power Features, covers the features that make Ami Pro special: document merge, the outliner, macros, design tools, the table generator, and power fields.

By the time you finish these chapters, you will be able to take full advantage of the program.

If you haven't installed Ami Pro yet, see Appendix A for step-by-step installation instructions. If you are new to Windows, refer to Appendix B for an introduction to Windows and Windows applications. Appendix C lists the standard icons and functions Ami Pro provides for the icon palette.

HOW TO USE THIS BOOK

This book is organized from simple to more complex. Depending on your level of expertise, you may discover sections that are largely review for you. If so, skim through these sections to review the material.

Throughout the book, we will put many of Ami Pro's features to use through tutorials, complete with numbered steps. Following these tutorials will allow you to learn features in context. Some of the work you do in a tutorial in one chapter will be continued in another chapter. It's always a good idea to save your work, but in those cases in which the document will be used again, saving the document will be part of the tutorial. At the beginning of the next section that uses the sample document, there will be a reference to the tutorial in which the original document was created.

MARGIN NOTES

Throughout this book, you will find notes in the margin, which expand on the subject under discussion, offer an interesting side comment, suggest a time-saving tip, or underscore a warning. The symbol next to each note shows the type of information it contains:

This symbol appears next to a note that contains more information about the topic covered in the paragraph beside it.

A note with this symbol provides a tip. For example, it may alert you to an additional option that will further enhance the operation being discussed in text.

This symbol is used for notes that warn you about problems that may occur.

CONVENTIONS USED IN THE TEXT

In this book, some conventions are used for keyboard keys. For a carriage return, you will see ⏎. For an arrow key, you will see →, ←, ↑, or ↓. In some cases, you will be instructed to press a key combination. For example, press Alt-F means to hold down the Alt key and press the F key (which is the universal Windows command to access the File menu). Press Ctrl-F means to hold down the Ctrl key and press F. Note that the Ami Pro documentation prefers to use a plus sign instead of a hyphen between keys, as in Alt + F.

Most of your keyboard entries in Ami Pro will be made typing the text in your documents. You can use the mouse for most cursor movement. There are also mouse-keyboard combinations. Ctrl-click and Ctrl-double-click mean that you should use the Ctrl key in combination with the mouse button. Shift-click means to press the Shift key while clicking the mouse button.

PART

1

Ami Pro Basics

CHAPTER 1

Getting Started
with Ami Pro

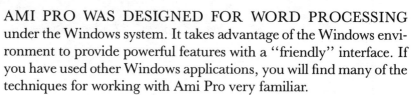

AMI PRO WAS DESIGNED FOR WORD PROCESSING under the Windows system. It takes advantage of the Windows environment to provide powerful features with a "friendly" interface. If you have used other Windows applications, you will find many of the techniques for working with Ami Pro very familiar.

This chapter covers the basics of getting Ami Pro up and running, including starting and exiting the program, understanding the components of the screen, and getting help from various sources.

STARTING AND LEAVING AMI PRO

Once Ami Pro is installed, you can begin word processing immediately. Like other Windows applications, Ami Pro is started from Windows. Follow these steps to start the program:

To install Ami Pro, follow the instructions in Appendix A.

1. Type **WIN** at the DOS command line and press ←┘.

Windows should start up. The next step is to locate the Ami Pro program group. You will see either the Program Manager window or a tiny icon with the words Program Manager beneath it.

If you are not familiar with the techniques for working with Windows, such as double-clicking on icons, see Appendix B.

2. If you see the Program Manager icon, double-click on it.

3. The Program Manager window should be visible. At this point, you must locate the Lotus Applications program group. If the Lotus Applications program group appears as a window, skip to step 4. If the group is not visible, use one of the following methods to display it.

   • If the Lotus Applications program group is visible in the Program Manager window as an icon, double-click on the icon.

   • Pull down the Window menu and select Lotus Applications from the list by clicking on it. If you have more

than nine program groups and do not see Lotus
Applications listed, click on the More Windows option
on the Window menu to display a list of all the
available program groups.

In the Lotus Applications program group, you will see an icon
labeled Ami Pro 2.0, which represents the program.

4. Double-click on the Ami Pro icon to start the program. You
will see the window shown in Figure 1.1.

Now that Ami Pro is running, you have access to all its powerful
features. But before you begin working with the program, you should
know how to leave it.

You can exit the program by using one of the following three
methods:

If you turn off your
computer before
giving the command to
exit Ami Pro, you risk
damaging your files.

• Double-click on the tiny square in the upper-left corner
of the Ami Pro window (called the *Control menu* or the
close box).

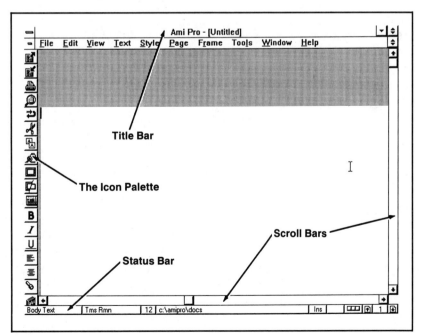

Figure 1.1: Ami Pro window

- Press Alt-F4. This is the standard keypress for closing any Windows application, including Windows itself.

- Pull down the File menu in Ami Pro and select Exit. To pull down the menu, press Alt-F; click on the word File in the menu bar; or press F10, then →, then ↓. To choose Exit from the menu, press the ↓ or ↑ key until it's highlighted, and then press ←; click on Exit with the mouse; or press the X key.

By providing a number of ways to interact with the program, Ami Pro's developers have made it flexible enough to suit all types of users. If you are an avid mouse user, you can employ all the pointing and clicking techniques. However, if you are a quick typist, using the keyboard commands will save you time.

If you added text or made any changes to the document in the Ami Pro window, the program will pause before closing to inform you that changes have been made and asking whether it should save the current document before shutting down the program.

ELEMENTS OF THE AMI PRO SCREEN

Many of the components of the Ami Pro screen, which are labeled in Figure 1.1, will be familiar to Windows applications users.

USING THE MENU BAR

Across the top of the screen is the menu bar with the names of the main menus: File, Edit, View, Text, Style, Page, Frame, Tools, Window, and Help. Clicking on a menu name pulls down a menu of options from which to choose.

The close box, or Control menu, in the extreme upper-left corner of the screen is also part of the menu bar. When a document is open, there are two close boxes: one for Ami Pro and one on the menu bar for the currently open document. Double-clicking on the Ami Pro close box will shut down Ami Pro. Clicking on the close box at the left end of the menu bar will close the current document.

After you pull down a menu from the menu bar, you can click on one of the options listed on the menu. Selecting an option followed by an ellipse displays a dialog box in which you provide more information before an action is taken. When you click on an option that is followed by a triangle, you will see a submenu of other options. Choosing options that aren't followed by either of these characters puts an action into effect immediately. To leave the menu bar without taking any action, just click somewhere within the document.

You can also access the menus by using the keyboard. Press the Alt or F10 key to activate the menu bar and highlight the first menu. Press ⬅ to pull down that menu, use the ↑ and ↓ keys to highlight the option you want to select, and press ⬅. To move to the menus to the right or left along the menu bar, press the → and ← keys. To leave the menu bar without making a selection, press Esc.

Not all the items in all the menus are available all the time. Dimmed items (items that are not as dark as the others) are not applicable to your current function, and you cannot select them with the mouse or keyboard.

Some items in the menus are accessed so often that the designers of Ami Pro decided to make them directly accessible from the keyboard. For example, to save a file, you can select Save from the File menu or you can just press Ctrl-S, without going through a menu. The keyboard shortcuts for options are listed on the menus as reminders, with a caret (^) to represent the Ctrl key and the other key to press at the same time. For example, on the File menu, ^S appears next to the Save option.

WORKING WITH THE TITLE BAR AND SCROLL BARS

The title bar identifies the program that is running and the file that is loaded. When the Ami Pro window is between its maximized and minimized sizes, sometimes called its *restore size*, the title bar is also the move bar. By dragging the move bar, you can reposition the Ami Pro window. Double-clicking on the move bar toggles the Ami Pro window between its maximized and restore size.

You can use the scroll bars to move to other parts of the document. The top of the vertical scroll bar at the right edge of the Ami Pro screen represents the top of the first page, and the bottom of the scroll bar represents the bottom of the last page. The horizontal scroll bar across the bottom of the screen moves left and right across the current page. Scrolling horizontally is useful when you're working with a wide document (printed on standard paper in landscape orientation, for example) or viewing magnified text or graphics.

The scroll bars consist of three principal parts:

- The arrows at the ends, which nudge the page along by small increments.

- The scroll box (also called the *elevator* or *thumb*), which moves proportionally through a distance (placing it halfway down will take you halfway through the document, for example).

- The slide bar (sometimes called the *gray area*), which the scroll box moves along. Click in the slide bar between the scroll box and the arrow to move approximately one full screen in the direction of the arrow.

USING THE ICON PALETTE FOR QUICK ACCESS

Ami Pro's icon palette provides quick access to important commands. You can issue a command by clicking on an icon—a visual representation of what the command does. For example, the first icon in the icon palette shows a floppy disk with an arrow leading away from it. This icon is used to load a document into Ami Pro. The next one, a disk with an arrow leading toward it, is the icon for saving the current file. A cynical person might point out the folly of creating a set of visual clues for someone literate enough to use a word processor, but it is much faster to click on an icon than it is to find and then select the same command on a menu.

You can move the icon palette to any position on the screen. Pull down the Tools menu and select SmartIcons. The ellipses next to this option indicates that selecting it displays a dialog box. The Smart-Icons dialog box that appears contains commands to hide the icon palette; move the palette to the top, bottom, right, or left on the screen; and create a floating icon palette that can be dragged anywhere on the screen and even resized and reshaped.

For some users, the icon palette will not be a friendly assistant but an intrusive nuisance. The icon palette can be banished by pressing Ctrl-Q. When it's gone, you can redisplay it by pressing Ctrl-Q again.

If you would prefer to have different commands available, you can customize the icon palette. Click on the Customize button in the SmartIcons dialog box to select from dozens of icons, each of which represents a command from one of the menus (the default palette contains only 26). Furthermore, you can select your own icons and assign macros to them. You will learn more about the icon palette and customizing it in Chapter 11.

GETTING INFORMATION FROM THE STATUS BAR

Ami Pro's status bar appears at the bottom of the screen. It provides useful information about the current document. From left to right, the status bar displays the following items:

When you define a style, it specifies text shape and color, paragraph outlining, tabs, distance between paragraphs, and any other formatting that can be applied to the paragraph.

- The current style. Each paragraph must have a style. Most of your paragraphs probably will be in the general default style called Body Text (which is the style you see in Figure 1.1). But you can have dozens of styles defined in your style sheet. Click on this item in the status bar to display a list of available styles. You can select a style from the list.

- The current font. Although there is a specified font for each style, you can choose a different font. Click on this item to see a list of available fonts that you can select. The current font is the font that will appear as you begin typing. It may be different from the font where the text cursor currently appears.

- The size of type in points (a point is equal to approximately $1/72$ inch). The size of the type is also set in the paragraph style, but you can override this setting. Click on this item to see a list of the available type sizes.

- The current path. Unless you change the setting in the Save As dialog box, this is where your file will be saved (when you choose the Save command). Click on this item in the status bar, and it will change to show the time and date. Click again, and you will see an indication of the cursor's position on the page. Click a third time to return to the path display.

Knowing the on-screen position of the text cursor can be helpful. For example, if you are filling out forms, you can measure the form to determine where on the page the printing should appear, put the cursor in that position, and enter the desired text. To see the location of the text cursor on the Ami Pro screen, click twice on the part of the status bar that shows the path (C:\AMIPRO-\DOCS is the default path).

- The typing mode. Click on this item to choose from three settings: Ins (Insert), Type (Typeover), and Rev (Revision Marking). In Insert mode, when you click in the middle of an existing paragraph and start typing, the new text will shove the old text out of the way so it remains intact. In Typeover mode, the characters you type within other text will replace the existing text. In Revision Marking mode, new text will be formatted in a special style, such as red and underlined (the default is blue italic), so it stands out from the old text.

- Caps Lock in effect. If you have pressed the Caps Lock key, you should see a light on your keyboard and the word Caps in the third section from the right end of the status bar.

The section near the right end of the status bar that contains three small squares toggles the icon palette on and off. Click on this area to remove the icon palette; click again to make it reappear.

At the far right end of the status bar, you see an upward-pointing arrow, a number, and a downward-pointing arrow. These are used to move from page to page. Click on the up arrow to go to the previous page or the down arrow to go to the next page. To move to a specific page, click on the number. This displays a dialog box in which you enter the number of the page you want to see.

GETTING HELP

Help with your Ami Pro work is available in several forms. Through Windows 3.0, you have access to an improved, context-sensitive hypertext Help facility that will answer nearly all your questions. *Context-sensitive* means that the Help information that appears applies directly to what you are doing at the moment. For example, if you have the Modify Styles dialog box open, Windows will display information about modifying styles.

Hypertext covers a wider scope than simply providing help with an application. It opens up possibilities for linking all the world's information (and greatest minds) to computers via cable and satellite.

Hypertext is a buzzword you've probably heard bandied about. In this context, it means that from a position in the Help text, you can call up a *gloss*—a more thorough explanation—by clicking on a keyword. Hypertext keywords are highlighted in green. For example, if you are reading information about the Modify Styles option and want to get more information on some aspect, look for a highlighted word that deals with that topic and click on it. You will see a new Help window that covers that topic. You can return to the original Help window by clicking on the Back button.

USING AMI PRO HELP

Any time you want to access Ami Pro's Help information, just press F1 or click on the Help menu. If you want more information about an error message that is displayed on your screen, press Shift-F1. For context-sensitive (also called *task-oriented*) help, pull down a menu and press Shift-F1. These methods work in all Windows applications.

Navigating through the Help System   When you access Help, the window that appears provides information that relates to your current activity. Figure 1.2 shows an example of a Help window for setting margins and tabs.

You might wonder why you would need help at all if the program is as user friendly as everyone says it is. The fact is that most of today's programs pack so many features that very few people can invest the time to fully understand all of them. Help not only gets you started with the program, but also provides support as you grow more experienced and want to take full advantage of the program's powers.

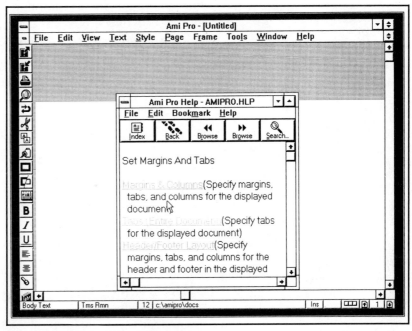

Figure 1.2: An Ami Pro Help window

The buttons along the top of the window allow you to maneuver through the Help system, as follows:

You can also access the Help Index by selecting Index from the Help menu.

- The Index button (on the far left side of the Help window beneath its menu bar) takes you to the Help Index. Through the Ami Pro Help Index, you can access information relating to any part of the program. The index is arranged alphabetically, so it's easy to find the item you want (provided you know what to call it).

- If you have clicked on a couple of hypertext words (highlighted in green on the screen), you may want to return to a previous screen. If so, click on the Back button.

- The Browse buttons allow you to move through a topic screen by screen. This is useful for learning about a range of options within a section of the Help Index. Click on the double-right arrow to move forward through the topic, or the double-left arrow to move backward.

- You can use the Search button to find help on a topic. Click on it to see a dialog box with an exhaustive list of Help topics. To display a Help window on one of these topics, double-click on the topic you want, or click on the topic and then click on Search.

Help for Beginners   Ami Pro's Help facility includes a set of relatively simple topics designed to get the beginner started with Ami Pro. To access this part of the Help system, pull down the Help menu and select Index. From the Help Index, choose Basics or How Do I?.

Lotus' Atlanta telephone number is (404) 851-0007. The product support line is (404) 256-2272. When you call, have your registration number handy. Lotus also operates a bulletin board to help users. The number is (404) 851-1371.

GETTING TECHNICAL ASSISTANCE FROM LOTUS

If you cannot find the information you need in the Ami Pro Help system or user's manual, you can call the Lotus product support group for assistance. Before calling, you should be prepared to discuss your problem.

If you are having trouble with some feature or calling to report a bug, write down all the steps you have gone through to create the problem situation. It's worth it to go through the steps a couple of times before calling to make sure you haven't made some small mistake. If you discover what you are doing wrong, you will save the cost of the call to Atlanta and you will understand Ami Pro that much better.

GETTING HELP FROM ON-LINE SERVICES

CompuServe has a special area for Lotus word processing programs, including Ami Pro, which you can reach by typing GO LOTUSWP at any prompt.

You can get assistance with Ami Pro through all the major on-line information and bulletin board services. You can leave a message about your problem in the area related to Ami Pro and wait for a response. Check for a forum or roundtable on Lotus products and see if it contains a section dedicated to Ami Pro. If you can't find anything specific, leave a message in an area having to do with word processing or desktop publishing.

Leaving a message on a bulletin board service will probably result in a response in a day or two. True, it won't get you out of an immediate jam, but the information will probably be in-depth and knowledgeable, and this might be your only option on a weekend or holiday when the technical support lines are closed.

CHAPTER 2

Writing with Ami Pro

WRITING WITH AMI PRO CAN BE AS SIMPLE AS TYPING the text in from the keyboard and correcting typographical errors as you see them. If your text needs heavier revisions, you can employ the program's wide range of editing techniques to make changes. To focus on what is important at each stage of the preparation of your document, you can display your text in one of Ami Pro's five views.

This chapter describes how to create and edit your documents. Then it takes you on a quick tour of Ami Pro's features that will demonstrate some of its capabilities.

CREATING A DOCUMENT

The purpose of a word processor is to get information into the computer's memory (RAM) and organize it in a useful way. Once it's in memory, it can be saved to disk, printed, formatted, and manipulated endlessly. But first and foremost, you must get that information into RAM.

TYPING AND CORRECTING TEXT

Usually, the way you get information into the computer's RAM is by typing. Let's create a document by typing information at the keyboard.

1. Start up Ami Pro using the method described in Chapter 1.

2. Type in the text shown in Figure 2.1.

If you are like most typists, you probably made some typing errors. There are several ways to correct simple mistakes:

- Use the Backspace key to erase characters as the cursor moves backward in the text.

Sweetness and Light
In the middle of the century, futurists boldly predicted that
America's grocery basket would contain many artificial foods,
specially processed and refined to be better than the real thing.
One of the basics to which they could point was saccharin, an
artificial sweetener developed in 1879, which, but for its bitter
aftertaste, could have replaced sugar in virtually all foods. A
group of chemical compounds known collectively as cyclamates,
developed in the 1930s, were only a little more expensive, but
sweetened without an aftertaste. Both of these artificial
sweeteners are stable, inexpensive, and many times sweeter than
sugar by weight.
     Since the 1960s, though, the news has been full of
reports that artificial sweeteners might be hazardous to
consumers' health. According to Sweet Talk, a book by Philip F.
Lawler about the sweeteners industry and the media, in 1969 the
secretary of the Department of Health, Education, and Welfare
ordered that cyclamates be banned. They were suspected of causing
cell changes in human kidneys and livers, and were implicated in
breaking down human chromosomes. More recently, in 1972, the
reputation of saccharin fell under a cloud as it was associated
with the appearance of cancers in test animals. By 1977, the
evidence against saccharin was so strong that the Food and Drug
Administration moved to ban the sweetener, and was only prevented
from doing so by overwhelming public outcry.

Enter Aspartame
The stage was set for the appearance of a new, safe sweetener.
This role was filled by aspartame, a product of the G. D. Searle
drug company. Discovered by accident in 1965, aspartame might
have been no more than a lab tech's footnote had not a researcher
accidentally violated laboratory protocol by tasting it. What he
tasted was sweet indeed.
     Aspartame is a compound containing aspartic acid and
phenylalanine, two naturally occurring amino acids that can be
found separately in many foods. Searle released the sweetener
under the name NutraSweet. It has been the center of controversy
ever since.

The Healthy Choice
NutraSweet is known to be hazardous to the health of victims of
phenylketonuria, a rare condition that makes it difficult for
sufferers to metabolize phenylalanine. This is the reason for the
warning to phenylketonurics that appears on the package of every
product that contains NutraSweet.
     Some consumer groups have accused NutraSweet of causing
such problems as panic attacks, mania, headaches, and seizures.
These attacks have presented the NutraSweet Company (the
manufacturers of NutraSweet) with a serious public relations
problem. To counter the rumors, NutraSweet was advertised to be
as safe as bananas and milk and called ``the good stuff.'' Even
the name NutraSweet seems to have been chosen to make aspartame
sound as if it were nutritious, though, in fact, it has virtually
no nutritional value.

1

Figure 2.1: Sample text for document

The principal value of NutraSweet is that it provides an alternative to sugar and saccharin. Sugar is the product of an industry with hazardous working conditions and a scandalous history recently exposed by a series of articles in the New Yorker. Sugar causes tooth decay and is associated with the physical diseases of hypoglycemia and diabetes. Saccharin may cause cancer of the bladder. No such charges can be leveled against NutraSweet. Instead, critics point to the possibility of changes in the brain's neurotransmitters. However, years of intensive study have failed to unearth any conclusive evidence of a link between NutraSweet use and headaches, or any of the other suspected neural problems mentioned earlier. NutraSweet releases methyl alcohol when it is metabolized, but scientists have determined that the amount of methyl alcohol released into the bloodstream is far less than the amount released when plain fruit juice is consumed.

Sweet, but Not Low
Interestingly, NutraSweet is neither less expensive nor lower in calories than sugar by weight. However, because it's about 180 times sweeter than sugar, far less is used to sweeten a product. The user takes in fewer calories. (By contrast, saccharin is hundreds of times sweeter than sugar and cyclamates are about 30 times sweeter.) This high level of sweetening allows manufacturers to use very small amounts of the sweetener in their products, resulting in a very small number of calories for the consumer.
One of NutraSweet's disadvantages is that it breaks down in liquids and when exposed to high temperatures. This instability prevented it from being used in soft drinks when it was first released, but it can now be found in most diet sodas and many other beverages. Diet soda left on the shelf too long can lose its sweetness, but as long as the inventory is carefully managed, this should not be a problem. Many diet soda makers have hedged their bets by mixing saccharin or sugar with the NutraSweet.

But Is It Smart?
The general scientific consensus is that NutraSweet is safe. But is it effective? Does it help users lose weight? Will it injure the sales of sugar? Food retailers should not be concerned that artificial sweeteners will drive sugar and products containing sugar off the market. Artificial sweeteners, while showing steady increases in use, have made no dent in the sales of naturally sweetened drinks and foods. The consumption of both sugar and artificial sweeteners has burgeoned over the years.
In fact, using NutraSweet may actually increase your craving for sugar, according to some studies. Other studies showed that dieters taking NutraSweet without their knowledge didn't gain weight, as might be expected if this paradoxical craving were real.

2

Figure 2.1: Sample text for document (Continued)

- To delete a character with the mouse, move the mouse cursor so that it appears to the left of the character and click the left mouse button to place the text cursor there. Then press the Del key to delete the letter to the right of the cursor.

- To insert characters, move the text cursor where you want the new characters to appear and type them. The existing text will move to accommodate the new text. As you learned in Chapter 1, this is called Insert mode, and you can tell Ami Pro is in Insert mode by the letters Ins in the status bar.

- To insert a character with the mouse, move the mouse cursor to the left of the character the new one should appear before and click. Then type the new character.

- If you want to replace one word with another one, double-click on the word to select it. A black rectangle will appear around the word, and the type will be reversed (white on black). Type the new word and press the spacebar once. Your old word will disappear, and the new one will take its place.

Having a mouse cursor and a text cursor that are independent of each other gives you flexibility in working with your documents. You can easily move the text cursor anywhere in your document by placing the mouse pointer in that location and clicking.

SAVING YOUR WORK

It's vitally important that you save your text early and often. Few things are more frustrating than suffering a power failure before you have time to save an hour's work. Ami Pro's Save command is on the File menu. It displays a dialog box in which you name the file and specify where it should be stored.

Follow these steps to save the sample text you typed:

1. Pull down the File menu and select Save. You will see the Save As dialog box, shown in Figure 2.2.

You use this dialog box to save a file that has not yet been named. Once the file is named, you can save it under the same name by selecting Save from the File menu or by using the keyboard shortcut Ctrl-S. If you want to save it under a different name or in a different format, use the Save As command on the File menu.

Ami Pro is set up to allow you very fast access to the commands necessary for word processing. You can access the menus with the mouse or from the keyboard. The items in the individual menus that are accessed most often are associated with special keypresses, such as Ctrl-S to save the current document.

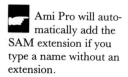

Figure 2.2: Save As dialog box

2. Make sure that Ami Pro is selected in the File Type list box. If some other name appears, click on the downward-pointing arrow at the right end of the box, scroll through the list until you see Ami Pro, and then click on it.

3. Type in the name of the file. Name our sample document **SWEET.SAM**.

Ami Pro will auto-matically add the SAM extension if you type a name without an extension.

The Save As dialog box contains several options relating to the way your file is saved. These options are discussed in Chapter 3.

EDITING TEXT

Along with the techniques for correcting typing errors described earlier, Ami Pro provides many other ways to edit your text. In editing your text, you will frequently need to move the text cursor to the characters you want to manipulate and select them. You can use the mouse cursor to position the text cursor and the standard mouse pointing-and-clicking techniques to select characters, or speed up your work by using the shortcuts described in the following sections.

CURSOR-MOVEMENT SHORTCUTS

You may prefer to use the cursor-movement keys to move the cursor quickly from one location to another. Table 2.1 lists the keystrokes, which you will recognize if you have worked with other word processing programs.

Ami Pro also features a speed cursor. When you press the ← or → key and hold it down, the text cursor will move character-to-character very rapidly. If you keep holding the key down (after about a second), the text cursor will begin racing along from word to word as if you were also

Table 2.1: Ami Pro Cursor-Movement Keystrokes

Keystroke	Cursor Movement
↑	One line up
↓	One line down
→	One character to the right
←	One character to the left
Ctrl↑	To before the beginning of the first word in a paragraph
Ctrl↓	To after the end of the last word in a paragraph
Ctrl←	One word to the left
Ctrl-→	One word to the right
Ctrl-PgDn	To the next page
Ctrl-PgUp	To the previous page
Home	To the left end of the line
End	To the right end of the line
Ctrl-. (period)	To the beginning of the next sentence
Ctrl-, (comma)	To the beginning of the previous sentence
Ctrl-Home	To the beginning of the document
Ctrl-End	To the end of the document
PgDn	Down one screen
PgUp	Up one screen

holding down the Ctrl key. This makes moving around in text much more efficient.

SELECTING TEXT

Selected text is highly vulnerable. If you press almost any key while text is selected, you will lose the selected text. If this happens, select Undo from the Edit menu to restore the text.

You can select text with your mouse by dragging the mouse pointer through it. To select units of text, you can use the following methods:

- To select a word, double-click on it.
- When the text cursor is at one end of the text you want to select, move the mouse cursor to the other end and press Shift and click (also called *Shift-click*).
- To select a sentence, hold down the Ctrl key and click on the sentence (also known as *Ctrl-click*).
- To select a paragraph, hold down the Ctrl key and double-click on the paragraph (also known as *Ctrl-double-click*).

You can also use the cursor-movement keys in combination with the Shift key to select text. Table 2.2 summarizes the text-selection methods.

USING TYPEOVER MODE

If you want new text you type to replace existing text instead of moving it over, switch to Typeover mode. There are two ways of changing from Insert to Typeover mode:

- Click the mouse cursor on the Ins indicator in the status bar at the bottom of the screen. The indicator will change to Type, which means that you are in Typeover mode. Click twice on the Type indicator to return to Insert mode.
- Press the Ins key (on the numeric keypad). The Ins indicator should change to Type. If a 0 appears on the screen and the insertion mode doesn't change, press the Num Lock key, then the Backspace key to delete the 0, and then press Ins again. To return to Insert mode, press the Ins key.

Table 2.2: Ami Pro Text-Selection Keystrokes

Keystroke	Text Selection
Shift↑	One line up
Shift↓	One line down
Shift→	One character to the right
Shift-←	One character to the left
Shift-Ctrl↑	Before the beginning of the first word in a paragraph
Shift-Ctrl↓	After the end of the last word in a paragraph
Shift-Ctrl←	One word to the left
Shift-Ctrl-→	One word to the right
Shift-Ctrl-PgDn	The next page
Shift-Ctrl-PgUp	The previous page
Shift-Home	The left end of the line
Shift-End	The right end of the line
Shift-Ctrl-. (period)	The beginning of the next sentence
Shift-Ctrl-, (comma)	The beginning of the previous sentence
Shift-Ctrl-Home	The beginning of the document
Shift-Ctrl-End	The end of the document
Shift-PgDn	Down one screen
Shift-PgUp	Up one screen

Typeover allows you to replace existing text with new typing. It's a powerful but dangerous tool. If you aren't careful, you could continue typing and obliterate useful as well as useless text.

In Typeover mode, the characters that existed where you typed the new text will be deleted. Usually, you will want to work in Insert mode, where you can easily delete any characters after making corrections. In this book, it is assumed that you are working in Insert mode.

CUTTING, COPYING, PASTING, AND RESTORING TEXT

When you need to move blocks of text around within or between your documents, use the Cut, Copy, and Paste commands on the

The Clipboard is available to all your Windows applications and can be used to move items between them. However, it stores only one item at a time, so whatever you put into the Clipboard replaces what was already there.

Edit menu. Cut and Copy move the selected text to the Clipboard, which is a chunk of memory that serves as a temporary storage area. The Cut command removes the selected text from the document; the Copy command places the selection in the Clipboard but also leaves it in the document.

The Paste command inserts the text that was last moved to the Clipboard at the location of the text cursor. Paste can be used to repeat text endlessly (as long as it's in the Clipboard) or to replace selected text with what is in the Clipboard.

These commands also have keyboard shortcuts:

Cut	Shift-Del
Copy	Ctrl-Ins
Paste	Shift-Ins

The Edit menu also contains two other kinds of Paste commands: Paste Link and Paste Special. These are used to place information into your text with a special link to some outside file or program. You will learn about linking files in Chapter 6.

Undo, the first option on the Edit menu, reverses the last change you made before selecting this option. For example, if you accidentally delete text, you can restore it by choosing Undo or using its shortcut, Alt-Backspace. If you decide that you liked the change after all, you can select Undo again, and the text will return to its original appearance— the way it looked before you selected Undo the first time.

To set the number of Undo levels, pull down the Tools menu and select User Setup. In the User Setup dialog box, click on the downward-pointing arrow at the right under Undo Levels. Click on the number of levels you want (1 through 4). You can also set undo levels to None, but then you will not have a simple way to recover from mistakes.

If you want to have several opportunities to reverse changes at one time, you can set your Undo levels to 4. With this setting, you will be able to undo up to four keypresses, providing a wide margin of error.

SWITCHING TEXT AND PARAGRAPHS

Although it is not listed on the Edit menu, Ami Pro also provides a move function that you can use to switch text around quickly. Drag through the text that you want to move to select it, place the mouse pointer where you want the text to appear, and then press Ctrl and click the *right* mouse button (the button that is opposite to the one you press to select text). The text will instantly be moved to the new location.

Ami Pro treats any string of text up to a carriage return as a paragraph. Any text that is in this format can be manipulated as a unit. One common editing task is to switch the order of text divided by carriage returns. Ami Pro provides two special keystrokes to accomplish this quickly:

Swap the paragraph   Alt-↑
containing the text cursor
with the paragraph above it

Swap the paragraph   Alt-↓
containing the text cursor
with the paragraph below it

VIEWING YOUR DOCUMENTS

There is more to the Ami Pro screen than you have seen so far. Ami Pro has several views and modes that are useful for each stage of developing your documents. Consider the typical steps in writing:

- You just want to get text down when you first sit down to write. You don't really care what it looks like, as long as it's text.

- Next, you want to have your text clear and easy to read so that it can be edited.

- You want to be able to see the text as it will appear when printed to make sure your design is tasteful and appealing.

- You want to see the facing pages in a page spread to be sure all the elements work together.

Put your writing aside for as long as possible before editing your own work so that you can take a more objective approach.

CHANGING YOUR POINT OF VIEW

Ami Pro provides four views in which you can edit and write, and one that shows facing pages. This means that rather than going through a series of paper printouts and wasting time, toner, and trees to check and adjust your text and layout, you can work within the various views.

Through the View menu, you can select from five views:

- Full Page: The primary purpose of Full Page view is to see the page as a whole so that you can check your format and see how the words will appear on paper without being distracted by the words themselves. You can make changes in this view, but it wouldn't be practical to write or edit in Full Page view unless you are working with extremely large letters.

- Working: In Working view, the text size is slightly reduced so an entire line of text will appear on screen at the same time. The default size is a 91 percent of Standard view. You can set the size of Working view by selecting View Preferences from the View menu. You can reduce Working view down to 10 percent, or about $^1/_{16}$ the size of Full Page view, and increase it up to 400 percent, or about half again as large as Enlarged view.

This view is called Standard because it's the same display size as other Windows applications. For example, a 12-point font will look about the same size in this view as a 12-point font in Windows Write or Excel.

- Standard: Standard view shows the text at full size. This means that if your lines are of the standard width (generally about 6 inches long from margin to margin), you will not be able to see the entire line on the screen at the same time. You will need to use the bottom scroll bar to shift from side to side as you read through the line.

- Enlarged: If you have difficulty seeing your text in Standard or Working view because of vision problems, or if you want to see details (such as type in a small typeface or the placement of frames on the page), select Enlarged view. In this view, the size of the text is about three times larger than it is in Standard view.

- Facing Pages: Facing Pages view is useful for seeing how facing pages will appear together. When you will print the document on two sides of the pages, this view shows the "spread" layout. As in Full Page view, in most cases, the text will be too small to read. You cannot make changes in this view. Use it to check the placement of text and graphics and white space without being distracted by the actual text.

Figures 2.3 through 2.7 show the sample document you entered at the beginning of the chapter in each Ami Pro view. You may want to use the View menu to see how the various views appear on your screen.

You can switch between all the views except Facing Pages by selecting a different view from the View menu. To leave Facing Pages view, you must click on the Cancel button that appears over the menu bar (see Figure 2.7).

WORKING IN DIFFERENT MODES

In addition to the views, there are three modes that can be accessed from the View menu:

- Layout: In Layout mode, which is the one you have seen so far, you see a true WYSIWYG (what you see is what you get) display, complete with correctly sized typefaces, color, frames, tables, pictures, headers, and so on. Figures 2.3

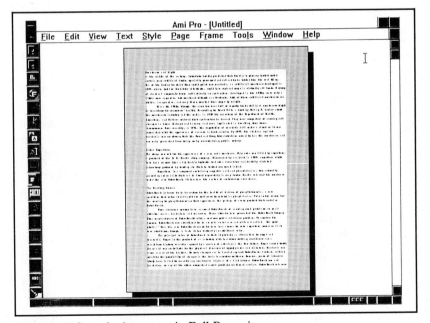

Figure 2.3: Sample document in Full Page view

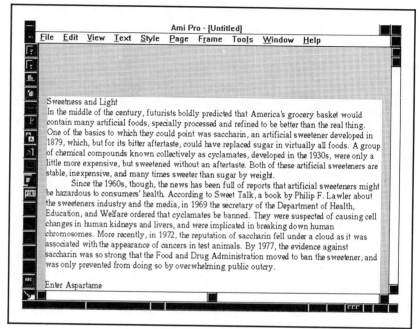

Figure 2.4: Sample document in Working view

through 2.7 show the screen in Layout mode. You can switch to any of the views in Layout mode.

- Outline: Use Outline mode to automate the process of assembling information, assigning it a level of significance, and organizing it in a logical way. You can see any text in Outline mode. For example, Figure 2.8 shows our sample document (with a few modifications) as an outline. Notice how Ami Pro assigns outline levels based on levels of heads, with the title as the highest division, the subhead as the next highest, and body text as the lowest unit of organization. Working, Standard, and Enlarged views are available in Outline mode.

- Draft: When you want to put down words and you don't care how they will look on the page, use Draft mode. As shown in Figure 2.9, Draft mode eliminates headers and footers, page breaks, and footnotes. Anchored frames

If you haven't written an outline since you were forced to in high school, you probably remember outlining as something to be avoided if humanly possible. However, taking the time and effort to outline will protect you from wandering and help you identify information that needs to be filled in before you can start writing. Chapter 10 covers outlining with Ami Pro.

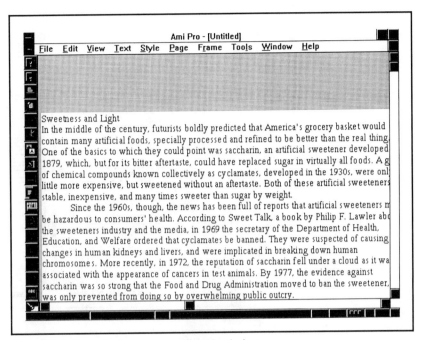

Figure 2.5: Sample document in Standard view

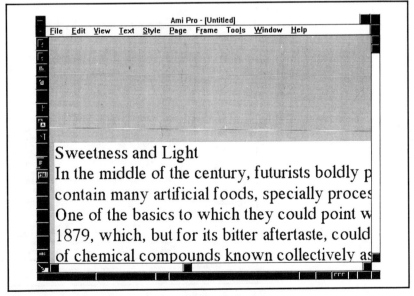

Figure 2.6: Sample document in Enlarged view

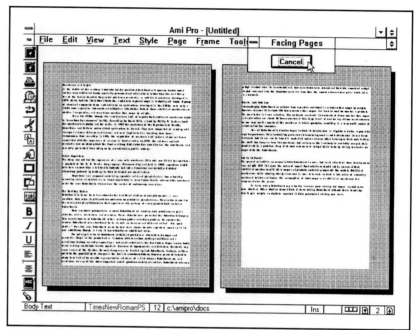

Figure 2.7: Sample document in Facing Pages view

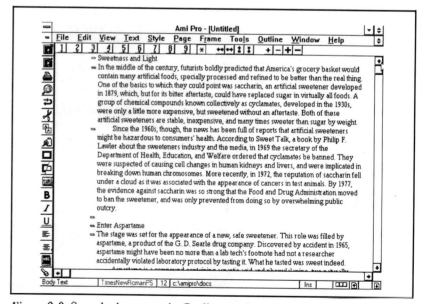

Figure 2.8: Sample document in Outline mode

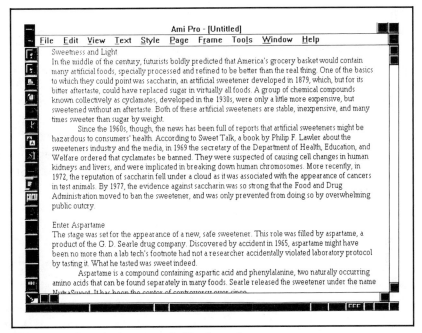

Figure 2.9: Sample document in Draft mode

(frames connected to the text rather than the page) will be displayed, but not other kinds of frames. You can see the Draft mode screen in Working, Standard, and Enlarged views.

A QUICK GLIMPSE OF AMI PRO'S FEATURES

In the following sections, you will get some hands-on experience with Ami Pro's multitude of features. Working with SWEET.SAM, the document you created earlier, you will assign styles, create a chart, and add a frame. By the end of the chapter, you will have a good idea of what Ami Pro offers.

INTRODUCING STYLES

In word processing, a style is a collection of formatting attributes applied to text to give it a distinctive look. You create well-designed

Courier, Times Roman, Helvetica, and Palatino are typefaces. Generally, you should try to stick to established body typefaces for most of your documents. Typefaces are discussed in Chapter 5.

If SWEET.SAM doesn't appear in the Files list box, try to remember where you saved it. The default is to save it to the DOCS directory under the AMIPRO directory. Try changing drives. You may have accidentally saved it to a floppy disk.

documents by using appropriate styles consistently throughout the text. For example, you do not want to use Courier for some body text and Times Roman for other body text, nor have some of your main heads centered Helvetica and others left-aligned Palatino.

To help you format your text uniformly, Ami Pro allows you to specify a single style for body text and other single styles for each level of heads. You can assign a particular style to the other elements of the document, such as headers and footers.

You select a style from the list that pops up when you click on the text style indicator in the status bar. Styles are imposed on paragraphs. Therefore, it isn't necessary for you to select the entire paragraph to apply a style to it. Just click on the text or use the arrow keys to move the text cursor to the paragraph. As long as the text cursor is within the paragraph, you can specify a style for it.

Follow these steps to apply a style to the title and subheads in your sample document:

1. If you closed the SWEET.SAM document, pull down the File menu and select Open. If Ami Pro isn't the format selected in the File Type box, select it. Then double-click on SWEET.SAM in the Files list box.

2. Move the text cursor to the paragraph title: *Sweetness and Light*.

3. Click on the first section of the status bar (the leftmost section), on the indicator that says Body Text.

You will see the menu of styles, called the Styles box, shown in Figure 2.10. This menu includes the options Body Text, Body Single, Bullet, Bullet 1, Number List, Subhead, and Title. Collectively, these styles make up a style sheet.

4. Click on the Title to give the first paragraph the Title style.

5. Click on the next paragraph, which begins *In the middle of the century....* The status bar should indicate that this is in the Body Text style. If it does not, click on the indicator and choose Body Text from the Styles box.

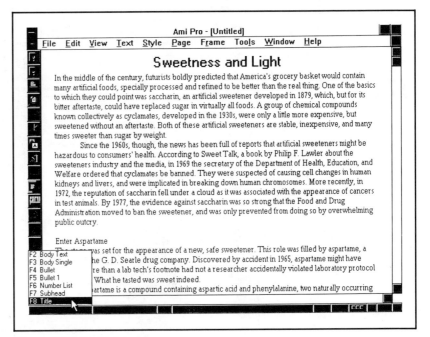

Figure 2.10: Styles box

6. Click on *Enter Aspartame.* This is a subhead, so click on the text style indicator in the status bar and select Subhead as the style.

Your screen should look like Figure 2.11. You can see that the Title style is larger and bolder than the rest of the text and in a different typeface. The Subhead style is a bold, italic font in the same typeface as the body text. These are just a few of the characteristics you can specify with a style.

APPLYING ATTRIBUTES TO TEXT

You can also change the appearance of individual sections of text by choosing attributes from the Text menu. It lists choices for bold-facing, italicizing, and underlining characters.

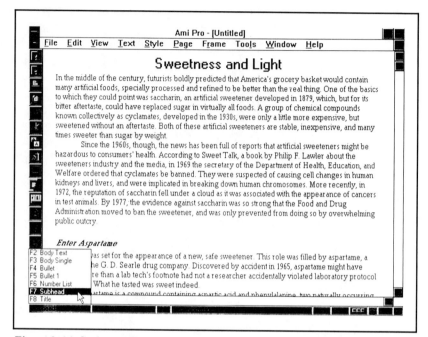

Figure 2.11: Style applied to paragraphs

As an example, we will italicize the names of the chemical components of aspartame in our document:

1. Using the mouse, place the mouse cursor ahead of the *a* in *aspartic acid* in the fourth paragraph of body text. Press the mouse button and drag to the right until both words are highlighted.

2. Release the mouse button.

3. Pull down the Text menu and select Italic. The text will appear in the italic font.

4. In the same sentence, you see the word *phenylalanine*, which also should be italic. Place the mouse cursor on this word and double-click to highlight it.

5. Press Ctrl-I. This is the keyboard shortcut for making text italic.

If you want to italicize every instance of a text string in a document, you can use the Find & Replace command on the Edit menu, as described in the next section.

FINDING AND REPLACING TEXT ATTRIBUTES

The Find & Replace command provides the quickest way to make global changes, which are changes to be made throughout a document. You can easily search for any text, such as a name you spelled wrong, and replace it with other text. Ami Pro's find-and-replace function is especially powerful because it works with text attributes as well as the text itself.

1. Move the text cursor t othe beginning of the document. Then pull down the Edit menu and select Find & Replace.

2. In the Find text box, type **NutraSweet?**.

3. Click the mouse pointer in the Replace With text box and type **NutraSweet?**.

The question mark serves as a wildcard. It stands for any characters that follow the text in the find-and-replace operation. This will result in commas, periods, and so forth being changed, too. But if the text isn't followed by another character, the wildcard is ignored and only the word is changed. See Chapter 4 for more information about using wildcards.

That's right, you're going to replace a text string with itself. We are changing the appearance, not the content, of the text string.

4. Click on the button marked Attributes. You will see the dialog box shown in Figure 2.12.

5. If Normal isn't already selected for Find Attributes, click on it.

6. Click on Italic under Replace Attributes in the lower half of the dialog box. This tells the program to search for *Nutra-Sweet* in normal text and replace it with *NutraSweet* in italics.

The Find Attributes and Replace Attributes options are both reset to Normal each time you open the Find & Replace dialog box.

7. Click on OK in the Find & Replace Attributes dialog box.

8. Click on Options in the Find & Replace dailog box.

9. In the Find & Replace options dialog box select Exact Attributes in the Replace Options sections.

10. Click on OK in the Find & Replace dialog box.

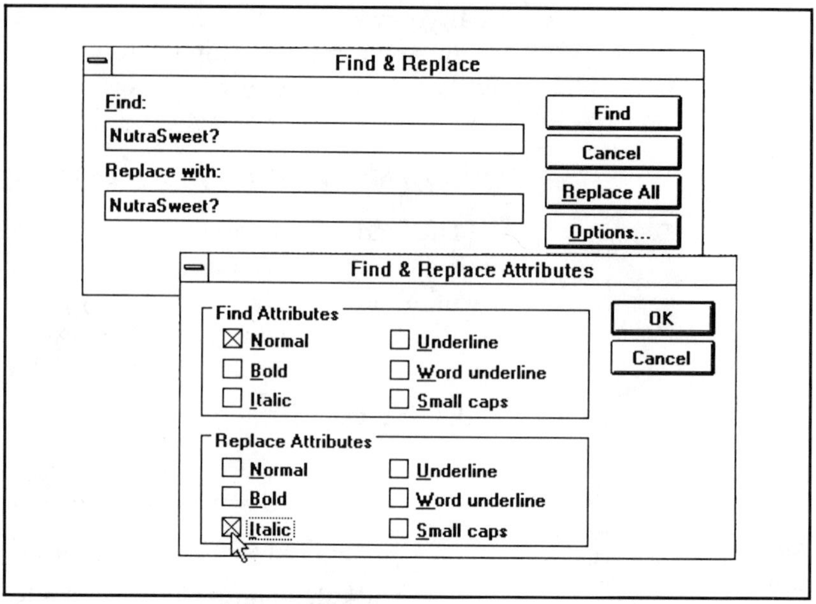

Figure 2.12: Find & Replace and Find & Replace Attributes dialog boxes

11. Click on Replace All in the Find & Replace dialog box. Instantly, all instances of *NutraSweet* will be replaced by the same text in italic.

ADDING A CHART

One of Ami Pro's special features is its charting capabilities. You can create all types of charts, such as bar, column, area, and pie, and incorporate them in your documents. In this section, we will use Ami Pro's Charting command (on the Tools menu) to create a bar chart. Ami Pro uses the Clipboard for importing numeric data into the charting part of the program.

In order to create the chart, we need data. We will type some values, place them in the Clipboard, and then generate a bar chart that graphs those values.

1. Press Ctrl-End to go to the end of your text.

2. Enter the following data: **49001, 27405, 48858, 10001**.

3. Drag the mouse pointer through the numbers so they are all selected.

4. Pull down the Edit menu and select Cut.

5. Pull down the Tools menu and select Charting. You will see the dialog box shown in Figure 2.13.

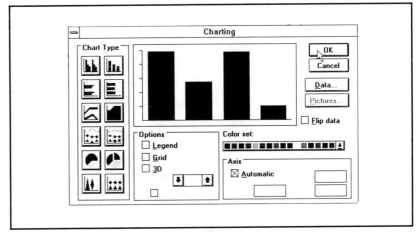

Figure 2.13: Charting dialog box

The Charting dialog box offers a variety of options, including 12 types of charts. The default type is bar, as shown under the title of the dialog box. You can change the chart type and other features, such as the color of the graph. Selecting chart types and other options is discussed in Chapter 8.

6. Click on the button marked Data at the right end of the Charting dialog box. You will see the dialog box shown in Figure 2.14.

You can alter the data in this box or enter the original data here without going through the preliminary step of placing information in the Clipboard.

7. Click on OK in the Charting Data dialog box to close the box.

Below and to the left of the dialog box you can see a frame—a shadowed, rounded-corner rectangle, which will contain the chart. You can make the outline of the frame invisible (so that the chart will appear to be an integral part of the text), but any time you place a graphic in the text, there must be a frame. Incidental text must also appear in a frame. You will learn more about frames later in this chapter and in Chapter 7.

Although you can enter an enormous amount of information in the Charting Data box, it's best to keep your charts as simple as possible.

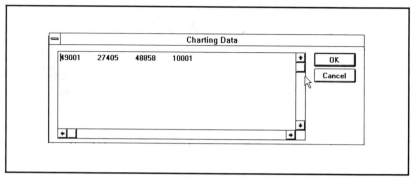

Figure 2.14: Charting Data dialog box

8. To see how the data looks in a three-dimensional chart, click on 3D in the Options box in the Charting dialog box.

9. Click on OK in the Charting dialog box to place the graph in the new frame. Your chart should look like the one shown in Figure 2.15.

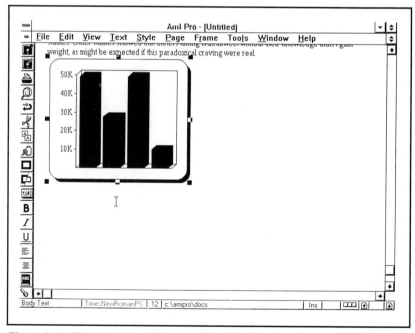

Figure 2.15: The chart in a frame at the end of the document

You can easily return to the Charting dialog box by double-clicking on the chart. From there, you could select a different chart type for the data and make other changes to improve the chart.

ADDING A FRAME

A frame is a powerful organizing tool used in word processing and page layout programs. It allows you to add layers of information to the page.

As an example, we will place a frame using the frame icon in the icon palette, and then add some text within it.

1. Place the mouse pointer on the scroll box in the vertical scroll bar at the right edge of the window.

2. Press the mouse button and drag the scroll box to the top of the scroll bar.

3. Release the mouse button. If your mouse pointer is too far from the scroll bar, nothing will happen. Try it again. If your mouse pointer was within about $1/16$ inch of the scroll bar, you should now see the very beginning of the document.

4. Click on the frame icon in the icon palette. In the default icon palette, it is the ninth icon—the one that looks like a frame.

If your icon palette is not along the left side of the screen, as shown in the figures in this book, you can move it there by pulling down the Tools menu, selecting SmartIcons, and clicking on the radio button marked Left in the Position box.

The shape of your cursor will change to resemble a frame. The upper-left corner of this frame is the *hot point*, or the point where clicking has an effect.

5. Place the mouse pointer to the right of the first subhead.

6. Press and hold down the mouse button while dragging the mouse pointer down and to the right, until you have a rectangle that resembles the one shown in Figure 2.16.

7. Release the mouse button, and a frame will appear, as shown in Figure 2.17.

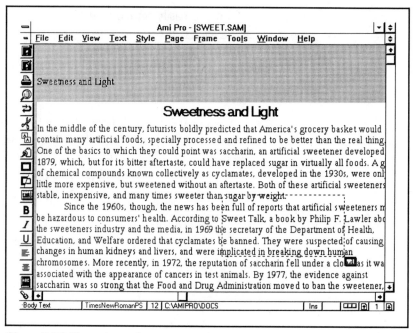

Figure 2.16: Dragging a frame rectangle

Another way to adjust the frame is to create a larger frame with no outline and place the frame you are going to use on top of this larger frame. The invisible frame will push all of the unwanted text out of the way.

You will notice that Ami Pro placed text to the right of the frame. When you insert a frame in the midst of text, Ami Pro must decide how to wrap text around the frame. In this case, it created a second column to the right of the frame, which contains the text that follows the text to the left of the frame. We will adjust the frame by enlarging it and changing its position so that it pushes unwanted text out of the way.

There are eight handles, which look like tiny black rectangles, around the frame. These handles are used to adjust the size and shape of the frame. The handles in the center of the sides adjust only that side (in this case, only the length of the frame). The corner handles are used for adjusting two sides at a time.

8. Place the mouse pointer on the handle at the center of the right side of the frame.

9. Press and hold down the mouse button and drag the pointer to the right until the frame is touching the right margin of the page, as illustrated in Figure 2.18.

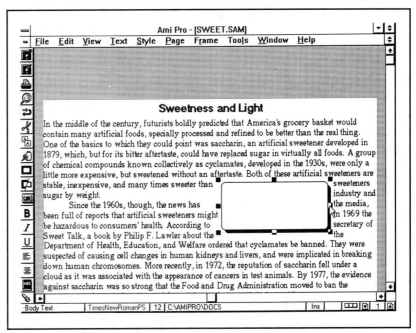

Figure 2.17: The frame appears after you release the mouse button

If you left too much space between the frame and the margin, you will have another column of text—possibly only the width of a single character. If this happens, adjust the frame size again.

10. Release the mouse button, and the frame will be adjusted to match the rectangle you dragged. The text that formerly appeared in a column to the right of the rectangle is pushed back into its proper location.

Next, we will place some text in the frame.

11. To prepare the frame for text entry, double-click on it. A text cursor will appear in the frame.

12. Type **Sugar causes tooth decay.** and press ←┘. Then type **No dangerous side effects have been conclusively linked to use of aspartame.**

13. To assign a style to the frame text, place the mouse pointer anywhere within the first paragraph (the text about tooth decay) and press the mouse button.

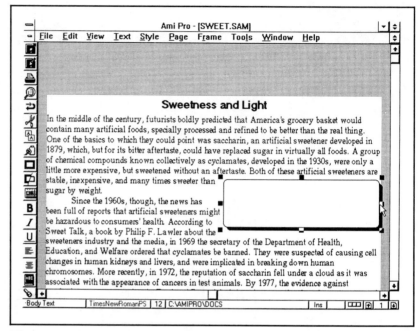

Figure 2.18: The frame stretched to the right margin

14. Drag into the second paragraph (the one about aspartame). You don't have to highlight everything in the two paragraphs as long as at least part of each is selected.

15. Click on the text style indicator in the status bar and select Bullet from the Styles box. Your screen should look like the one shown in Figure 2.19.

You will learn more about frames and how to modify them in Chapter 7.

PLACING A HEADER AND A FOOTER

We'll complete our tour of Ami Pro's features by placing a header and footer on the page. Headers, sometimes called running heads, contain text that appears at the top of each page in a document; footers include text that goes at the bottom of every page. Traditionally,

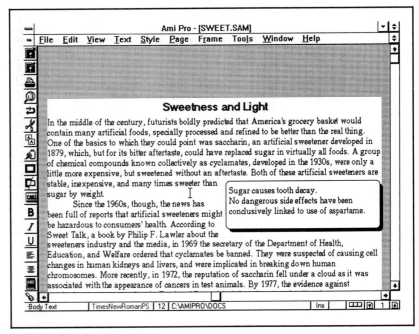

Figure 2.19: The finished frame

text goes in the header and page numbers go in the footer, although you can set up your headers and footers in whatever way you desire.

To enter a header or footer, click within the header or footer area on the screen and type the text.

Follow these steps to add a header and footer to our document:

1. Click in the shaded area above the white page area, and a blinking text cursor will appear there. This is where the header will appear—in the margin above the text. If you don't see this area, click on the arrow at the top of the scroll bar at the right side of the window until the screen stops moving.

2. Type the header: **Sweetness and Light**.

Figure 2.20 shows the header entered in the document. The text is a little difficult to see because of the shading that Ami Pro uses in the margins.

You can change the header or footer at any time, even when you are on the last page of the document. Just click on the header and make your changes. The header will be altered throughout the document.

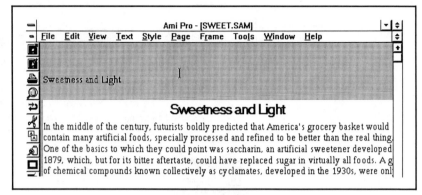

Figure 2.20: The header entered in the header area

By default, the header is left aligned. You can use the Alignment option on the Text menu to center, right align, or justify the text. Let's center our header.

3. Click anywhere in the header.

4. Pull down the Text menu and select Alignment.

5. In the Alignment dialog box, select Center. (The keyboard shortcut for centering is Ctrl-C.)

Next, we will set the page number to appear in the footer area. You tell Ami Pro to number your pages by selecting Page Numbering from the Page menu.

6. Click on the arrow at the bottom of the scroll bar on the right side of the window until you can see the shading in the bottom margin. If you go too far, you will find yourself at the top of the second page. If this happens, click on the arrow at the top of the scroll bar until you return to the bottom margin.

7. Click on the margin. You should see a blinking cursor.

8. Pull down the Page menu and select Page Numbering. This displays the Page Number dialog box.

9. Click on OK to accept the default page numbering settings.

11. Press Ctrl-C to center the page number.

12. Press Ctrl-S to save your work.

You have now created a document and enhanced it with styles, text attributes, a chart, framed text, and a header and footer. This is just a preview of what Ami Pro can do.

The next chapter covers the fundamentals of handling your Ami Pro files, from recalling existing documents to using Ami Pro's File Manager for efficient file management.

CHAPTER 3

Managing and Printing Your Documents

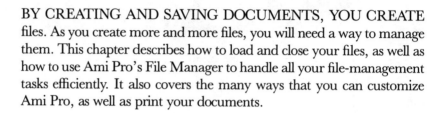

BY CREATING AND SAVING DOCUMENTS, YOU CREATE files. As you create more and more files, you will need a way to manage them. This chapter describes how to load and close your files, as well as how to use Ami Pro's File Manager to handle all your file-management tasks efficiently. It also covers the many ways that you can customize Ami Pro, as well as print your documents.

LOADING A DOCUMENT

You can load a document into Ami Pro in one of three ways:

- Open a file, creating a new Ami Pro window to contain it.

- Import a file.

- Copy a file to the Windows Clipboard and paste it into another text file in an existing window or into an empty window.

If you have more than one file open in Ami Pro and you want to go directly to a document that is hidden from view, pull down the Window menu and select the file name of the document you want to see.

Usually, you will simply open a file. If you open a document while there is already one on the screen, Ami Pro will open a new window for it.

To open an existing document, select Open from the File menu or click on the icon in the icon palette that shows an arrow leading away from a disk. You will see the dialog box shown in Figure 3.1.

If the name of the file you want is listed in the Files list box, double-click on it to load it into a new window, or click on the file name and click on OK. Another way to select a file is to double-click on the File Name text box, type in the name of the file you want to load, and click on OK.

The other options in the Open dialog box allow you to change the drive and directory, import files, replace the current file, show a description of the file, and insert a file into another one. These options are described in the following sections.

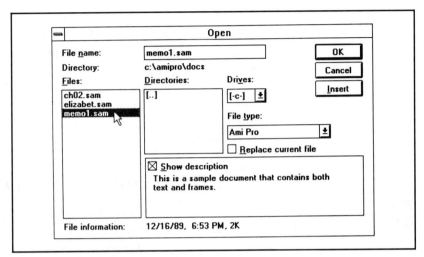

Figure 3.1: Open dialog box

CHANGING YOUR DIRECTORY AND DRIVE

If the Files list box does not show the name of the file that you want to open, the file may be in a different drive or directory. To change to another directory, double-click on its name in the Directories box, or click on its name and then click on OK.

The [..] designation in the Directories box indicates that the current directory has a parent directory. Double-click on [..] to move up to the parent directory and display its files. For example, in Figure 3.1, the current directory is C:\AMIPRO\DOCS. Double-clicking on [..] will take you to C:\AMIPRO and display a list of its files and subdirectories, which will also include [..]. Double-clicking on that [..] will take you to the parent directory of C:\AMIPRO, which is the root directory.

To change drives, click on the downward-pointing arrow on the right side of the Drives list box (next to the Directories box). You will see a list of all the available drives. Click on the designation of the drive you want to use.

IMPORTING FILES

Through the Open dialog box, you can directly import files created in many popular word processor formats, such as DCA/RFT,

If you are on a network, have your hard disk partitioned into several logical drives, or simply have a lot of disk drives attached, the Drives list might be a long one. If the list is too long to fit in the list box, you will also see a scroll bar.

Importing files is described in detail in Chapter 6.

DisplayWrite, Enable, Manuscript, Word, MultiMate, Samna Word, Windows Write, Word for Windows, WordPerfect, and WordStar. You can also import files created with some spreadsheet and database programs.

The File Type box indicates that Ami Pro is the file format of the names currently listed in the Files box. To see a list of files of another type, click on the downward-pointing arrow on the right side of the File Type box.

REPLACING THE CURRENT FILE

If the Replace Current File box in the Open dialog box is checked, you will lose the text in the current Ami Pro window when you open a new file. If there have been any changes to the existing file since the last time you saved it, Ami Pro will pause to ask whether you want to save the changes before replacing it with the new file.

If you want to make a document window fill the Ami Pro window, click on the Maximize box or open the Control menu and select Maximize. If you have several files open and maximized, you can flip through them as if they were papers on your desktop by selecting Next from the Control menu.

If the Replace Current File box isn't checked, the file you are opening will appear in a new window, as shown in Figure 3.2. In the example shown in the figure, the new file, MEMO1.SAM, is loaded into a new window with the old file, Untitled, in the background. Untitled is a file that is always opened when Ami Pro is started up, so that you have a place to write immediately. (Ami Pro won't save the file under the name Untitled; this title indicates that the file has not been named and saved.)

SHOWING THE FILE DESCRIPTION

When you save a file for the first time, you are given the opportunity to enter a description of the file. The DOS limitation of eight characters for a file name makes it difficult to create descriptive names. With some programs, you can use the three extra characters in the extension, but Ami Pro requires all its files to end with the extension SAM. Until Windows allows the use of 32-character file names, this descriptive paragraph is the best way to keep track of your files.

If you typed a descriptive paragraph for the file you are opening, you can select the Show Description option (below the Directories box), to see that description.

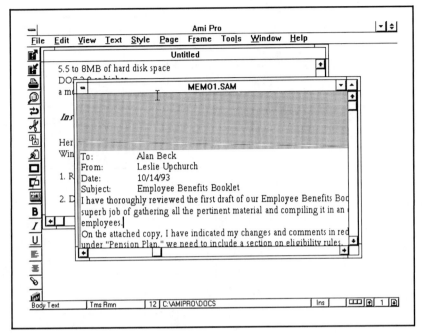

Figure 3.2: The new file loaded into a new window

INSERTING A FILE INTO ANOTHER FILE

Through the Open dialog box, you can easily insert the text of another file within the current file. To insert a file, select it in the Files box, and then click on Insert instead of OK.

The Insert option is handy for pasting an entire document into another. Since the Clipboard is so volatile, some people prefer to use the slightly more complicated route of copying important or frequently used text into a file of its own rather than pasting from the Clipboard.

OPENING MULTIPLE WINDOWS OF THE SAME DOCUMENT

You can open two or more windows showing the same document, although you can save only one of them. Open the document, pull down the Ami Pro Window menu, and select New Window. Ami

Pro will pause to warn you that your file is already open, and you cannot save any changes in this one. Click on the OK button in the dialog box, and the new window will open, as shown in Figure 3.3.

Although this window can be edited, it cannot be saved. Therefore, you need to make sure that you make all permanent changes in the other window. Click on the original window to bring it to the foreground. You will note that changes made in one window won't appear in the second window unless you reload the file.

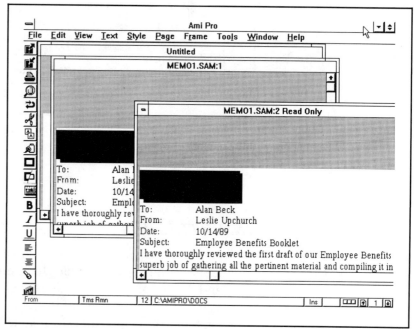

Figure 3.3: The new view of the document

CLOSING FILES

After you have finished working with a file, you will want to close it. You close a file by clearing it from memory. If you want to be able to retrieve that file again, you will need to save it to disk before clearing it.

If you find yourself dumping files because your hard disk is full and you don't want to save old versions of a file, consider saving them to a high-density or a high-capacity floppy disk before clearing them. If the floppy disk becomes full, file it away and start using another. This kind of backup only costs about a dollar per megabyte, as opposed to about $10 per megabyte for hard-disk storage.

Although password protection can guard your file to some extent, any encryption can be broken if the person intent on breaking it has enough resources at hand.

SELECTING OPTIONS FOR SAVING A FILE

As you learned in Chapter 2, to save a file to disk, select Save from the File menu or click on the icon in the icon palette that shows an arrow leading toward a disk. If you have never saved the file before, you will see the Save As dialog box (see Figure 2.2).

In the File name text dialog box, type a file name of up to eight characters for the current file. Before you save the file, you can change to another directory and drive to store the file there, in the same way you can switch directories and drives in the Open dialog box.

You can also select from the following options in the Save As dialog box to control how the file is saved:

- Keep Format with Document: If this option is not checked, the saved document will lose all formatting.

- Password Protect: If the file you are saving is confidential, you can choose this option to save it in a scrambled, encrypted format under a password. Then the file cannot be opened without first entering the password.

- Ami Pro 1.2 Format: Choosing this option saves the file in the format of the earlier version of the program. Use it if the file is being shared with people who haven't yet upgraded to Ami Pro 2.0.

- Document Description: This box is where you can enter a paragraph of text that explains briefly what the file is about. Then, if you check Show Description in the Open dialog box, this paragraph will appear when you select to open the file.

- File Type: This option allows you to save the file in the format of another program. Click on the arrow at the right of the box to display a list of the alternate formats to which Ami Pro can export files. Because the list of file types is so long, there is a scroll bar for scrolling through it.

If you want to change the file name or any other attribute of the file, select Save As instead of Save from the File menu.

If you have already saved the file, you will not see a dialog box when you select Save from the File menu or click on the save icon. The file will automatically be saved under its own name in its own format.

DISPOSING OF A FILE

⊙ Although it is an effective way to drop a file and all its changes, you shouldn't reset, reboot, or turn off the computer, especially while it is accessing a disk. Doing so could leave lots of temporary files open and scramble your FAT (file-allocation table), potentially making the files on your hard disk inaccessible.

While working on a file, you may decide that you have made too many errors and want to start from scratch. You can dispose of the file in one of two ways:

- Drop the file without saving it by selecting Close from the File menu and responding No when you are asked if you want to save the changes.
- Reload the same file from disk, minus all the changes you have made since you last saved it. To do this, select Revert to Saved from the File menu.

If you select Revert to Saved, you will see a dialog box that says

This will undo all the changes you have made since you last saved. Are you sure?

Click on Yes if you are sure you want to lose all your changes.

USING THE FILE MANAGER

You could use the Windows 3.0 File Manager, but it's easier to work with your files using Ami Pro's version. Windows also offers the option of returning to DOS to do your file-management work (double-click on the DOS icon in the Main program group).

Ami Pro offers a very useful function for managing your files, which is accessed through the File Management option on the File menu. Figure 3.4 shows the Ami Pro File Manager window. Like other windows, it includes a menu bar, Maximize and Minimize boxes, and a Control menu.

The window lists the files in the current directory, along with a description if one was entered for the file. In Figure 3.4, the list includes CH02.SAM, which the File Manager recognizes as a non-Ami Pro file despite its SAM extension, and a letter and memo that are Ami Pro files. MEMO1.SAM has a description.

From this window, you can navigate through your drives and directories, manipulate your files, and view file information.

NAVIGATING THROUGH DRIVES AND DIRECTORIES

You can change the drive and directory very easily through the File Manager by double-clicking on the new drive or directory. As in all

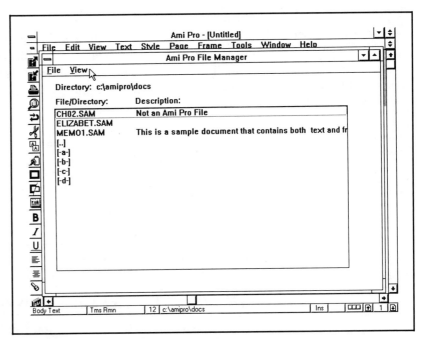

Figure 3.4: Ami Pro File Manager window

The double dot always refers to the parent of a directory, even in DOS. If you find yourself several directories deep in the hard disk, just keep clicking on [..] in Windows or entering CD .. on the command line in DOS to return to higher level directories. Eventually, you will wind up in the root directory, which has no parent directory.

Windows list boxes, [..] refers to the next directory up the path. The complete path appears at the top of the File Manager window.

WORKING WITH FILES

You can manipulate the files listed in the File Manager window by selecting options from its File menu. This menu offers the following actions:

- Copy: Makes a copy of a file in another location.
- Move: Copies the file to a new location and then deletes the original file.
- Rename: Changes the name of the file.
- Delete: Removes the file.
- Attributes: Toggles the read-only attribute of files.

Although DOS will accept a large number of characters as part of a file name, including nonprinting characters such as ASCII 255, you should make the name comprehensible by limiting yourself to letters and numbers, the underscore character, and the hyphen. Use the Document Description option in the Save As dialog box to enter additional information about the file.

Click on the files you want to work with, and then pull down the File menu and select the action you want to take. If the File Manager needs more information before performing the action, it will display a small dialog box. Figure 3.5 shows an example of the dialog box that appears when you select to copy files.

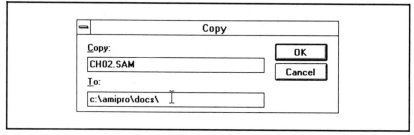

Figure 3.5: File Manager's Copy dialog box

VIEWING DIFFERENT KINDS OF FILES

Pull down the View menu, and you will see that the File Manager is set to show only the files with the S?M extension (extensions in which the first letter is *S*, the last letter is *M*, and the middle letter might be any character) in the File Manager window.

The wildcard characters ? and * are very powerful features in DOS. A question mark stands for any single character, and an asterisk stands for any number of characters.

You can change this listing to list all files in the directory, or use the Partial option to indicate which files you want to see. The Partial dialog box will accept wildcard designations, so you can be less specific about the names of the files to be listed. For example, you could enter *.TXT to see all files with the TXT extension, or E*.* to see all files that start with the letter E.

VIEWING FILE INFORMATION

The last option in the File Manager View menu is Doc Info. This displays the dialog box shown in Figure 3.6.

The Doc Info dialog box provides the following information about your files:

- The file name
- The file's location (directory)

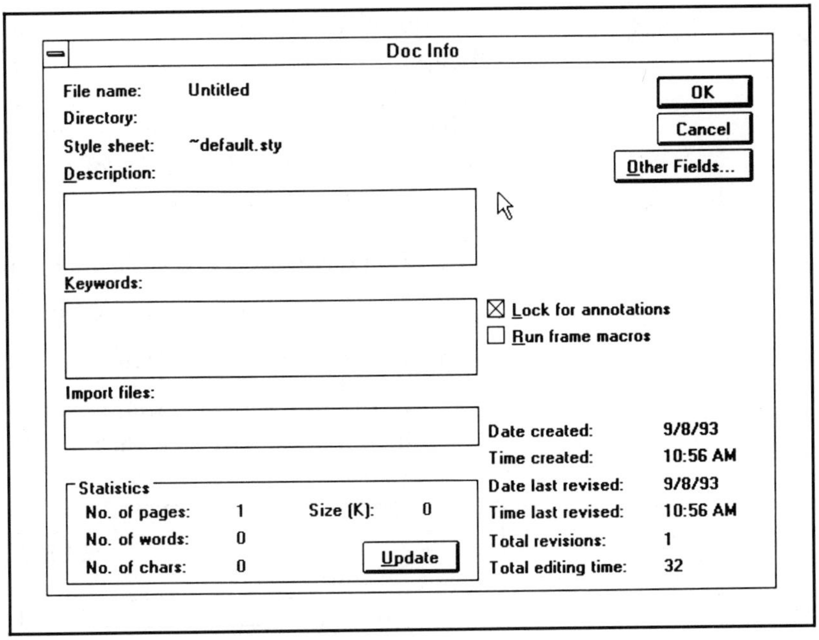

Figure 3.6: Doc Info dialog box

You can use this dialog box to learn more about a file in the File Manager window, but you can't use it to provide information. If you want to alter the document description, use the Doc Info option on the Ami Pro File menu.

- The style sheet associated with the file

- The descriptive paragraph associated with the file

- Keywords

- Import files

- Vital statistics, such as the number of pages, words, and so on

- Whether the file is locked for annotations (a locked file cannot be altered)

- Whether frame macros will be run when the document is open (you can attach frame macros that will be run automatically when the file is opened)

- Creating and editing information, such as the date of creation, date of last change, and so on

If you would like to keep more information about files, you can add up to eight more fields to the Doc Info dialog box. Click on the Other Fields button to see the dialog box shown in Figure 3.7.

Here you can enter whatever information you would like to see. If you want to change the names of these fields to something more descriptive, follow these steps:

1. Pull down Ami Pro's File menu and select Doc Info.
2. In the Doc Info dialog box, click on Other Fields.
3. In the Doc Info Fields dialog box, click on Rename Fields.
4. In the Rename Doc Info Fields dialog box, type the new field names, and then click on OK.

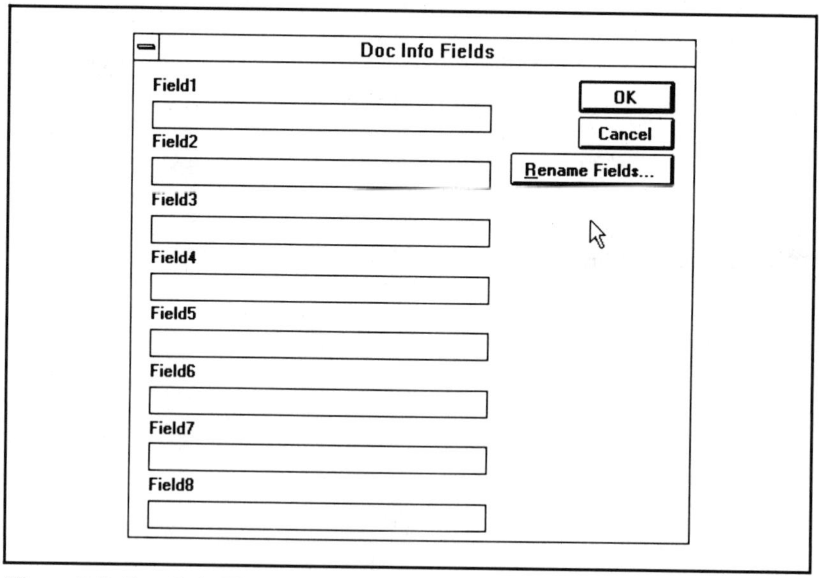

Figure 3.7: Doc Info Fields dialog box

CUSTOMIZING THE WAY AMI PRO WORKS

Ami Pro allows you to customize the way it works to suit your needs. Customizing Ami Pro should make it seem friendlier to you.

Ami Pro can be adjusted in a wide variety of ways. It would be possible to alter the screen so that it looks very different from the one in the figures in this book. It will be easier to follow the examples in this book if you do not make any changes to the program's setup.

When you're getting to know the program, take the time to try out different working arrangements.

ADJUSTING THE PROGRAM SETUP

Through the User Setup option on the Tools menu, you can customize Ami Pro in a variety of ways. This option displays the dialog box shown in Figure 3.8.

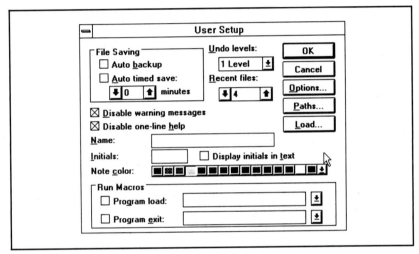

Figure 3.8: User Setup dialog box

The selections in the User Setup dialog box allow you to make the following changes:

- Select automatic backup, so that Ami Pro saves your files at the time intervals you specify.

- Specify the number of Undo levels (1 to 4).

- Disable warning messages and on-line help.

- Enter a default color for notes.

- Enter your name and initials to personalize Ami Pro.

- Specify which macros should run when you start up Ami Pro and which macros to run when the program exits. (See Chapter 11 for more information about marcos.)

Selecting a large number of undo levels will encourage you to experiment without worrying about making errors. Saving often will give you the freedom to experiment because you can always choose Revert to Saved from the File menu to start over from the last version.

The User Setup dialog box also contains the Options, Paths, and Load buttons, which display dialog boxes for specifying other program setup options.

Specifying Default Paths   Clicking on the Paths button in the User Setup dialog box displays the dialog box shown in Figure 3.9. Here you can specify where Ami Pro should look for the following types of files:

- Your documents (C:\AMIPRO\DOCS is the default)
- Your style sheets
- Your macros

You also can select where to place your backup files if automatic backup is turned on.

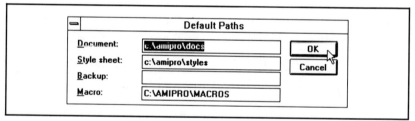

Figure 3.9: Default Paths dialog box

Choosing Load Defaults   Click on the Load button in the User Setup dialog box to specify the defaults that will be in place when Ami Pro is started up. You will see the Load Defaults dialog box, shown in Figure 3.10.

Appropriately enough, DEFAULT.STY is the default style sheet.

You can specify the mode and view and whether the screen is maximized. The list box in the lower-right corner of the box allows you to choose the default style sheet.

Choosing Other Setup Options   When you click on the Options button in the User Setup dialog box, you will see a dialog box with choices that affect how your text appears and the speed of the program, as shown in Figure 3.11.

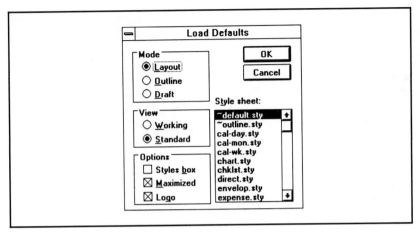

Figure 3.10: Load Defaults dialog box

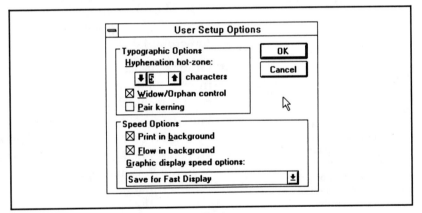

Figure 3.11: User Setup Options dialog box

You can set the following Typographic options:

- The width of your hyphenation hot zone, which can be set from 2 to 9 characters. The *hyphenation hot zone* is where Ami Pro will begin looking for a place to break a word for hyphenation. A wider hyphenation zone allows Ami Pro the most leeway in specifying where lines are broken and generally results in a better fit.

- Control of widows and orphans. *Widow/orphan control* prevents a single line at the beginning of a paragraph from appearing at the end of a page or column (a widow), or prevents a single line at the end of a paragraph from appearing at the top of the page or column (an orphan).

- Pair kerning, if you are using a PostScript printer. *Pair kerning* allows Ami Pro to adjust the amount of space between certain pairs of letters to improve their appearance in printed text.

Pair kerning takes a lot of processor time. Use it for only the final draft of a manuscript.

The Speed options in the User Setup Options dialog box include the following:

- Print in background, which allows you to continue editing and writing in the foreground while printing in the background.

- Flow in background, which makes Ami Pro format the text in the background while you write and edit in the foreground.

- Graphic display speed options, which you can scroll through in the box at the bottom of the dialog box. The choices include maintaining the screen snapshot on the hard disk (Save for Fast Display), keeping it in RAM (Conserve Disk Space), or creating and keeping it on the hard disk only when the document containing the pictures is open (Save While Open).

Pictures imported into Ami Pro are displayed on the screen. The picture displayed is called a *screen snapshot*, a low-resolution representation of the final printout. Unless you are almost out of disk space, using Save for Fast Display, the default graphic display speed option, makes the most sense.

CUSTOMIZING YOUR PRINTER SETUP

The Printer Setup option on the File menu allows you to make certain specifications about your printer, such as the orientation it will use, without having to exit Ami Pro and use the Control Panel in the Main program group. When you select Printer Setup, you will see the Select Printer dialog box, shown at the top of Figure 3.12. Click on the Setup button to see a dialog box for your printer. The lower dialog box in Figure 3.12 is for a PostScript printer.

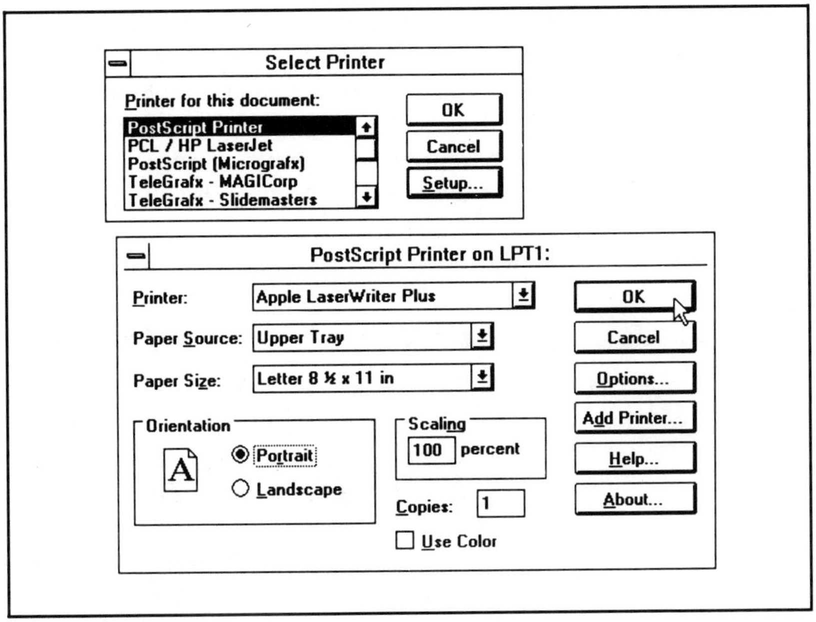

Figure 3.12: Printer Setup dialog boxes

SETTING VIEW OPTIONS

You can select what you see on the Ami Pro screen by choosing Preferences from the View menu. This displays the View Preferences dialog box, shown in Figure 3.13.

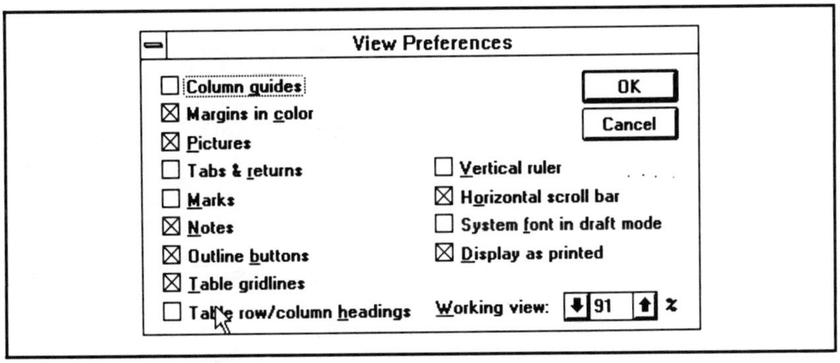

Figure 3.13: View Preferences dialog box

Through this dialog box, you can turn display of various on or off the items on your screen. For example, if you would like to be able to identify the end of a paragraph, click on the check box next to Tabs & Returns. This will place a distinctive paragraph mark at the end of paragraphs. In the box in the lower-right corner of the dialog box, you can adjust the magnification of Ami Pro's Working view, which is described in Chapter 2.

PRINTING YOUR DOCUMENTS

Printing within a Windows application is very simple because Windows handles all printer operations. When you are ready to print a document, open it and choose Print from the File menu. You can change the settings in the Print dialog box, or just click on OK to print the document.

Follow these steps to print the sample document you created in Chapter 2:

1. Open the SWEET.SAM document.

2. Pull down the File menu and select Print. You will see the dialog box shown in Figure 3.14.

This dialog box allows you to print your document in several different ways. For now, accept the default settings. Ami Pro's other printing options are described in the following sections.

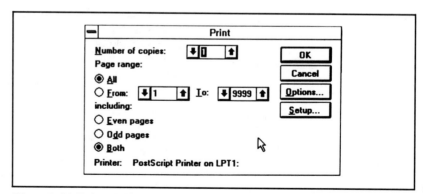

Figure 3.14: Print dialog box

If you are printing to a PostScript laser printer, pull down the Control menu and select Control Panel. Double-click on the printer icon and click on Configure in the dialog box that appears. Find the Timeouts area. Make sure the Transmission Retry text box is set to 999. This prevents Windows from giving up too soon on a complex document that is taking longer than usual to be interpreted by the printer.

If you are using a laser printer to print on both sides of pages, print odd pages, select Options, click on Reverse Order, flip the stack of pages over, and print the even pages. If you are printing on fanfold paper, print odd pages on one side, turn the whole stack of fanfold paper over, and print the even pages on the back.

3. Make sure your printer is turned on and on-line, and then click on OK.

Ami Pro will begin printing the pages, and you can see the results of the work you did in the previous chapter.

PRINTING COPIES AND SPECIFIC PAGES

In the Print dialog box, you can specify how many copies will be generated by entering a value other than 1 in the Number of Copies text box. Ami Pro will print all the copies of each page together, unless you select Collate in the Print Options box, as described below. For example, if you choose to print two copies of a document, Ami Pro will print two copies of page 1, two copies of page 2, and so on.

If you do not want to print all the pages in the document, select From in the Page Range section and use the arrows on the sides of the From and To boxes to specify the first and last pages of the printout, or double-click on the boxes and type in page numbers. You can print any range of pages from 1 to 9999.

You can also select to print out even or odd pages. This is useful when you are printing double-sided pages. The default in the Including section is to print both odd and even pages.

SPECIFYING WHAT AND HOW TO PRINT

Ami Pro provides printing options that allow you to specify exactly what you want to print and how it will be printed. Click on the Options button in the Print dialog box to see the Print Options dialog box, shown in Figure 3.15. In this dialog box, you can choose from the following options:

- Reverse Order: Prints from the last page to the first.
- Collate: When used with multiple copies, causes each copy of the document to be printed in its entirety before the next copy prints.
- Crop Marks: Prints lines that show the size of the actual page. When you are producing a page that is smaller than

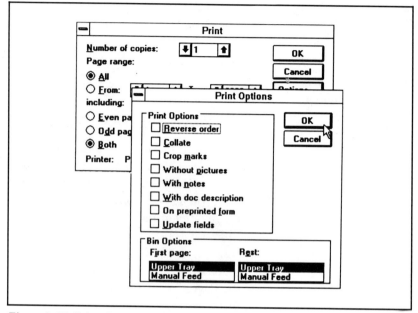

Figure 3.15: Print Options dialog box

Printing collated copies takes more time than printing uncollated copies, particularly with a laser printer, because the printer must be sent the complete page each time it is printed. For uncollated pages, the program can send all relevant information to the printer and then command it to make a given number of copies of the page.

Use the Without Pictures option when you are printing a proof copy of a document.

the sheet of paper you are printing on, you can use crop marks to tell the printer where the page should be trimmed.

- **Without Pictures:** Prints just the text of the document without graphics, which saves a great deal of time.

- **With Notes:** Causes all notes to be printed at the end of the document. The initials of the person who entered the note appears in the text at the position of the note. (Adding notes to documents is described in Chapter 4.)

- **With Doc Description:** Prints a cover page for the document that contains the document description you entered in the Save As dialog box.

- **On Preprinted Forms:** Prevents protected text, lines, and shades associated with frames and tables from printing. Use this if you are printing on preprinted forms and your document includes these items just to ensure the text will be placed properly on the form.

- Update Fields: Updates power fields at the time of print-out. (Using power fields is discussed in Chapter 13.)

- Bin Options: Selects the bin from which paper for the print-out will be taken. You can specify where the first page is taken from and where the remainder of the paper is taken from. For example, you can use this to print a cover sheet on letterhead or other higher quality paper.

CHANGING THE PRINTER SETUP

To access the Control Panel, which is also available in the Main program group, pull down the Ami Pro window Control menu and select Control Panel.

If you need to change your printer setup before printing, click on the Setup button in the Print dialog box. This displays the Print Setup dialog box, which is the same as the dialog box that appears when you click on the Setup button in the Select Printer dialog box (see Figure 3.12).

The options in this dialog box depend on the printer you selected when you set up Windows. You can select a different printer by clicking on the downward-pointing arrow at the right end of the Printer list box.

Here are some options that may appear in the Print Setup dialog box:

- Paper Source: Sets the paper source. Click on the downward-pointing arrow at the right end of the list box to see your options.

- Paper Size: Sets the paper size. Click on the downward-pointing arrow to see a list of sizes and their dimensions.

Setting the Orientation causes the printer to make the adjustment. If you select Landscape, you don't have to turn the paper 90 degrees. Windows will make all necessary adjustments to print sideways on the paper.

- Orientation: Specifies which direction the printer will print.

- Scaling: Adjusts the size of the printout. It's only available with PostScript printers. You can print scaled pages (pages altered in size equally in the horizontal and vertical dimensions) from 25 percent to 400 percent of the page size.

- Graphics Resolution: Allows you to adjust the printout resolution (sharpness or clarity) to 75, 150, or 300 dots per inch. Usually, printing at a lower resolution will result in a faster printout.

- Cartridges: Specifies the cartridge installed in your LaserJet-compatible printer. Click on the downward-pointing arrow in the list box to see the available cartridges.

- Memory: Sets the amount of RAM available in your printer. Click on the downward-pointing arrow to select a different amount from the list box.

- Copies: Allows you to select the number of copies of each page the printer should produce.

- Use Color: Allows you to select whether a page should be printed in color (for color printers).

The buttons in the dialog box also depend on the selected printer. The buttons you may see are described in the following sections.

Printing in color frequently takes up to four times as long as printing in black and white. You might want to restrict drafts to black and white and save color for the final product.

Add Printer and Fonts Buttons   If you want to install a different printer, click on the Add Printer button to display the Add Printer dialog box. You will be prompted to insert a disk containing the new printer file into drive A or to type the letter of the drive that holds the printer disk. This disk may be the printer disk from your Windows installation, or it may be a disk that came with your printer. When you click on the OK button in this dialog box, the installation will take place.

The Fonts button allows you to select downloadable fonts for your LaserJet-compatible printer.

Printing to a file is a very useful if you have access to a Post-Script printer but don't own one. You can print to a file, copy the file to a disk, take the disk to a computer attached to a PostScript printer, and use the command COPY filename.ext PRN. The computer will send the data from the file directly to the printer, as if it were a disk drive.

Options Button   The Options button displays a dialog box that allows you to select whether to print to a printer or to a file. If you select File, you are provided with a text box to enter the file name.

The Job Timeout option in this dialog box tells the computer how tolerant it should be of the printer's tendency to take time off. The default is zero seconds. If your printer fails frequently—seems to just die in the middle of a job—and you see a dialog box in Windows complaining that it can't get information to the printer, enter a value in the Job Timeout box.

The Margins option specifies the amount of space allowed at the edge of the page. Selecting None requires greater memory from your printer.

You can choose to download the file header once at the beginning of a session or download it with each printout. If you are printing huge volumes of files, use the former to save time (the header takes about 20 seconds to download). The default selection is to download each time.

There are two visible buttons in the Options dialog box:

- Header: Directs the header information to a file or to the printer. Header information is part of the PostScript program file that establishes parameters.

- Handshake: Allows you to select a hardware handshake or a software handshake. (*Handshake* is the term used to describe how the computer and the printer interact.)

Finally, there is the hidden button. The only way to access the Error Handler button is to press Alt-E while the Options dialog box is open. The Error Handler dialog box will appear, giving you the option of sending error messages to the printer or to a file. If it is directed to the printer, the printer will generate a page with the error handler information printed on it. If it is directed to a file, a file will be created with the error handler information in it.

Help Button The Help button provides a special group of Help screens specifically related to your printer. For example, a step-by-step procedure for downloading the header file once at the beginning of a print session is provided.

Now that you know the basics of how to create and print documents with Ami Pro, you are ready to use the features for improving your documents. The following chapters describe how to work with your text.

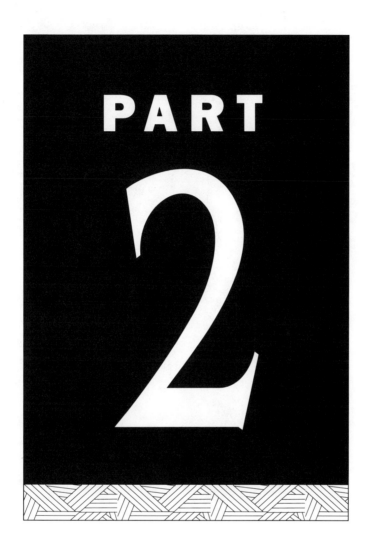

PART

2

Working with Your Documents

CHAPTER 4

Working with Longer Documents

WHEN YOU ARE WORKING WITH DOCUMENTS THAT will be longer than a few pages, your requirements are more demanding. You will need a way to handle portions of your document and go to specific places in your text. Ami Pro provides features that take care of these aspects, as well as a find and replace function, spelling checker, and thesaurus. You can even protect text from being changed.

In this chapter, you will learn how to use Ami Pro's features to manage your longer projects.

HANDLING BIG PROJECTS WITH MASTER DOCUMENTS

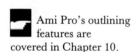
Ami Pro's outlining features are covered in Chapter 10.

If you are working on longer writing projects, such as books, monographs, or theses, you will find it much more convenient to keep your individual parts separate, maintaining individual chapters, sections, or other divisions. It helps you to organize your information, particularly if you are using an outline. And your work will be faster because the computer will have to work less. It takes less time for the machine to deal with ten 10,000-word pieces, for example, than it does to process a single 100,000-word piece.

A master document is often called a *publication* in desktop publishing programs.

When you divide a project into sections, you still need a way to manage the whole document the sections will form. You must ensure that the files print sequentially and that page numbers are updated properly as you move from section to section. In Ami Pro, you can easily manage the files by incorporating them into a master document. Then you can set up a table of contents and index for your master document.

CREATING FILES FOR A MASTER DOCUMENT

In this section, we will create three simple documents that contain three different styles. These will serve as the files for a master document. We will also mark an index entry so that we can generate an index for the document.

Follow these steps to create the files:

1. Select New from the File menu and click OK in the New dialog box.

2. Type the following lines, pressing ◄─┘ after each one.

   Chapter 1

   Subhead 1

   Body Text

3. With the text cursor below *Body Text*, pull down the Page menu and select Breaks.

4. When the Breaks dialog box appears, make sure Insert Page Break is selected (with a black dot in the button to the left of the text). If it isn't, click on the button. Then click on OK.

5. You will find yourself on page 2. Go back to page 1 by clicking above the scroll box in the scroll bar until you see the text you entered.

6. Click on *Chapter 1*, or use the cursor-movement keys to move the text cursor to it, place the mouse pointer on the text style indicator in the status bar (which says Body Text, unless you have changed to another style), and click on it.

The F8 beside Title on the styles list means that you could simply press the F8 function key rather than go through the menu to select this style. The F7 next to Subhead indicates that pressing F7 applies this style.

7. Select Title. If Title isn't listed, you have changed from the default style to some other style. Pull down the Style menu and select Use Another Style Sheet. In the dialog box that appears, double-click on the ˜DEFAULT.STY style sheet in the Change to list box.

8. Click on *Subhead 1* (or use the cursor-movement keys to move to it).

9. Press F7 to apply the Subhead style to this text.

10. Drag the mouse pointer through the text *Body Text* to select it.

11. Pull down the Edit menu and select Mark Text.

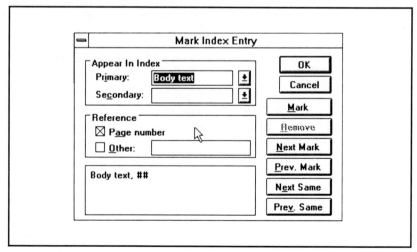

As with all index generators, Ami Pro requires that you specially mark index entries before it can generate an index.

12. In the dialog box that appears, select Index Entry to see the dialog box shown in Figure 4.1.

13. Click on OK in the Mark Index Entry dialog box to close the dialog box and mark the word as an index entry.

14. Press Ctrl-S to save the text and type the name **CHAP01.SAM** in the Save As dialog box.

15. To create the second file, drag the mouse cursor over the *1* in *Chapter 1* at the top of the page and type **2**, so the text says *Chapter 2*. Note that the text you type takes on the style of the surrounding text.

16. Pull down the File menu, select Save As, and save the text as **CHAP02**.SAM.

17. Change *Chapter 2* to **Chapter 3**.

18. Select Save As from the File menu and name this file **CHAP03.SAM**.

You should now have three files on your disk in the current directory named CHAP01.SAM, CHAP02.SAM, and CHAP03.SAM. Each file contains a title, a subhead, and an index item.

Figure 4.1: Mark Index Entry dialog box

CREATING A MASTER DOCUMENT

After you have set up some of the files for a project, you are ready to create the master document for them. Open a new document and define it as the master by selecting Master Document from the File menu. Then, in the Master Document dialog box, specify the files you wish to include. We will do this now to create a master document for our three files.

A quick way to close a window is to double-click on the Control-menu box, often called the *close box*.

1. Pull down the File menu and select Close to close the window containing CHAP03.SAM.

2. Pull down the File menu and select New to open a new, untitled document.

3. Pull down the File menu and select Master Document. The Master Document dialog box will appear.

4. Click on CHAP01.SAM in the Files list box, and then click on the >>Include>> button.

5. Click on CHAP02.SAM, then the >>Include>> button.

6. Click on CHAP03.SAM, then the >>Include>> button.

All three files should now appear in the Master Doc Files list box, as shown in Figure 4.2.

You can add a file anywhere within the Master Doc Files list, not just to the end. To do so, click on the file name in the Master Doc Files list box that should follow the new file. Then select the file you wish to add in the Files list box and click on Include. The newly added file will be placed ahead of the file you highlighted in the Master Doc Files list.

To remove a file from the master document, click on the name of the file in the Master Doc Files list box and click on the Remove button.

CREATING A TABLE OF CONTENTS AND AN INDEX

Through the Master Document Options dialog box, accessed by clicking on the Options button in the Master Document dialog box, you can generate a table of contents and an index for all the files associated

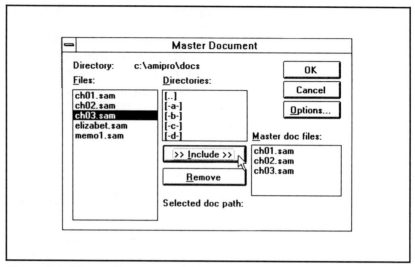

Figure 4.2: Master Document dialog box with three files included in the master

with the master document. The table of contents can be generated immediately because it's based on styles. It will look for a specific style to stand for a chapter title, major head, subhead, and so on.

You can specify the format for the table of contents through the TOC Options dialog box, which is displayed when you select TOC Options from the Master Document Options dialog box.

Follow these steps to set up a table of contents and index for our sample master document:

1. In the Master Document dialog box, click on Options to display the Master Document Options dialog box, shown in Figure 4.3.

2. In the Master Document Options dialog box, click on Generate TOC, and then click on Generate Index.

Ami Pro needs to know where to store the table of contents and index it creates. Type a name for the file in the Output File text box. If you do not want to save it in the current directory, shown below the Output File box, use the Directories list box to choose another one.

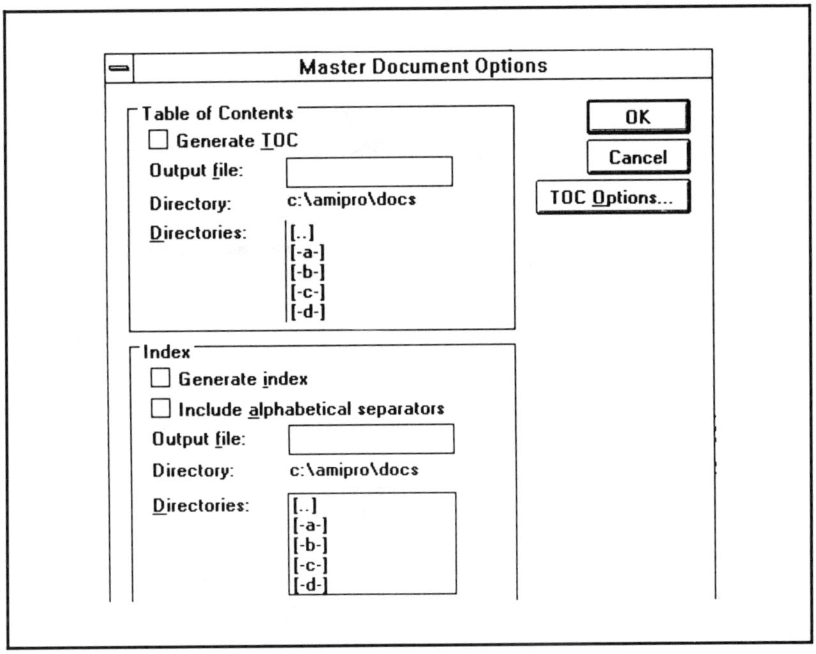

Figure 4.3: Master Document Options dialog box

3. Click on the Output File text box in the Table of Contents area and type **CHAPTOC**.

4. Click on the Output File text box in the Index area and type **CHAPIND**.

5. Click on the TOC Options button to display the TOC Options dialog box, shown in Figure 4.4.

In the TOC Options box, you can assign a style and page number to each level of table of contents' entries. When you choose to have the page number appear for a level, you can specify a separator, or leader, to appear between the entry and the number and right align the number. If you type a character in the Separator box (typically, periods are used to create dot leaders), Ami Pro will insert the leaders between the heads and the page numbers.

6. In the Level 1 area, click on the Page Number box, the Right Align Page Number box, and finally the Style text box.

You may want to include the page numbers of only chapters and major heads and just list the secondary heads. Also, although you may be accustomed to seeing leaders, often they detract from the appearance of the page. Create a sample table of contents, like the one in this section, to see whether you really want a string of dots between the name of the section and the page number.

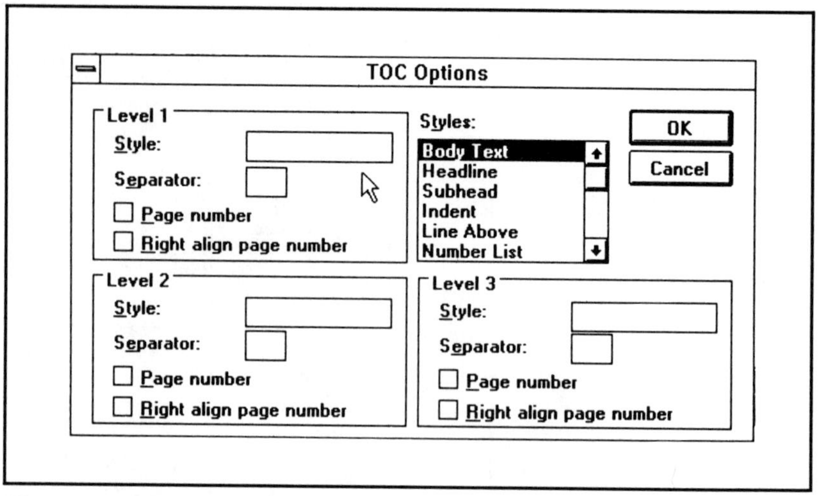

Figure 4.4: TOC Options dialog box

7. Click on title in the Styles list box in the top-right area of the dialog box to assign this style to level 1 entries.

8. In the Level 2 area, click on Page Number, Right Align Page Number, and Style. Then click on Subhead in the Styles list box.

9. Click on OK in the TOC Options dialog box, then in the Master Document Options dialog box, then in the Master Document dialog box.

You can now generate the table of contents and index at any time, as described in the following section.

GENERATING THE TABLE OF CONTENTS AND AN INDEX

After you have selected the options for your table of contents and index, you can produce them by selecting the TOC, Index option from the Tools menu. Here are the steps:

1. Pull down the Tools menu and select TOC, Index. You will see the dialog box shown in Figure 4.5.

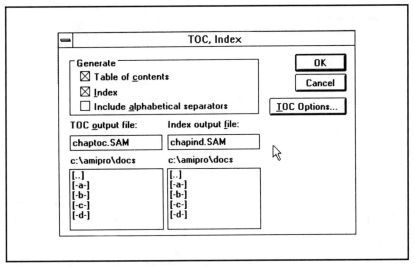

Figure 4.5: TOC, Index dialog box

This dialog box also includes a TOC Options button, which displays the same dialog box as the TOC Options button in the Master Document Options dialog box (Figure 4.4). This allows you to change the format of the table of contents before generating it.

2. Click on OK.

3. When Ami Pro asks whether you want to save the untitled document (the master), click on Yes.

4. In the Save As dialog box, give the file the name **CHAPMD.**

After CHAPMD.SAM has been saved to disk, Ami Pro will proceed to create your table of contents and index.

Anytime you want to generate another table of contents or index, just load the master document file (CHAPMD.SAM in this example). When you select Master Document from the File menu, you will find all the information already in place.

SPEEDING TO A LOCATION IN THE TEXT

Trying to locate something in your document can be frustrating. This is especially true when your document has had a chance to age a bit and slip from your memory. You can scroll through the document with the scroll bar, move from page to page by clicking on the up and down arrows in the status bar, and move quickly through the text using keyboard and mouse shortcuts. However, none of these techniques will take you to a specific place in the text.

If you want to go to a particular place in a document, you can set bookmarks, use Ami Pro's Go To command, or add line numbers. These techniques are described in the following sections.

Another way to locate a particular piece of information is to use the Find & Replace command on the Edit menu. Finding and replacing text are described later in the chapter.

FINDING YOUR PLACE WITH BOOKMARKS

While you are working on a book or long manuscript, you may find that you are missing information or need to check on some of your material. When you will need to return to a specific portion of your document for any reason, you can leave an electronic bookmark there.

To add a bookmark, move the cursor to where you want to place it and select Bookmarks from the Edit menu. You will see the dialog box shown in Figure 4.6.

Type a name for your bookmark in the Bookmark text box. The name can be as long as the width of the text box, so be as descriptive as possible. The name can include any characters except spaces. After you enter the name, click on Add to establish the bookmark.

You can also use Ctrl-H, the Go To command, to go to the next bookmark. If you want to go to bookmarks sequentially, use Ctrl-H. If you want to go to a specific bookmark, use the Bookmarks dialog box.

When you want to return to the text that contains the bookmark, pull down the Edit menu and select Bookmarks. If you have set many bookmarks, the list box will have a scroll bar. If necessary, use it to scroll through the list until the bookmark you want to move to appears. Double-click on the name of the bookmark, or click once to select it and then click on the Go To button. The text cursor will instantly go to the bookmark, regardless of its position in the document.

After you no longer need a bookmark, you can delete it. In the Bookmarks dialog box, click on the name of the bookmark you want to delete, and then click on the Remove button. The bookmark will disappear from the list, as well as from your text.

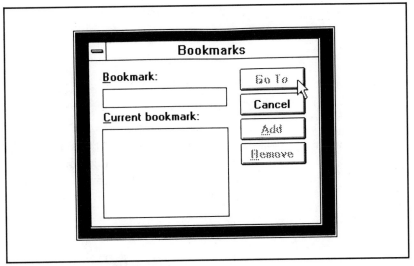

Figure 4.6: Bookmarks dialog box

GETTING THERE WITH THE GO TO COMMAND

The Go To command will take you to a specific place in the text. You can use it to go to a page number and the first or last page in the document. It will also take you to the next occurrence of the following items:

- Bookmark
- Header text
- Floating header/footer mark
- Layout change
- Footer text
- Next field
- Footnote mark
- Note
- Footnote text
- Frame

- Tab ruler

- Hard page break

- Tab ruler mark

Another way to open the Go To dialog box is by clicking on the page number area at the right end of the status bar.

To use Go To, press Ctrl-G or pull down the Edit menu and select Go To. You will see the dialog box shown in Figure 4.7.

Click on the option that corresponds to where you want to go. If it is a page number, scroll through the Page Number box until that number appears, or double-click on the text box and type the page number, and then click on Go To. If you want to move to one of the Next Item choices, click on the item and then click on the Go To button (or press Ctrl-H).

NUMBERING LINES

The methods described so far take you to a particular place in text by displaying it on your screen. Ami Pro also provides line numbering, which makes it easier to find information in the printed text as

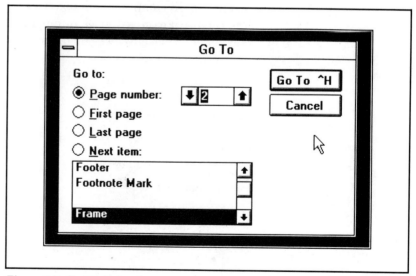

Figure 4.7: Go To dialog box

well as in the on-screen version. When you turn on line numbering, the line numbers appear in the left margin of the document, a short distance from the text.

To number lines, open the file that you want to contain line numbers and select Line Numbering from the Page menu. You will see the Line Numbering dialog box, as shown in Figure 4.8.

In this dialog box, you can set numbering for every line, every other line, or every fifth line. Or, you can replace the 1 in the text box in the Every 1 Lines option to specify which lines you want to number.

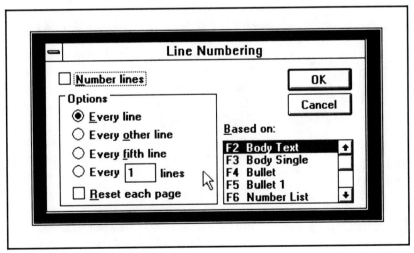 You may have to scroll to the left side of the screen to see the numbers.

The default setting is for the line numbering to increase throughout the document. If you want the numbering to begin with 1 on each page, click on the Reset Each Page box to turn on this option.

To actually add the line numbers, click on the Number Lines check box at the top of the dialog box. Finally, select the style of the line numbers themselves by clicking on a style in the Based on list box.

Click on OK. You will see line numbering on the screen, as shown in the example in Figure 4.9. The numbering will also appear on the printed pages.

Figure 4.8: Line Numbering dialog box

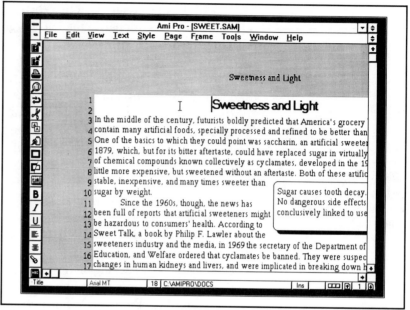

Figure 4.9: Numbered lines in text

FINDING AND REPLACING TEXT

When you need to find certain text and replace it with other text, or just locate a particular text string, use the Find & Replace command on the Edit menu (or use the keyboard shortcut, Ctrl-F). In the Find & Replace dialog box, type the text you want to find and the replacement text (if any). Both text strings can be up to 40 characters long. Then click on Find to just locate the text, or Replace All to substitute your replacement text for every occurrence of the original text automatically.

For example, suppose you have written a memo in which you have referred to the president of your company as a "low-down skunk," but later you decide that it would be more politic to call him an "exalted humanitarian." To save your job, you fill in the Find & Replace dialog box as shown in Figure 4.10, and then click on the Replace All button.

Your worries are over, unless you accidentally misspelled *low-down skunk* somewhere in the text. Ami Pro will not find anything except the exact text you enter in the Find text box, and your boss may not

If you want to just find text and not replace it, don't fill in the Replace With text box. Just click on the Find button.

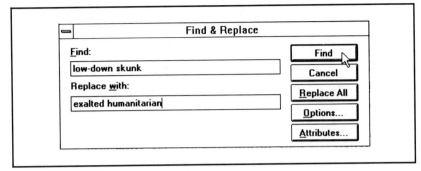

Figure 4.10: Find & Replace dialog box

Remember that whenever you change text automatically, you must go back and reread it.

take kindly to being referred to as a *low-down skink*. However, you can use wildcards to search for text, as described in the following section.

Rather than choose Replace All, you can replace text on a case-by-case basis by clicking on Find after filling in the Find and Replace with boxes. Then you can choose to keep or replace each instance as Ami Pro finds it. Controlling the find and search operation is described shortly.

WIDENING YOUR SEARCH WITH WILDCARDS

If you are familiar with DOS, you have probably used the question mark and asterisk wildcards. For example, DIR C?T will locate files whose names are three characters long, begin with C, and end with T, including CAT, CRT, and CST. DIR C* will locate any file in the current directory that starts with the letter C, including CALIFOR, CSCAN, and CESIUM.

The wildcards work almost the same way in the Find & Replace dialog box as they do in DOS. For example, *t* will locate any word that starts with *t*, such as *the*, *there*, and *televise*. You can also use the * wildcard to subsitiute for the initial characters in a word. For example, *e will locate the same word as the previous example.

When you use wildcards in your replacement text, the text that is replaced with the wildcard will be unchanged. For example, if you enter *c?n* in the Find box and *b?t* in the Replace with box, you will change every instance of *can* to *bat*.

If you are using wildcards in your find and replace operation, you will have to turn off the Whole Word Only option, as described below.

REFINING YOUR SEARCH
WITH FIND AND REPLACE OPTIONS

You can refine your find and replace operations by making selections in the Find & Replace Options dialog box. Click on Options in the Find & Replace dialog box to see the dialog box shown in Figure 4.11.

You can turn off or on the following Find and Replace options:

- Whole Word Only: Finds the text only if the text is surrounded by spaces or separators (periods, commas, and other punctuation). For example, with Whole Word Only selected (the default setting), specifying *for* in the Find text box will find only that word. But if this option is turned off, Ami Pro will find any word that contains those letters in that order, such as *fortitude* and *affordable*.

- Exact Case: Looks for text that matches the case of the text in the Find text box. For example, with Exact Case selected, searching for *FOR* will find only those uppercase letters, not *For*, *for*, *fOr*, or *fOR*.

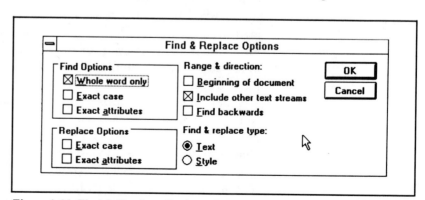 If you followed the exercise in Chapter 2, you used the Find & Replace Attributes dialog box to replace normal text with italic text.

- Exact Attributes: Finds the text only if it matches the attribute specified in the Find & Replace Attributes dialog box, which is displayed when you click on this option. For example, if you are looking for a boldfaced word, choose Exact Attributes, and then check the Bold box in the Find Attributes section of the Find & Replace Attributes dialog box.

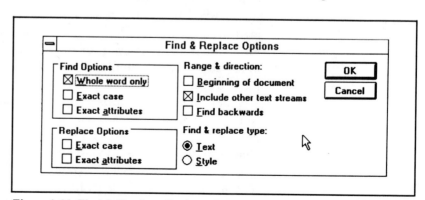

Figure 4.11: Find & Replace Options dialog box

The Range & Direction options in the Find & Replace Options dialog box specify which text will be searched, as follows:

You can select both Beginning of Document and Include Other Text Streams.

- Beginning of Document: Searches for text from the beginning of the document and proceeds to the end. It searches only the text in the main part of the document, ignoring footnotes, headers, and so on.

- Include Other Text Streams: Searches all the text in the document, including the footnotes and other *streams* (types of text) that are not part of the main text of the document.

- Find Backwards: Searches backwards from the text cursor to the beginning of the document. It searches within only the stream in which the cursor is located. For example, if the cursor is in the header text, the headers will be searched back to the beginning of the document. If the cursor is in the main document text, the search will be limited to the main document text.

If none of these boxes is selected, the search will proceed from the current cursor location to the end of the text.

Below the Range & Direction section of the Find & Replace Options dialog box are the two choices for the type of find and replace operation. You can select Style to search for styles as well as text. This will help you locate, for example, all the chapter headings in a text or all the figure captions.

CONTROLLING THE
FIND AND REPLACE OPERATION

While Ami Pro is finding and replacing text, you will see the dialog box shown in Figure 4.12. Unless you have selected Replace All, you can take charge of the operation by clicking on the buttons in this dialog box, as follows:

- Replace & Find Next: Re- places the Find text with the Replace with text.

- Replace Remaining: Quickly replaces all the rest of the Find text without any further confirmation.

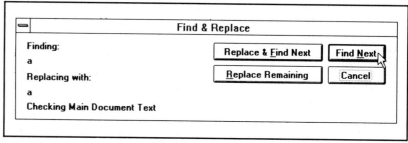

Figure 4.12: Find & Replace dialog box with found text

- Find Next: Skips this instance of the text and looks for the next.

- Cancels: Halts the find and replace operation.

USING THE SPELLING CHECKER

Programmers have developed astounding compression techniques to reduce the size of spelling checker files; if you open such a file with a text editor, it might not look like a dictionary to you.

A spelling checker is now a standard feature in a word processor. Basically, it compares each word in your document against a look-up table laid out a little bit like a dictionary. Unfortunately, a spelling checker cannot eliminate the need for you to read a document before printing it and sending it out into the world. A word can be misspelled so that it looks like another word that is spelled correctly. For example, *form* for *from* and *to* for *too* are two common mistakes. Therefore, you should always reread your writing and ask someone else to read it, just to be sure.

CHOOSING SPELLING CHECKER OPTIONS

In Ami Pro, a *text stream* is the type of the text in the document. For example, footnote text is a text stream and header text is another text stream.

Ami Pro's Spell Check command is on the Tools menu. Alternatively, you can click on the ABC icon in the icon palette to access the spelling checker without going through a menu. When you select Spell Check, you will see the dialog box shown in Figure 4.13.

By default, Ami Pro will check the spelling in all the text, from the beginning of the document. You can check from the current location to the end of the document by clicking on the Beginning of Document check box to deselect it. If you turn off Include Other Text Streams, Ami Pro will check the spelling in only the stream where the text cursor is currently resting.

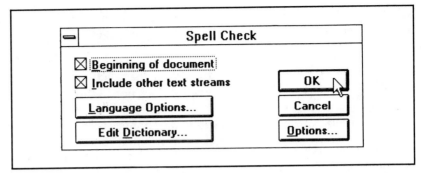

Figure 4.13: Spell Check dialog box

The Language Options button allows you to select a different language file, if you are writing in one of the languages supported by Ami Pro. The Edit Dictionary button lets you edit your personal dictionary, looking for misspelled words that inevitably will worm their way into it. You will learn how to edit your personal dictionary in the next section.

If you click on Options, you will see the Spell Check Options dialog box, shown in Figure 4.14. You can control how the spelling check works by selecting and deselecting the options in this dialog box:

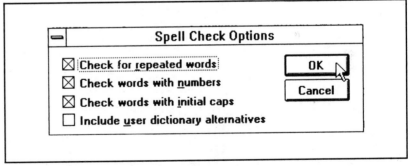

Figure 4.14: Spell Check Options dialog box

- Check for Repeated Words: Looks for identical words that appear together, such as *the the* or *is is*.

- Check Words with Numbers: Checks the spelling of the text part of words that are in combination with numbers.

Turn off Check Words with Initial Caps to avoid frequent halts when you are editing a page full of names. Also, since the user dictionary isn't compressed, using it takes longer than using the standard dictionary, so you might want to leave it deselected unless you are in a specialized technical field where you use many words that are not in Ami Pro's dictionary.

- Check Words with Initial Caps: Checks words that begin with a capital letter, including proper names.

- Include User Dictionary Alternatives: Provides suggestions from your user dictionary when Ami Pro encounters a word it does not recognize.

You can make changes in the Spell Check Options dialog box, and then click on OK, or click on Cancel to accept the default settings. Click on OK in the Spell Check dialog box to begin the checking process.

SKIPPING AND CORRECTING WORDS

When Ami Pro finds a word that is not in its dictionary, you will see the dialog box shown in Figure 4.15. The word appears at the top of the box and in the Replace with box. In the Alternatives list box, you can see the words Ami Pro suggests as alternative spellings of the highlighted word.

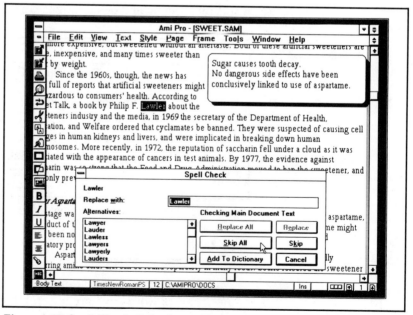

Figure 4.15: Spell Check dialog box with an unrecognized word

If the word is actually spelled correctly, you have three choices: Skip All, Skip, or Add to Dictionary. Skip All will add the currently selected word to a temporary dictionary that will disappear when this spelling check is completed. Skip continues the process without changing the word, but the spelling checker will stop on it again the next time it appears. Add to Dictionary enters the word in a personal dictionary file for specialized words. If you think the correctly spelled word occurs only one time in the document, choose Skip; there is no point in wasting RAM by clicking on Skip All or disk space by clicking on Add to Dictionary. If it is used frequently, but just in this document, choose Skip All. Choose Add to Dictionary if the word may appear in your other documents.

If Ami Pro has found a genuine error, correct it in the Replace with box, or click on one of the suggestions in the Alternatives list (you can scroll through the list to see all the possibilities). Once the correction is made, the Replace All and Replace buttons become selectable. Replace puts the text in the text box in place of the highlighted text in the document. Click on Replace All to have Ami Pro automatically change all occurrences of the word, without consulting you.

If you have a repeated word in your document, you will see the message box shown in Figure 4.16. Click on OK, and you will be returned to the Spell Check dialog box. From there, you can change the second instance of the word or skip it if it is repeated intentionally.

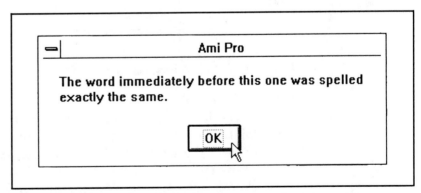

Figure 4.16: Message box alerting you to a repeated word

EDITING YOUR USER DICTIONARY

After you have added words to your user dictionary (by choosing Add to Dictionary in the Spell Check dialog box), you should regularly read that dictionary because you may have accidentally added misspelled words to it.

Click on Edit Dictionary in the Spell Check dialog box to open a new window containing a file with your personal dictionary, as shown in the example in Figure 4.17. To remove a word from the dictionary, drag through the word with the mouse pointer and press Del.

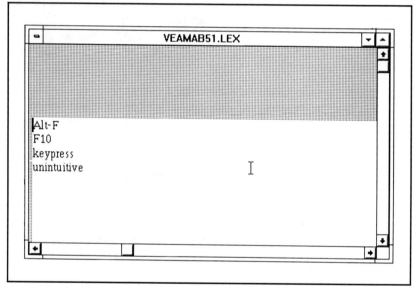

Figure 4.17: A user dictionary displayed for editing

You can also add words to the file while it is displayed. If your profession has a special vocabulary, enter as many words as you can think of into the user dictionary. Then use the Spell Check command to check the spelling in the user dictionary. When Ami Pro comes across a word it doesn't recognize, click on Add to Dictionary. Then close the version of the user dictionary on your screen without saving it. This will prevent you from entering words in the user dictionary that already exist in the regular dictionary.

VIVID, STIRRING, DRAMATIC WRITING WITH THE THESAURUS

Almost every writer finds that sometimes the word that immediately springs to mind isn't the right word for the particular situation. Thesauruses not only assist you in finding the right word, but they can also help you learn synonyms and antonyms, thus actually increasing your vocabulary.

To use the thesaurus, highlight the word you want to find a synonym for by dragging through it with the mouse cursor. Then pull down the Tools menu and select Thesaurus to see the Thesaurus dialog box. Figure 4.18 shows an example of the dialog box that appears when the highlighted word is *commence*.

The Thesaurus dialog box displays the word being looked up, its alternative meanings (if there are any), and the synonyms for the currently selected meaning, listed alphabetically. The first synonym appears automatically in the Replace with text box. At the bottom of the dialog box, you can see the dictionary meaning of the word in the Replace with box.

Use the thesaurus to help make your writing clearer and more cogent. Search for the word that is the most precise, not the longer, stuffier one.

An interesting sidelight for the theologically preoccupied: Looking up *creator*, *patriarch*, and *originator*, I was unable to make the thesaurus come up with the word *God*. So I entered this word directly in the Replace with text box and looked it up. I discovered that—at least in Ami Pro's thesaurus—there is no *God*.

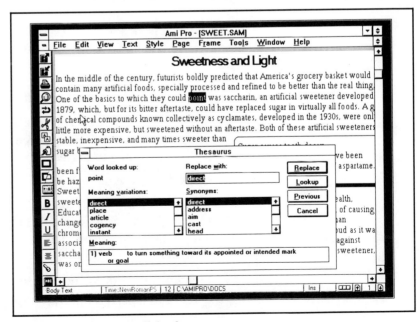

Figure 4.18: Thesaurus dialog box

Another use for a thesaurus is as a cure for the "tip-of-the-tongue" syndrome. If you can't think of the right word, type the closest word you can come up with in the Replace with box and click on Lookup. The Thesaurus dialog box will then show alternative meanings and synonyms for that word. Lookup always looks up the word that appears in the Replace with text box. This means that you can enter your own word or click on any of the words in the list boxes.

Occasionally, you will discover that you are in a blind alley—the word you are searching for doesn't lie down the chain of references you are pursuing. In this case, you can back up by clicking on Previous. The Replace with box will show the previous word you looked up, and its synonyms will be listed again.

PROTECTING TEXT

In some cases, you may want to make sure that no changes are made to text. You might want to protect parts or all of a document from being edited by yourself or someone else. This can be especially useful if you are working on a network and others may access your files.

To protect text from editing, select the text you do not want changed, choose Mark Text from the Edit menu, and then choose Protected Text.

To see just how protected your text can be, follow these steps:

1. Clear the screen by selecting all the text and pressing Del.

2. Type three sentences: **This text is not protected. This text is protected. This text is not protected.** (Try to guess which text we are going to protect.)

3. Click the mouse pointer just after the first period of the text on the screen.

4. Hold down the Shift key and click the mouse pointer just after the second period. The entire second sentence should be highlighted.

5. Pull down the Edit menu and select Mark Text.

6. Select Protected Text from the Mark Text menu. The text is now protected.

7. Click the mouse pointer on the text. Note that the text cursor cannot be placed within the protected text.

8. Use the cursor keys to move to the text. You won't be able to.

9. Place the mouse cursor in the middle of the first sentence and drag to the middle of the third sentence. Note that you can select protected text.

10. Press the Del key. Note that you can delete protected text. It's not very well protected, is it?

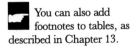 The best way to protect text is to click on the Lock for Annotations box in the Doc Info dialog box (accessed by choosing Doc Info from the File menu).

You can't absolutely protect text. Marking it and selecting Protected Text will prevent anyone from moving to the text with the cursor keys or placing the text cursor within the text by clicking with the mouse. However, you can delete it by placing the text cursor after it and pressing the Backspace key or by cutting it, as you did in the above example. You can also copy and paste it.

ADDING NOTES TO DOCUMENTS

You may want to leave notes to yourself or others in some of your documents. For example, you might leave a note about something you need to add later or about suggestions you would like to make to the writer.

To add a note, select Insert from the Edit menu, and then select Note. Type your note in the dialog box that appears. When you are finished, double-click on the close box.

You can print the notes in the document, as described in Chapter 3.

The note is indicated by a tiny colored rectangle at the text cursor position where you chose to insert the note. To read the note, double-click on the colored rectangle that indicates the note position. Click once on the close box to see your additional options. You can delete the current note by selecting Remove This Note, or you can remove all notes by selecting Remove All Notes.

CREATING FOOTNOTES AND ENDNOTES

You can also add footnotes to tables, as described in Chapter 13.

Footnotes and endnotes are used to provide references and supplementary information in technical reports, research papers, and other types of documents. Ami Pro provides the Footnotes option on the Tools menu for inserting footnote reference numbers and text.

INSERTING FOOTNOTES

To create a footnote, click where you want the reference number to appear (next to the text that you want to associate with the footnote), pull down the Tools menu, and select Footnotes. You will see the dialog box shown in Figure 4.19.

Make sure Insert Footnote is selected and click on OK. The text cursor will appear in a footnote area at the bottom of the current page. Type the text you want to appear in the footnote. To return to the main text, scroll up and click where you want to resume typing.

The footnote superscript reference number will appear in the text, and the footnote will be at the bottom of the page. As you continue to add footnotes, Ami Pro will number them sequentially throughout the document. If you move the text, the footnote will go to the bottom of its page, and all the footnotes will be renumbered to match the new order.

To edit a footnote, either scroll down to it or select Footnotes from the Tools menu and choose Edit Footnote. To delete a footnote, drag through the superscript footnote reference number in the text to select it, and then press the Del key. When the reference number is deleted, the footnote text is also removed.

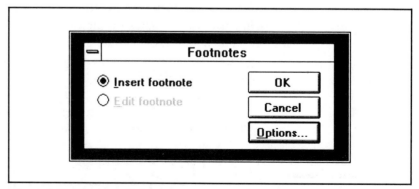

Figure 4.19: Footnote dialog box

FORMATTING FOOTNOTES AND ENDNOTES

You can alter the appearance of your footnotes or move them to the end of the text to create endnotes. To see your options for working with footnotes, select Footnotes from the Tools menu and click on the Options button in the Footnote dialog box.

In the Footnote Options dialog box, shown in Figure 4.20, click on the Make End Notes check box to make the footnotes appear at the end of the document.

The default numbering system for footnotes begins with 1 at the beginning of the document and continues to the end of the document. You can check the Reset Number on Each Page option to restart footnote numbering on each page. Change the number in the Starting Number text box to begin with a number other than 1.

Footnotes are separated from the rest of the text by a line. In the lower section of the Footnote Options dialog box, you can specify the separator line and its length (by default, it extends from the right margin to the left margin). You can also set the footnote's indentation from the right edge of the paper.

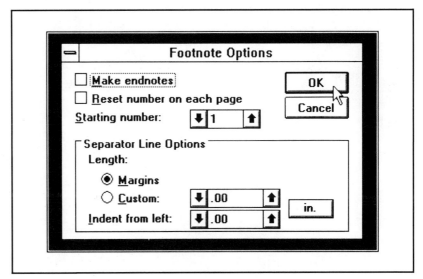

Figure 4.20: Footnote Options dialog box

CHAPTER 5

Styling Your Text

IN A PROFESSIONAL DOCUMENT, THE APPEARANCE of the text is just as important as its contents. The typeface, character styles, paragraph formatting, and page layout all convey a message to the reader.

This chapter begins with an introduction to fonts and typefaces, which are an integral part of your document's style. Then you will learn more about using Ami Pro's style sheets and creating your own styles to format your text consistently. Page formatting is covered in the final sections.

FONT BASICS

In the simplest terms, a font is a group of characters that look good together. But the individual members of a font share much more than a harmonious appearance. Most people have no trouble telling one font from another.

COMPARING FONTS

In a typeface, very large and very small bowls and exaggerated ascenders and descenders are the mark of older faces that are useful for conveying a sense of tradition and age; smaller variations in the lengths of ascenders and descenders and uniform bowl sizes are generally associated with newer faces, and they communicate newness and modernity.

Fonts are identified by the size and shape of their *descenders* (the part of the *g, j, p, q,* and *y* that drops beneath the baseline), the height of their *ascenders* (the part of the *b, d, f, h, k, l,* and *t* that extend above the x-height, which is the height of the lowercase *x* in a typeface). They are also distinguished by the size and shape of their *bowls* (the holes that appear in the *a, b, d, e, g, o, p,* and *q*). Typically, these bowls are treated in a similar way—some fonts have exaggerated bowls and others have nearly no bowls at all.

Let's put two different fonts on the screen and compare their features.

1. Start Ami Pro and type the following text: **bxg.**

2. Drag the mouse pointer through the text to highlight it, and then select Copy from the Edit menu to place the three letters in the Clipboard.

3. Press the → key to move the cursor to the right end of the text, then ↵.

4. Pull down the Edit menu again and select Paste. You should now have two lines of text that are identical.

5. Move the text cursor to the beginning of the first line, hold down the Shift key, and press the → key until both lines of text are highlighted.

6. Pull down the Text menu and select Font. You will see the dialog box shown in Figure 5.1.

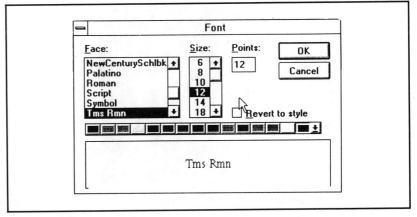

Figure 5.1: Font dialog box

Your list of fonts may be different from the one shown in Figure 5.1. The fonts you have available depend on the printer you selected and the font packages you have installed.

This dialog box contains a list of fonts, a list of sizes, a text box showing the currently selected size (points), a Revert to Style text box, and a palette of colors. The large box at the bottom shows an example of the currently selected font.

Through the Font dialog box, you can change the font, size, and color of the selected text. Select the Revert to Style option to return the selected text to the font, size, and color specified in the paragraph style. For now, however, we will just change the size so we can examine the characters more closely.

7. Double-click on the Size box to select it and type **99**.

8. Click on OK.

You should now have 99-point text on your screen, as shown in Figure 5.2. The status bar in the figure shows that the text is Times Roman (Tms Rmn). If your status bar shows another font, pull down the Text menu, select Fonts, and choose Times Roman from the list box.

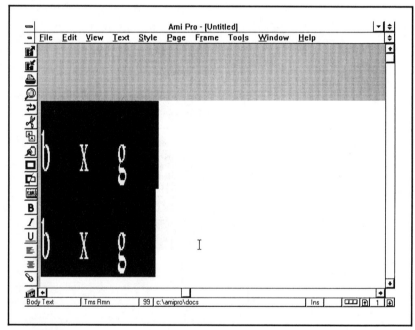

Figure 5.2: 99-point Times Roman

Times Roman is a *serif* font. Serifs are the little completion lines that appear at the top of the *b* and the "feet" and "hands" of the *x*. This is also a *weighted* font, in which some lines are thicker than others; for example, the lower-left-to-upper-right bar of the *x* is thinner than the other bar. The weight is *oblique*, which means that the thick and thin lines are diagonally opposed, like the parts of the *x*. Another similarity among fonts is the style of the bowls in the characters, as in the lower part of the *b* and both parts of the *g*.

Times Roman and Helvetica are sometimes called by other names, such as Dutch and Swiss.

Now let's compare the Times Roman text with text in another typeface.

9. Drag the mouse through the bottom row of letters to select them, pull down the Text menu, and select Font again.

10. Scroll through the Face list box looking for fonts named Helvetica (or Helv), AvantGarde, Geneva, Franklin, Swiss, or something similar. As you locate these fonts, click on them to see examples in the box at the bottom of the Fonts dialog box.

11. Select one of these fonts and click on OK to apply it to the highlighted text.

You now have a line of Times Roman and a line of Helvetica (or similar) text on your screen, as shown in Figure 5.3. Helvetica is a *sans serif* (without serifs), unweighted font. Its bowls are much rounder, but the *g* doesn't use the lower bowl at all; it has a hook. Also notice how the bowls seem to be "stuck on" the Helvetica letters, while they're integrated into the design of the Times Roman letters.

Although *font* and *typeface* are used interchangeably by desktop publishers, there is a distinct difference in the meaning of these terms. A typeface, or just *face*, describes a design, such as Helvetica or Times Roman. A font is a certain style and size in that typeface. You might specify 14-point Helvetica Italic or 10-point Times Roman Bold as fonts.

Family is another term used to refer to a group of type. Some families include not only the four styles (bold, italic, plain, and underline), but other special groups. For example, the Stone family includes serif typefaces and a sans serif typeface, as well as small caps and other special groups of type.

If you are in the market for typefaces, the Stone family is a good choice because it includes a variety of styles, as well as other specifically designed features that make all the members of the family look good together.

CHOOSING WHICH TYPEFACE TO USE

Choosing the correct typeface involves many of the same decisions as choosing the right words. A face communicates a message before the reader even begins reading. Times Roman, widely used in newspapers, is probably the most transparent face, which means that it

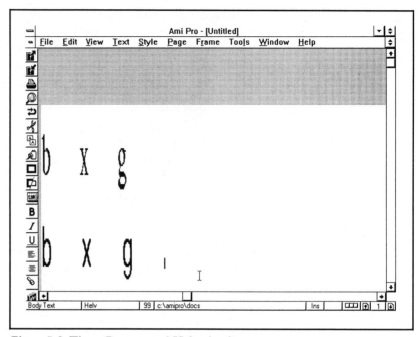

Figure 5.3: Times Roman and Helvetica fonts

can be used for a wide range of text, from obituaries to fashion news. It's an all-purpose face.

Omni magazine is published in a sans serif font because it is about the future, written for people who spend a lot of time thinking about trends, science, science fiction, and lifestyles. The *New Yorker*, on the other hand, uses a very traditional face for its pages, communicating tradition, comfort, and values of old money and old school ties.

There are formal and informal typefaces. A face like Vagabond looks as if it were designed for writing on barns and outhouses. Park Avenue, a prissy face by any measure, would look good in an advertisement for a milliner—if in fact milliners still advertise—or a wedding invitation. There are script fonts that look like fine calligraphy and script fonts that look like the writing on a doctor's prescription pad. Each has its place, and many look ludicrous when placed next to each other.

Yet another distinction among typefaces is whether they are *body faces* or *display faces*. Display faces are used occasionally in heads, titles, captions, and other places where the publisher wants to call attention to the text. Body faces take a step into the background and almost disappear from the reader's consciousness as they're read.

In general, you should use an attractive serif font, such as Times Roman, for most body, or paragraph-style, text. Palatino is a face you might reserve for important letters and typeset documents. The face is elegant without looking contrived, but it may be too elegant for informal letters and school papers. If you are writing something to make people feel at home, such as a list of friendly rules for guests at your bed and breakfast, consider a font like Vagabond, which has a Will Rogers-like charm about it.

Helvetica or another sans serif font is fine for use as a display font. These fonts attract the eye but aren't highly readable. A font is said to be readable when you can read it for page after page in comfort.

To pick an appropriate typeface for your document, ask yourself what is being communicated, how much reading is involved, and what values you want to support.

Bookman and New Century Schoolbook are two serif fonts that are widely available, however, they give many readers a cringing flashback to textbooks from school days.

USING AMI PRO'S STYLES

In Ami Pro, a style is a collection of formatting options that is given a name. A style is applied to a paragraph. Although you can change formatting within a paragraph, such as the font or alignment, the format specified in the style will be the default for that paragraph.

You have been introduced to styles in Chapters 2 and 4 and worked with three different types: Body Text, Title, and Subhead. You also have seen how styles are used in constructing a table of contents. When we told Ami Pro to create a table of contents and defined the first level as Title and the second level as Subhead, Ami Pro searched through the master document file by file and noted the location of all the discrete pieces of text marked with those styles.

By using styles, you can apply a broad range of formatting to your documents in one step. You can use the styles and style sheets provided with Ami Pro or create your own.

A style is a kind of shorthand. It allows you to sum up a dizzying list of specifications in a single name.

USING EXISTING STYLE SHEETS

When you open a new file, Ami Pro automatically uses the ˜ DE-FAULT.STY style sheet for the text. However, Ami Pro supplies dozens of other style sheets. To see the other style sheets you can select from, pull down the Style menu and select Use Another Style Sheet. You will see the dialog box shown in Figure 5.4.

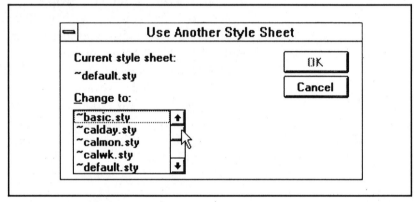

Figure 5.4: Use Another Style Sheet dialog box

Scroll through the list of style sheets in the Change to box. To see how your text appears in that style, select it and click on OK in the dialog box. If you select another style sheet while a file is open, that style sheet will automatically be used for that file each time you open it.

MODIFYING A STYLE THE EASY WAY

Be very careful about changes to ˜ DEFAULT.STY. It's easy enough to save styles for specialized uses under new style sheet names.

You can easily modify an existing style by using the Define Style option on the menu. To see how this works, we will work with the two lines of large text that we used to study font features.

1. Drag through the letters (the two *bxg* lines) to select them. Then pull down the Text menu, click on Font, and click on the Revert to Style check box.

2. Place the text cursor somewhere in the series of letters, and click on the text style indicator on the status bar.

3. With Body Text selected, pull down the Text menu and select Font.

4. In the Font dialog box (Figure 5.1), select Helvetica or Modern for the face and 18 points for the size. Then click on OK.

5. Pull down the Style menu and select Define Style. You will see a dialog box asking for confirmation:

   Changing Body Text to have attributes of the selected paragraph's text. Are you sure?

6. Click on the Yes button.

The Body Text style is now defined as 18-point Helvetica or Modern. However, it isn't permanent, and this style is attached to only this particular document. If you modify a style in the default style sheet while a file is open, the style is stored with the file rather than with the style sheet, so it will always be available to that file, but not to other files. If you want to use that style with another document, you must save it as a style, as explained later in this chapter, and load it as a style sheet while the other file is open.

Since we do not want to save these changes to the ˜DEFAULT-.STY file, close the file without saving it.

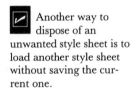 Another way to dispose of an unwanted style sheet is to load another style sheet without saving the current one.

7. Pull down the File menu and select Close. Respond No when you are asked if you want to save the changes.

CREATING NEW STYLES

For more complex formatting, you will want to create your own styles. Through the Create Style option on the Style menu, you can define all the characteristics you want your text to have.

Generally, it is easier to base a style on an existing one rather than design it from scratch. To save time, pick the style that most closely resembles the style you want to create.

As an example, we will create styles to be used for something writers are almost universally familiar with: a rejection slip.

Before you create any new styles, you should take the time to think about what your style should say and how the style should say it. In our example, we want to give the impression of solidity and professionalism; we want to communicate the image of a group of tweedy, learned academics carefully discussing the rejected work over brandy and cigars on a Sunday afternoon. We will design styles that reflect this image.

First we need to enter the text for a sample letter:

1. Close your current document without saving it and open a new file.

2. In the new document, type the following text:

   Arachnoid

   2372 Variable Foot Path

   Iambic, Pennsylvania

   Thank you for sending your work to Arachnoid. The editors have considered it carefully, and while we regret to inform you that it isn't quite what we are looking for, we wish you luck in placing it elsewhere.

CREATING A LOGO STYLE

Before you create a new style sheet, you need to select an existing style sheet on which to base it. You can use the default style sheet (˜ DE-FAULT.STY) or choose another one from the Use Another Style Sheet dialog box (displayed by selecting Use Another Style Sheet from the Style menu). For our example, we will use ˜ DEFAULT.STY.

1. Click on the name *Arachnoid* at the top of the letter.

2. Pull down the Style menu and select Create Style. You will see the dialog box shown in Figure 5.5.

If you already have a style designed for you by a professional, you can use Ami Pro's Create Style option to recreate that style.

You do not have to drag through the text to create a style for it. As long as the text cursor is located somewhere in the text, the style will be applied to that paragraph.

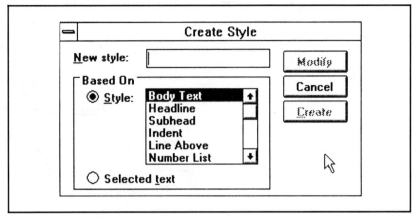

Figure 5.5: Create Style dialog box

In this dialog box, you give your style a name and select a style to base it on. You can click on the name of the style that you want to base it on in the Style list box, or you can select some text by dragging through it and specify the style based on the selected text.

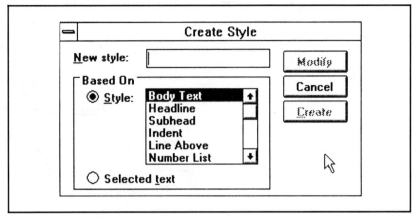 Pick a descriptive style name based on the primary use of the text.

3. Type **Logo** in the New Style text box, and the Modify button will become selectable.

4. Make sure Body Text is selected in the Based On list box, and then click on the Modify button. You will see the dialog box shown in Figure 5.6.

This dialog box has several pages for defining the formatting associated with your new style. The first page is the Font page. Only fonts that can be printed on the selected printer will be listed.

The F9 that appears in the upper-left corner of the Modify Style dialog box indicates that you can apply the style you are creating to a paragraph by clicking on the paragraph and pressing F9.

5. Click on Roman if you don't have a PostScript printer; click on Times-Roman (Tms Rmn) if you do.

6. Click on Bold in the Attributes area.

7. Double-click on the text box under Points and type **50**. This point size results in letters about ¾ inch high.

8. Click on Alignment in the Modify box on the left side of the dialog box. You will now see the Alignment page, as shown in Figure 5.7.

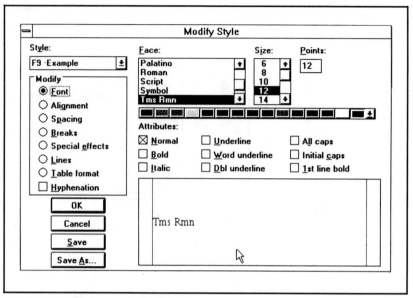

Figure 5.6: Font page of Modify Style dialog box

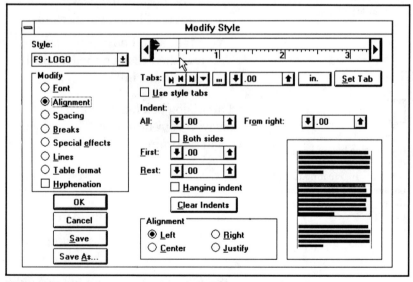

Figure 5.7: Alignment page of Modify Style dialog box

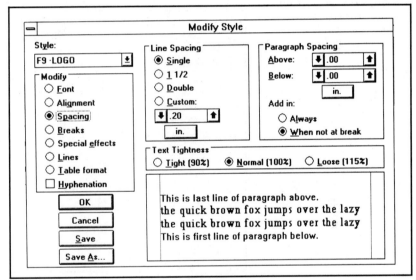

Later in the chapter, you will learn how to set the margins and tabs for the style using the Alignment page of the Modify Style dialog box.

In the Alignment page, you can set the tabs, margins, and alignment for the paragraph. Paragraphs can be left or right aligned (with smooth margins on the right or left), justified (with smooth margins on both the right and left), or centered.

9. In the Alignment box at the bottom of the Alignment page, click on Center to center the Logo style.

10. Click on Spacing in the Modify box. You will see the Spacing page, as shown in Figure 5.8.

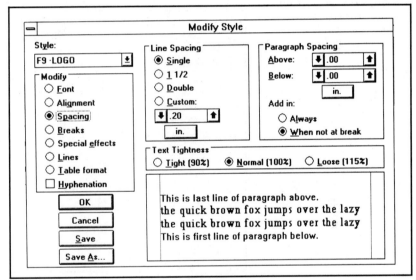

Figure 5.8: Spacing page of Modify Style dialog box

The space between lines will change to match the type size. Generally, text appears best when it is leaded at 120 percent of the type size, as in 10-point type with 12-point leading. Our 50-point type will automatically be set for 61.2-point leading.

Here you can set the spacing above and beneath the paragraph, the line spacing (also known as the *leading*—which rhymes with *breading*), and the tracking (shown here as Text Tightness). We will place an inch of space above the paragraph and a half of an inch below it. Also, we will set our logo to be loose, which places some additional space between the letters in a word.

11. In the Paragraph Spacing section, click on the up arrow at the right end of the Above text box until the value in the box is 1.00.

12. Click on the up arrow at the right end of the Below text box until the value is .50.

13. Make sure the Always button in the Paragraph Spacing section is selected.

14. Click on the Loose button in the Text Tightness area of the dialog box.

15. Click on Breaks in the Modify box, and you will see the Breaks page, shown in Figure 5.9.

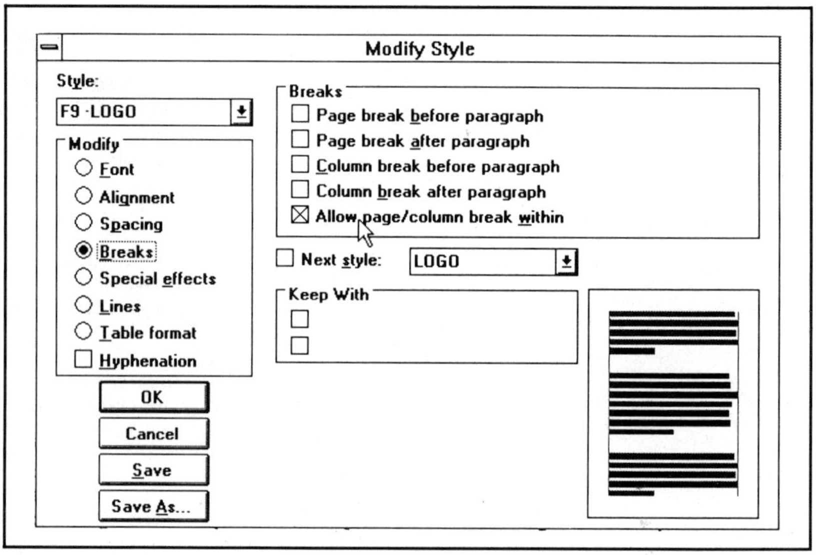

Choosing Always for Paragraph Spacing of a normal paragraph, can have unexpected effects. Generally, you won't want extra space added to a paragraph when it appears at the top of a page, but the sample logo is an exception to that rule.

Figure 5.9: Breaks page of Modify Style dialog box

The selections in the Breaks page have to do with breaking pages and columns in the midst of paragraphs. Note that Allow Page/Column Break Within is selected. If you turn it off, as you will for the logo, the Keep With options become available. These options ensure that the paragraph will always appear on a page with another paragraph—the one immediately before, the one immediately after, or both. Use them for text that must always appear with another item, such as section headings that should never appear alone at the bottom of a page.

Next Style has no effect when you press ← in the middle of a paragraph. If you do this, both paragraphs will automatically have the same style.

The Next Style option in the Breaks page sets the style that will be used for the next paragraph after you press ←. For a body text style, you will generally keep the next paragraph in the same style. For other styles, you might want to use a different style for the next paragraph. For example, you might specify an unindented paragraph style to follow a heading.

16. Click on the Allow Page/Column Break Within option to turn it off. None of the other options on this page relate to the Logo style, so make sure nothing is selected.

17. Click on the Lines button in the Modify box to display the Lines page, shown in Figure 5.10.

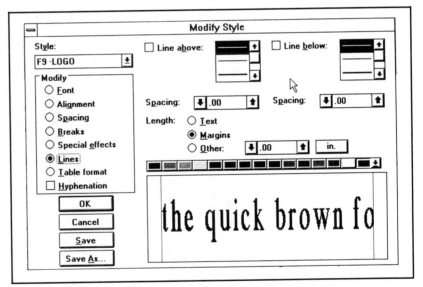

Figure 5.10: Lines page of Modify Style dialog box

If you set the length of the lines to some arbitrary value, the lines will always be that length, regardless of the length of the text. Be sure to check all the incidences of the style to make sure that the line length is always appropriate.

This page contains options for creating borders around paragraphs. You can select the style of the line above and/or below the paragraph and specify the spacing above and below the text in the Spacing text boxes, or use the Length options to set the lines to be as long as the text, margins, or the length you specify in the Other text box. You can also set the color of the lines.

18. Click on the check boxes for Line Above and Line Below, and then scroll through the line styles in the list boxes until you see a thick line with thin lines above and below. Click on this set of lines.

There are no more modifications for our logo style. We have used most, but not all, of the pages in the Modify Style dialog box. You'll learn how the other options work later in the chapter.

19. Click on OK to close the Modify Style dialog box.

20. If the text cursor isn't already in the *Arachnoid* text, click on it.

21. Click on the text style indicator in the status bar and select Logo as the style.

The text is now in your new style, as shown in Figure 5.11. The vertical line at the left of the text is the text cursor.

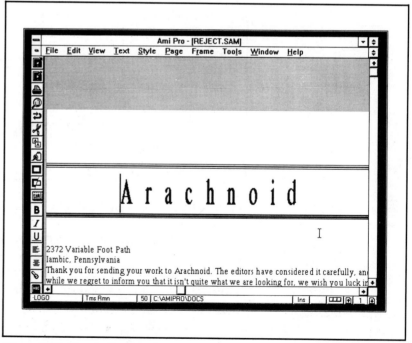

Figure 5.11: Text in Logo style

CREATING AN ADDRESS STYLE

Now we will create a style for the address portion of the letter. This will be a simpler style, in the same typeface but smaller, centered on the page. Follow these steps:

1. Click on the first line of the address.

2. Select Create Style from the Style menu and in the Create Style dialog box, type **Logo Address**. Make sure Body Text is selected in the Based On box.

3. Click on Modify in the Create Style dialog box.

4. In the Font page of the Modify Style dialog box, choose the same font as you selected for Logo (Roman or Times Roman) and make the size 10 points.

5. Select Alignment in the Modify box, and then click on Center in the Alignment box.

6. Click on OK in the Modify Style dialog box.

7. Drag through the two lines of the logo address to select them, click on the text style indicator, and select Logo Address as the style.

The address should take on all the attributes you specified.

FORMATTING THE BODY OF THE LETTER

Finally, we will create a style for the body of the letter to make it look a little more formal:

1. Click on the body of the rejection slip.

2. Create a new style based on Body Text. Call it **Form Letter**, so you can use it for all your rejection replies.

3. Click on the Modify button in the Create Style dialog box.

4. On the Font page, select the same font that you used for the logo and address (Roman or Times Roman).

5. Click on Alignment in the Modify box to display the Alignment page, and choose Justify in the Alignment box.

6. Click on the upward-pointing arrow in the All list box in the Indent section (under the Tabs section) and set it to 1.25. Then click on the Both Sides check box. This gives the letter 1¼-inch right and left margins.

7. Click on Spacing in the Modify box, and in the Paragraph Spacing section, double-click on the Above text box and type **.17**. This sets a pica (¹⁄₆ inch) of space between the top of the text and the paragraph above it. Make sure When Not at Break is selected.

8. Click on OK to close the Modify Styles dialog box.

9. If the text cursor is not already in the body of the letter, click somewhere within it.

10. Click on the text style indicator and select Form Letter as the style.

Your completed rejection slip appears as shown in Figure 5.12.

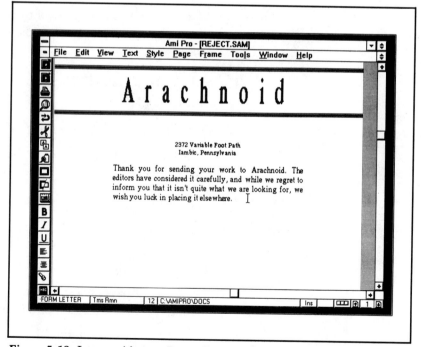

Figure 5.12: Letter with new Logo, Logo Address, and Form Letter styles

CHANGING THE STYLE OF SPECIFIC TEXT

You can change the appearance of text without using styles and regardless of the style currently applied. For example, if you wanted to italicize the word *Arachnoid* in our sample form letter, you would select it, pull down the Text menu, and click on Italic. Alternatively, you could just select it and press Ctrl-I.

However, you should not use the Text menu to change anything except for incidental text. If you find yourself formatting subheads or some other repeating item in the text, you are doing unnecessary work. Furthermore, if you later need to change the style of that repeating element, you will have to go back through the text and select each element separately. In the process, you may miss one or make a mistake and change one so it doesn't match the others. If you use styles instead, any change you make to the style of one element will be made to similar elements throughout the document.

SAVING A STYLE SHEET

You have done all the work of creating styles, but they are temporary unless you save them. The Save as a Style Sheet command is on the Style menu. Now we will save our sample styles so you can use them with future forms.

1. Pull down the Style menu and select Save as a Style Sheet.

2. In the dialog box that appears, type **FORMLTR.STY** as your style sheet name.

3. Pull down the File menu, select Save, and save your rejection slip as **REJECT.SAM**.

USING THE RULER TO SET INDENTS AND TABS

Although our sample styles did not use tabs or indents, when you are creating your own styles, you may want to include these settings. For example, you can set apart text in numbered or bulleted lists by making the margins of the lists narrower than the rest of the text.

You can create up to 22 tabs on a ruler.

Setting Tabs   In the Alignment page of the Modify Style dialog box (Figure 5.7), the faint vertical line through the ruler shows where the mouse pointer is over the ruler. The tiny flagged mark is a tab. It is a left tab. There are four other kinds of tabs available. Look at the buttons immediately beneath the ruler:

- The button at the far left that looks as if it is depressed is the left tab button. When you use a left tab, the text will always be aligned on it to the left.

- Next is the right tab button. A right tab aligns text to the right.

- The third button provides a decimal tab, which aligns text on a period (for aligning columns of figures that contain decimals). If the text or value has no period or decimal point, it will be right aligned.

- The fourth button is for center tabs. If you have a column of entries that contain one-digit numbers and very brief text, you might center align that column.

- The last button provides leaders. If you create a leader tab, it will be connected to the column to its left with a series of periods or a line. By clicking on the leader button, you can create one of four leader schemes: line, dashes, small dots, and no leader.

Figure 5.13 shows how the various types of tabs appear in text.

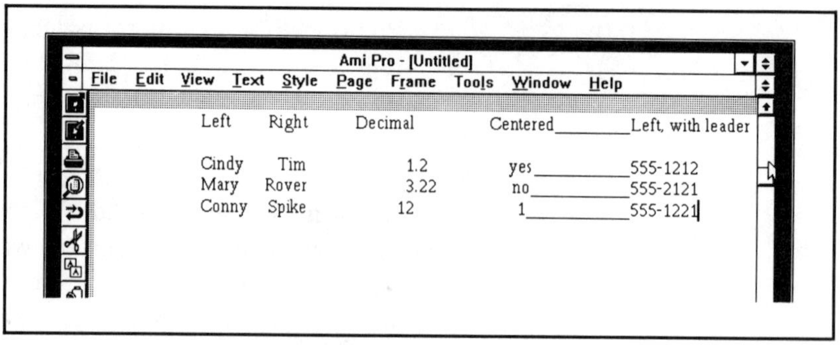

Figure 5.13: Various kinds of tabs

In the text box that appears next to the leader button, you can type in a tab location.

The next button in the row (which says *in.*) is used to set the unit of measure. Its default is inches (in.), but if you're more comfortable setting tabs in centimeters, click on this button once. Click again for picas (about ¹⁄₆ inch), and again for points (about ¹⁄₇₂ inch). When you change the default measurement, the ruler changes to reflect the new measurement.

To move along the ruler (only about 3¹⁄₂ inches are visible at one time), click on the arrows that appear at either end of the ruler.

To set tabs, adjust the leader by clicking on the leader button, then click on the tab alignment button, and then click in the upper half of the ruler. You can also set tabs from the document, but they won't apply to the style, just to the individual paragraph you set them within.

Setting Margins and Indents   Margins determine the default width of the paragraph. The margins, like the tabs, can be adjusted from the Ami Pro window for an individual paragraph, but you must use the Alignment page of the Modify Style dialog box to change the default margins for a style. There are two margins—left and right—and two indents. You can indent the first line of a paragraph or all of the lines in a paragraph other than the first line (sometimes called an *out-dent*).

To see how to set tabs and indents with the ruler in the Alignment page of the Modify Style dialog box, follow these steps:

1. Select Create Style from the Style menu, enter **Tabs** as the name of the style, click on the Modify button, and then click on Alignment in the Modify box.

2. Move the mouse pointer to the ruler until you see the line. Then move the pointer to the upper half of the ruler, so it is above the score line that runs horizontally through the ruler, and click the mouse button.

The tab disappears when you drag the mouse pointer out of the ruler area.

3. Place the mouse pointer on the tab, press and hold down the mouse button, and drag the tab downward or upward until the mouse pointer leaves the ruler.

4. Scroll to the extreme left end of the ruler and note that there is a split arrowhead.

The top half of the split arrowhead is the first-line indent pointer, and the bottom is the paragraph indent marker. You can simply drag the margin and indent pointer.

5. Place the mouse pointer below and slightly to the right of the bottom half of the lower half of the arrowhead, press the mouse button, and drag to the right. If only the lower half follows your mouse pointer, you are doing it right. If not, try again.

6. When you have successfully moved the bottom half away, place the mouse pointer above and to the right of the top half of the arrowhead, press the mouse button, and drag the mouse to the right. The top half of the arrowhead should move, leaving behind a thin vertical bar. If this doesn't happen, try again.

Your ruler should now look similar to the one shown in Figure 5.14.

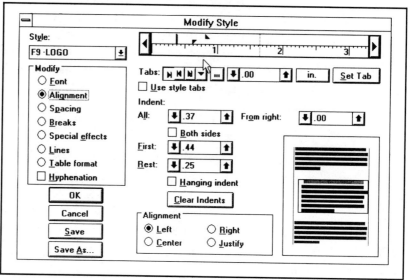

Figure 5.14: Split margin marker in the ruler

The vertical bar marks the paragraph margin. It is located at .37 inch from the page margin. The first line indent is .44 inch from the paragraph margin. The indent for the rest of the paragraph is .25 inch from the paragraph margin. You can see these figures in the text boxes in the Indent section of the dialog box in Figure 5.14:

- All shows where the paragraph margin falls relative to the page margin.

- First indicates the location of the first-line indent.

- Rest shows the indent for the rest of the paragraph.

Also, the box in the lower right of the dialog box contains a visual representation of the paragraph alignment that results from these settings.

Use the From Right text box to set a right margin. Once again, this is relative to the page margin. You can center the paragraph within the page margins by clicking on the Both Sides check box. When this option is checked, the paragraph margin is set the same on the right and left sides.

The Hanging Indent option sets the first line of a paragraph to appear at the left, with subsequent lines indented below it. You will often see this kind of indent in a dictionary or a glossary. It is also useful for lists with numbered or bulleted items. You must enter a positive value in the Rest text box for this option to work.

Removing Tabs and Indents If you want to eliminate all the indents, click on the Clear Indents button. It will set all the indent values to zero. To remove tabs, drag them off the ruler. Follow these steps to delete the indent and tab settings and then remove the Tabs style:

1. Click on the Clear Indents button.

2. One by one, remove each of the tabs you might have set. To do this, place the mouse pointer on the tab markers and drag them up or down off of the ruler.

3. Click on Cancel in the Modify Style dialog box.

4. Pull down the Syle menu and select Style Management. You will see the Style Management dialog box, shown in Figure 5.15.

5. In the Style Management dialog box, click on Tabs, then the Remove button, then OK.

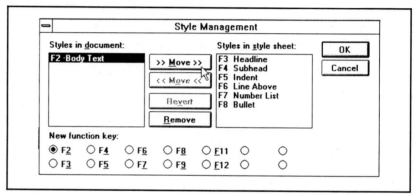

Figure 5.15: Style Management dialog box

You will learn more about using the Style Management dialog box later in this chapter.

CREATING A STYLE
WITH BULLETED AND NUMBERED ITEMS

The Special Effects page in the Modify Style dialog box allows you to create numbered, lettered, or bulleted paragraphs. You can scroll through the list of bullets until you find the one you want to use. Click on that bullet, and the Bullet check box will automatically be checked.

Let's create styles for bulleted and numbered lists to see how the options in the Special Effects page work:

1. Select New from the File menu, click on OK in the New dialog box, and then click on the Maximize box so that the blank page fills the window.

The DEFAULT-.STY style sheet already contains two bulleted text styles and a numbered list style. Ami Pro also provides a separate style sheet for numbered lists.

2. Type the following text:

   The decline in Atlantic fisheries is primarily related to

   Over fishing

   Pollution

   Here are a few things we can do to reduce the decline in this vital natural resource:

   Sign treaties with nations to reduce fishing in the western Atlantic

   Enact and enforce laws against releasing toxins into the Atlantic

3. Pull down the Style menu and select Create Style.

4. Type **Bulleted List** as the style name and click on the Modify button.

5. In the Modify section of the Modify Style dialog box, click on Special Effects.

6. In the Special Effects page, click on Bullet and select the first bullet if it is not already selected.

7. Click on the Alignment button in the Modify section of the dialog box.

8. To set up a hanging indent, double-click on the Rest text box, type **.1**, and then click on OK.

9. Drag through the lines of text that read *Over fishing* and *Pollution* and select Bulleted List from the Styles box.

Bullets (tiny dots) now appear at the left end of the paragraphs you selected. If these paragraphs had been longer than a single line, the second line would be indented slightly so that only the bullet would be at the left margin.

10. Select Create Style from the Style menu, name the style **Numbered List**, and click on the Modify button.

11. Click on Special Effects, and then click on Number in the Special Effects page.

12. Click on the down arrow next to the Number text box to see the numbering schemes available. Select Arabic numerals if they are not already selected.

13. Type a period and a space in the Text text box. In this style, the number will be followed by a period.

14. Make sure the Text box is checked and look at the sample box to see how the style appears. If the period isn't there, click on the Text box twice.

15. Click on the Alignment button in the dialog box.

16. Double-click on the Rest text box, type **.1**, and click on OK.

17. Drag through the lines of text that begin *Sign...* and *Enact...* and select Numbered List from the Styles box.

A number appears at the left end of the paragraphs you selected. The number is at the left margin, and additional lines are indented.

USING OTHER STYLE MODIFICATION OPTIONS

There are a couple of options for creating styles that we have not used.

The Table Format page contains options for setting up a table style, as described in Chapter 13.

Use the Hyphenation option to have Ami Pro automatically hyphenate words that might otherwise be moved to the next line. This usually produces a smoother right margin in left-aligned text and more even spacing in justified text.

DESIGNING YOUR OWN STYLES

Although you should use a single face for body and incidental text, you can specify a different size or use a different style for items that should stand out, such as margin notes.

You have a multitude of choices for your styles, and you should experiment with designing effective ones. Above all, your design should be coordinated. To accomplish this, select a single typeface for body text. This same face should be used for incidental text, such as text in frames, headers, and footers.

Use another typeface for display text, such as chapter heads, subheads, table heads, and so on. Differentiate among these levels of heads by using different sizes of the face.

Don't use very similar faces for these two duties. There should be some contrast between these faces or they will clash. If you want the display and body text to look similar, use the same face but in a different style, such as Times Roman for body text and a bold or bold italic version of Times Roman as the display face.

Avoid overuse of typefaces on a page. More than two faces on a page almost invariably makes the page look muddled. As mentioned at the beginning of the chapter, each face tells its own story, lending a certain feeling to a text printed in that face. Too many faces on the page means that too many subconscious messages are being sent.

PAGEGREAT!, a book-disk combination from Logic Arts, contains styles and page layouts designed for the use with Ami Pro.

MANAGING YOUR STYLES

You can manage your styles using the options in the Style Management dialog box, which is displayed when you select Style Management from the Style menu. The Style Management dialog box (Figure 5.15) lists the styles that are in the document and the ones that are in the style sheet, along with buttons for managing the styles.

If you want to be able to use a style that is in the document with other documents, you must move it into the style sheet. To do so, select the style in the Styles in Document list box and click on the >>Move>> button.

When you click on a style name, the function key that applies that style will be highlighted as a radio button in the lower part of the dialog box. If you want to change the function key associated with a style, click on a different button from the one that is highlighted.

To delete a style, select it and click on the Remove button. When you remove a style that has been applied to text, the text reverts to the style that the deleted style was based on. The name of the deleted style will appear in red in the status bar. Red text in the status bar (gray on a monochrome monitor) indicates a condition that is no longer supported.

DISPLAYING A STYLES LIST

If you want to see a window containing a list of styles, pull down the Style menu and select Select a Style. A window will open showing the name of the style sheet in its title bar. The list of styles will be visible

Since the styles are displayed in a window, you can adjust the size of the display simply by placing the mouse pointer on an edge or corner segment and dragging.

inside the window. If the list is longer than the window can contain, a scroll bar will appear.

If the window gets in the way of the text in the Ami Pro window, you can resize it so that it is very small. To close the window, double-click on its close box in the upper-left corner. You can redisplay the window by pressing Ctrl-Y.

CHANGING THE APPEARANCE OF THE PAGE

Styles affect the appearance of individual paragraphs. The layout of the page affects the entire document. Through the Modify Page Layout option on the Page menu, you can define margins and columns, as well as page size and orientation. You can also add lines, headers, and footers.

As an example, we will create a page layout for a college paper.

1. Select New from the File menu and click on OK in the New dialog box to open a new file.

2. Pull down the Page menu and select Modify Page Layout. You will see the dialog box shown in Figure 5.16.

You can select Insert Page Layout from the Page menu to insert a new page layout at any time. Selecting this option displays the same dialog box as selecting Modify Page Layout.

The Modify Page Layout dialog box is similar to the Modify Style dialog box. The first page that appears is Margins & Columns. You switch to other pages by clicking on the corresponding option in the Modify box. The Pages box below the Modify box allows you to select which pages you want to affect. You can modify the page layout for all pages or just the right or left ones. This lets you create a setup for a document with facing pages. Usually, you will want to mirror facing pages. For example, you may want to provide wider margins on the binding side, which will be on the right edge of left pages and the left edge of right pages. Our paper will be printed on a single side of the paper, so we'll leave All selected in the Pages area.

You can set the number of columns on the page in the Number of Columns area. The value in the Gutter Width text box determines

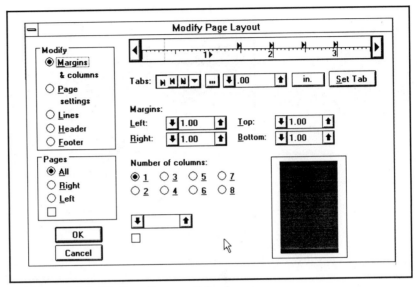

Figure 5.16: Modify Page Layout dialog box

It's risky to select columns and justified text. Unless the columns are wide, you will have spacing problems. Long, unhyphenable words will appear on either end of broad white spaces, making the page look like a tributary of the Amazon—full of lakes and channels.

the amount of white space between columns. Column balance makes all the ends of columns of equal length (the alternative is to have the last column short, if there isn't enough text to fill all the columns).

You've already seen how to adjust margins using the ruler in the Modify Style dialog box. In the ruler in the Modify Page Layout dialog box, the margins are marked by tiny black arrowheads in the lower half of the ruler, which you can drag with the mouse. You can also adjust the top and bottom margins.

3. Set all four Margins boxes to 1.5 inches.

4. Click on Page Settings in the Modify box. You will see the Page Settings page, as shown in Figure 5.17.

In this page, you can specify the page orientation and the size and shape of the page.

5. Make sure Letter is selected in the Page Size section and Portrait is selected in the Orientation area.

6. Click on Lines in the Modify box. You will see the Lines page, as shown in Figure 5.18.

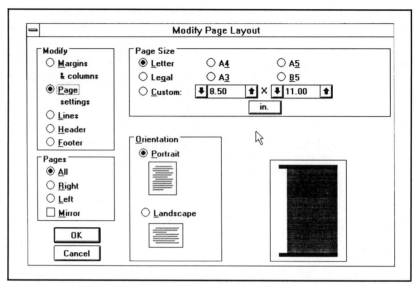

Figure 5.17: Page Settings page of Modify Page Layout dialog box

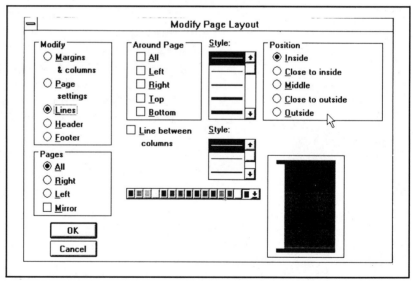

Figure 5.18: Lines page of Modify Page Layout dialog box

Lines can make the page look boxy and claustrophobic. However, they can be useful for frames and to separate unjustified columns. Generally, lines are a difficult thing to use tastefully on a page. If you can get along without a line, you should.

Here you can specify the location and appearance of lines. In the Around Page section, you can select which part of the page on which to place the lines. The Position section offers five choices that affect the position of lines relative to the margins. Inside places lines within the margins, and Outside places them at the extreme edge of the page. The other settings are intermediate positions between the edge of the page and the margins. If you want to place a line between columns, click on the Line Between Columns check box.

7. Make sure no lines are selected in this page.

8. Click on Header in the Modify box. You will see the Header page, as shown in Figure 5.19.

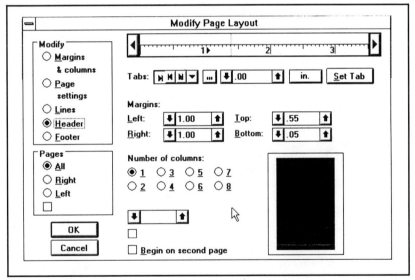

Figure 5.19: Header page of Modify Page Layout dialog box

The header is like a separate section of text (a text stream, as described in Chapter 4), and it has all the formatting options available to the page. You can specify tabs, margins, and columns. If you are creating a document with facing pages, you may want to set up a different header for right and left pages. Click on the page you are designing a header for in the Pages section.

You can also set up floating headers for different section of a document, as described in Chapter 12.

If you want to make the header start on the second page, leaving the first page without one, click on Begin on Second Page. This is the preferred format for most papers and manuscripts.

9. Adjust the margins as follows: right and left margins to 1.5 inches, top to .55 inch (the distance from the outside edge of the paper), and bottom to .05 inch (the distance from the text).

10. Click on the Begin on Second Page check box.

11. Click on Footer in the Modify box.

The Footer dialog box is identical to the Header dialog box. The settings are the same, except that they affect the format of the footer text that appears on the bottom of all, right, or left pages.

12. Adjust the footer margins as follows: right and left margins to 1.5 inches, top to .05 inch (the distance from the text), and bottom to .55 inch (the distance from the outside edge of the paper).

13. Click on OK in the Modify Page Layout dialog box.

The page layout you created will apply to all pages that follow the current page. You can type some text and print the document to see how your settings look on the actual page.

CHAPTER 6

Importing and
Exporting Files

USING THE IMPORT AND EXPORT FUNCTIONS OF Ami Pro is a little like conducting the business of shipping exotica across oceans and national borders. Instead of a translator, you use filters. Instead of paying a duty, you have to pay in time for the information to be prepared in a format that Ami Pro will accept. Although other programs operate under DOS or Windows, just like Ami Pro, they use a different set of values. Ami Pro acts as your agent in information exchange.

In this chapter, you will learn how to import text from other programs, export Ami Pro documents in other file formats, and import graphics files. You will also learn how to use Ami Pro's special pasting commands to bring in files.

IMPORTING AND EXPORTING TEXT

By using Ami Pro's text importing capabilities, you can bring text files from other programs into Ami Pro programs. You can also export Ami pro files to use with other programs.

IMPORTING TEXT FILES

Importing a text file into Ami Pro is as easy as opening one of your Ami Pro files. You can bring in text created in any application for which Ami Pro has a filter. Ami Pro can import files in the following formats:

AdvanceWrite	MultiMate
ASCII	Navy DIF
dBASE	Paradox
DCA/FFT	PeachText

DCA/RFT	Rich Text Format
DIF	Samna Word
DisplayWrite 4	SmartWare
E-Mail	SuperCalc
Enable	Symphony
Excel	Windows Write
Exec MemoMaker	Word for Windows
Lotus 1-2-3	WordPerfect
Manuscript	WordStar
Microsoft Word	WordStar 2000

To import a file, start Ami Pro and choose Open from the File menu. Change to the appropriate file type to list the files that are in the format you want to import, and then select the file when it appears in the Files list.

You can import text into a new or existing Ami Pro document. For example, to import a file that is in Microsoft Word format, open a new Ami Pro file or the existing one you want to add the text to, pull down the File menu, and select Open. Then click on the downward-pointing arrow at the right end of the File Type box, use the scroll bar to locate Microsoft Word, and click on it. If necessary, use the Drives and Directories boxes to change to the directory where you placed the file. Click on the name of the file in the Files list box, make sure the Replace Current File check box isn't checked, and then click on Insert.

If you are importing a document file from a word processor that keeps style and font files separate from document files, and these files are not in the same directory as the document file, you will see a dialog box asking for the location of the font and style files. You can either enter the path to the files or select Ignore Fonts to load the document without fonts or styles.

When you import a spreadsheet, Ami Pro displays a dialog box requesting the range to import. Enter the range or click on the button marked Entire File to load the whole spreadsheet.

Always use the Insert button when you are importing text into an existing document. Otherwise, you will lose all the text in the document.

If you want to practice importing a text file and don't have one handy, create one in Windows Write and save it in *Microsoft Word format* in the DOCS subdirectory of the AMIPRO directory.

Frames were intro-
duced in Chapter 2
and are the subject of the
next chapter.

You can also import text directly into a frame in an Ami Pro document. Just select the frame (when it is selected, it will have handles
around it) before you use the Open dialog box to insert the file into
the document.

EXPORTING AMI PRO DOCUMENTS

You can export
drawings you
created in Ami Pro by
saving them in the appro-
priate format. When a
drawing frame is selected,
use the Save as Drawing
option in the Save As
dialog box to save the
drawing as an AmiDraw,
Windows metafile, or
Windows bit-map file.

If you or someone else needs to use an Ami Pro document with
another program, you can save it in that program's format. Ami Pro
can export files in the same formats in which it can import files,
except for the spreadsheet formats (dBASE, DIF, Excel, Paradox, or
SuperCalc).

To save a file in another format, pull down the File menu and select
Save As. In the Save As dialog box, scroll through the File Type list to
locate the format in which you want to save the file and click on it. Type
a name for the file in the File Name text box, and then click on OK.

You will see a dialog box similar to the one shown in Figure 6.1.
Click on OK to convert paragraph styles and export in the file format
you selected.

If you are exporting an Ami Pro file to Microsoft Word, you will
see a dialog box asking for the location of your Word printer file. You
can either enter the path to your Word directory or click on the button marked Ignore Fonts to export the file without font information.

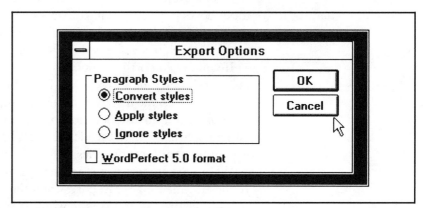

Figure 6.1: Export Options dialog box

The text in the file will be converted to the other format, but any pictures or frames in the document will not be included. The text in frames will be exported as only text, appended to the end of the file.

IMPORTING GRAPHICS

Ami Pro can import graphics in either bit-map or draw formats. You can import graphics in the formats listed in Table 6.1.

The format of the graphics file determines how the image is formed. A bit-map is a picture made up of dots corresponding to bits of memory in the computer mapped out in a grid. PCX, BMP, and TIF files are examples of bit-map formats.

Vector graphics are stored not as pictures of what is on the screen but rather as directions to draw a picture. Instead of having specific bits set to ones or zeros in the drawing, the vector format file contains a formula that indicates which bits should be turned on. EPS and DRW are two vector formats.

Table 6.1: Graphics Formats Supported by Ami Pro

File Type	File Name Extension
AmiDraw	SDW
AmiEquation	TEX
Computer Graphics Metafile	CGM
DrawPerfect	WPG
Encapsulated PostScript	EPS
Freelance	DRW
Hewlett-Packard Graphics Language (HPGL)	PLT
Lotus PIC	PIC
PC Paintbrush	PCX
Tagged Image File Format (TIFF)	TIF
Windows Bitmap	BMP
Windows Metafile	WMF

The advantage of a vector image over a bit-map graphic is that vector images are produced at the highest resolution available for the output device—whether it is a computer monitor at about 72 dots per inch, a laser printer at 300 dots per inch, or a typesetter at 1200 dots per inch. A bit-map image printed on a typesetter will retain the 72 dots per inch resolution of screen graphics, resulting in a very blocky printout. A vector drawing might look slightly blocky on the screen, but will become increasingly smooth when output on a laser printer or typesetter.

A metafile is a file that can accommodate either bit-map or vector graphics. Metafiles are necessary in Windows because the Clipboard must be capable of handling either a graphic from Windows Paintbrush or from a draw program like Micrografx Designer. CGM and WMF are two metafile formats.

To import an image, pull down the File menu and select Import Picture. You will see the dialog box shown in Figure 6.2.

At the bottom of the dialog box there is a Copy Image check box. If this is checked, Ami Pro will copy the image and import the copy. This way, you can change or even destroy the original drawing, and the graphic in the Ami Pro document will remain as you originally imported it.

If you don't select Copy Image and you later delete or modify the graphics file, the image will also be deleted or modified in the Ami

To practice importing graphics, you can use any .BMP or .PCX file. Create a graphic with Paintbrush and save it in one of these formats, or use a Windows background (scroll through the File Type list box, select Windows Bitmap, and change to your Windows directory in the Directories list box).

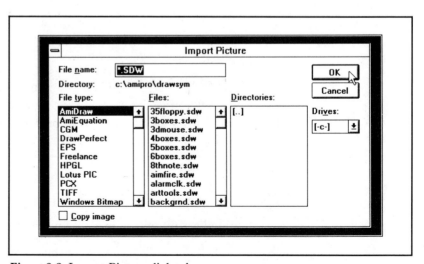

Figure 6.2: Import Picture dialog box

Pro document. If you want the changes you make in the graphics file to be reflected in the Ami Pro document, do not check Copy Image.

The graphic image will be imported into the selected frame. If no frame is selected, a frame will be created. Figure 6.3 shows an example of two graphics imported into a document.

Another way to import a graphic is to bring it into Ami Pro as a drawing. Select Drawing from the Tools menu, and then choose Import Drawing from the File menu. This option allows you to import AmiDraw (SDW), Windows Metafile (WMF), or Windows Bitmap (BMP) pictures into a drawing frame.

Working with frames and using Ami Pro's drawing features are described in Chapters 7 and 8.

MODIFYING IMAGES

After you have imported a graphic image, you can crop it and adjust the way it is processed. You can also change its size within the frame by using the Graphics Scaling command on the Frame menu, as explained in the next chapter.

Figure 6.3: Graphics files imported into a document

Cropping an Image   When you have an image in a document, you can crop it so that only part of the image is visible. To crop a picture, double-click on the frame and place the mouse pointer on the image inside frame. Then press the mouse pointer and drag the image until the part of the image you want to show is displayed.

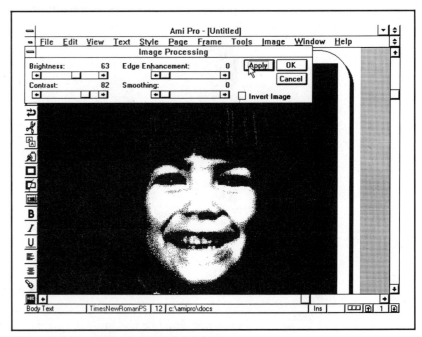

Image Processing is not available for draw, vector, or purely black-and-white images.

Processing the Image   If you are working with a gray-scale or color image, you can use the Image Processing command on the Tools menu to adjust its brightness and contrast. Double-click on the image within the frame to select it, pull down the Tools menu, and select Image Processing. You will see the Image menu added to the menu bar.

From the Image menu, select Processing to display the Image Processing dialog box, shown in Figure 6.4. This dialog box contains four main controls for adjusting the appearance of the image.

You can adjust the brightness of the picture by changing the Brightness value. This is a uniform adjustment applied to the entire picture. The image shown in Figure 6.5 has been adjusted from a brightness of 63 to 71.

Figure 6.4: Image Processing dialog box

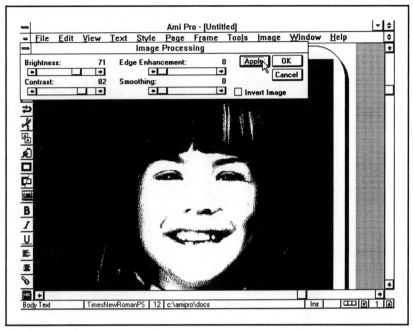

Figure 6.5: Higher brightness

The Edge Enhancement option detects edges throughout the picture and sharpens the contrast, bringing out detail. The Edge Enhancement in the image shown in Figure 6.6 has been adjusted from 0 to 25.

Use the Contrast option to adjust the whiteness of light areas and the blackness of dark areas. A higher value results in a sharper image; a lower value creates a flatter, less distinct image. The image shown in Figure 6.7 has been adjusted from a contrast of 82 to 100.

Setting a value for Smoothing tends to make areas of this picture that would ordinarily be in high contrast less sharp and more smoothly graded from one gray level to the next (opposite to Edge Enhancement). Figure 6.8 shows an image with its smoothness increased from 0 to 100. The higher the contrast, the more dramatic smoothing will be.

The Invert Image check box turns the image into a photographic negative of itself. Figure 6.9 shows the results of inverting an image.

Set the Image Processing dialog box options, and then click on the button marked Apply. This allows you to see the effects of your changes while keeping the dialog box open for further experimentation. Click on OK only when you are finished using the dialog box.

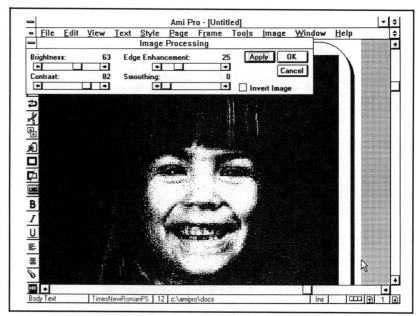

Figure 6.6: Higher edge enhancement

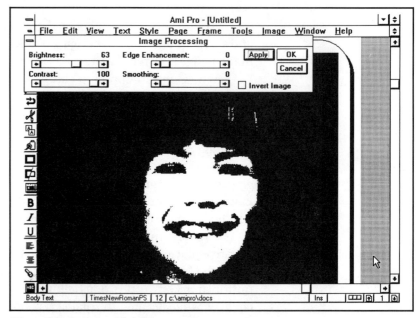

Figure 6.7: Image with high contrast

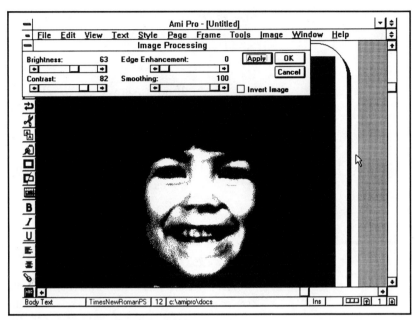

Figure 6.8: Highly smoothed image

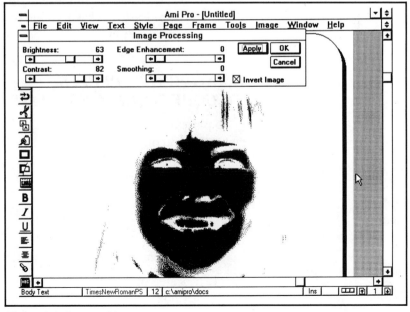

Figure 6.9: Inverted image

Using Other Image Options   The other options on the Image menu allow you to manipulate the imported image as follows:

- Revert: Returns the image to its original condition.

- Halftone: Allows you to select printing options. Choose Fastest Printing, Best Picture Quality, Automatically Selected, or Posterize (which reduces the number of gray-scale tones).

- Leave Image: Leaves the Image Processing function and removes Image from the menu bar.

PASTING FROM OTHER APPLICATIONS

Another way to bring data from other types of files into Ami Pro is by copying and pasting through the Clipboard. Often, the graphic image or text can be copied to the Clipboard from the other application and then pasted into an Ami Pro document with the Paste command on the Edit menu. To paste items in a special format, use the Paste Special or Paste Link command on the Edit menu, as described in the following sections.

USING PASTE SPECIAL TO COPY SPECIAL FORMATS

To paste a copy in Ami Pro in a special format, use the Paste Special command on the Edit menu. To see how this type of paste operation works, we will copy a Paintbrush image to the Clipboard and then bring it into an Ami Pro document.

Normally, Paintbrush is kept in your Accessories program group.

1. Open the program group that contains Paintbrush.

2. Start up Paintbrush by double-clicking on it.

3. Pull down the File menu and select Open.

4. Locate your AMIPRO directory using the Directories list box.

Because BMP (bit-map) is the file format normally selected in the Open From section of the File Open dialog box, a list of BMP files appears in the Files list box.

5. Scroll through the bit-map files until you see GAME.BMP, and then double-click on this name. A tiny square with a picture in it will appear in the Paintbrush window.

6. Click on the top-right icon (the one that looks like a pair of scissors cutting a rectangle) in the icon bar.

7. Move the mouse cursor to the top-left corner of the bit-map image. When the mouse pointer looks like a cross and is as close as possible to the upper-left corner of the image, press and hold down the mouse button.

8. Drag to the lower-right corner of the image. You shouldn't be able to move the mouse pointer beyond the lower-right corner of the image.

9. Pull down the Edit menu and select Cut to place the bit-map in the Clipboard.

10. Close Paintbrush by double-clicking on the close box.

11. Start Ami Pro, open a new document, and accept ~DEFAULT.STY as the style sheet.

12. Click on the Maximize box in the upper-right corner of the window to make the new window fill the Ami Pro window.

13. Type the text **Welcome to Ami Pro**.

14. Pull down the Edit menu and select Paste Special. You will see the dialog box in Figure 6.10.

15. Double-click on Bitmap (the only option for a Paintbrush file).

The bit-map image will appear in your document within a frame, as shown in Figure 6.11.

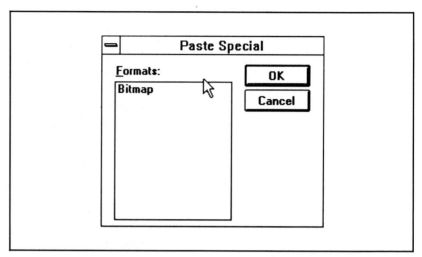

Figure 6.10: Paste Special dialog box

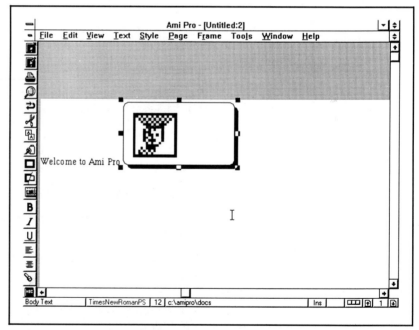

Figure 6.11: GAME.BMP file pasted into an Ami Pro frame

You can use the Paste Special command to paste other types of files into your Ami Pro documents and establish links between files. For example, if you selected a column of figures in an Excel spreadsheet, copied them to the Clipboard, and then chose the Paste Special command in Ami Pro, you would see a list of pasting options, as shown in Figure 6.12.

You could paste the numbers from the spreadsheet as a bit-map, which would make the section of the text look exactly the way Excel looks in Windows. Or you could paste the section as text, which would make the information look like Ami Pro text.

If you choose Object Link in the Paste Special dialog box, the copy of the Excel cells in the Ami Pro document will be linked to the original Excel spreadsheet. If the figures are changed in Excel, they will be automatically updated in Ami Pro. You can also link Ami Pro files to other files by using the Paste Link command, as described in the next section.

Ami Pro and Excel support OLE (Object Link Exchange) and DDE (Dynamic Data Exchange). As of this writing, very few applications have OLE or DDE. More will certainly appear in the future, but currently you will be limited in your use of these powerful features.

LINKING DOCUMENTS WITH PASTE LINK

Dynamic Data Exchange (DDE) refers to the linking of information between files. With DDE, instead of cutting and pasting again and

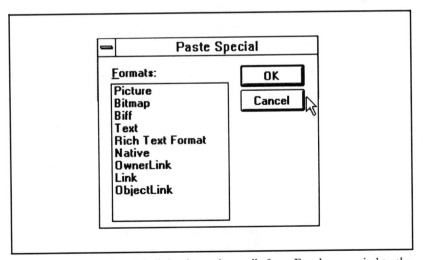

Figure 6.12: Paste Special dialog box when cells from Excel are copied to the Clipboard

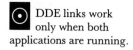

DDE links work
only when both
applications are running.

again to make sure your information is up-to-date, you can copy and paste once, setting up a dynamic link that will be maintained by Windows.

To paste a file with a DDE link, use the Paste Link option on the Edit menu. For example, if you want to link some inventory figures you have in an Excel spreadsheet with a sales report you are creating in Ami Pro, copy the Excel spreadsheet cells to the Clipboard and click in the text in Ami Pro where you want the cells to appear. Pull down the Edit menu and select Paste Link. The text from the Clipboard will appear, but there is more here than a simple transfer of information.

If you change any of the figures in the copied area of the spreadsheet, the figures in your Ami Pro document will be automatically updated to reflect those changes. However, if Excel isn't running, the value won't be changed. You need to start Excel to make sure you have the latest information.

To access options for the link you have established, select Link Options from the Edit menu. You will see the dialog box shown in Figure 6.13.

The Update option updates the information in the text associated with the highlighted link in the Links list box.

Selecting Unlink is like hanging up the telephone. The connection is broken, and no further updating will take place. Choosing Deactivate is like putting someone on hold. The link is still there, but no updating will take place unless you reconnect by selecting Update.

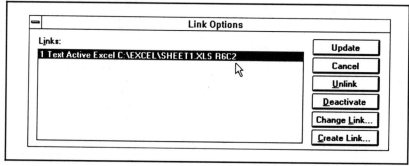

Figure 6.13: Link Options dialog box

The Change Link button displays the dialog box shown in Figure 6.14, which allows you to enter a different application or cell reference in the link (like hanging up and calling someone else).

The Create Link button in the Link Options box displays the same dialog box as Change Link, except that all the text boxes are blank. In this case, the Link dialog box is used to establish a link that didn't exist before. This setting allows you to create a dynamic link without first running the application and cutting and pasting. Specify the exact location of the information and click on OK. Ami Pro will warn you if the program is not currently running. If this happens, click on OK to let Windows start the other application.

Each time you load the linked document into Ami Pro, you will be asked whether you want to retain the links with the outside application. If you specify No, the links will be severed. If you select Yes, the other application will be started up, the links will be reinstated, and the information will be updated automatically.

If the program is already running and you see a dialog box saying it is not, establish the link through the Clipboard.

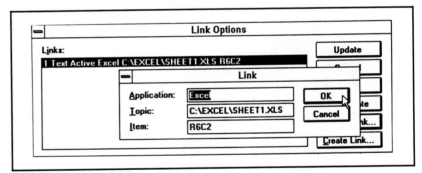

Figure 6.14: Link dialog box for changing links

PART

3

Working with Graphics

CHAPTER 7

Using Frames

WHEN YOU WORK WITH GRAPHICS IN AMI PRO, YOU are working with frames. Ami Pro places frames around charts and drawings automatically to separate the graphics from the text. You can easily add your own frames and modify them in many ways. In this chapter, you will learn how to create and adjust frames for text, pictures, and charts.

CREATING FRAMES

Frames serve to define charts, graphics, and special text on a page. You can use them to contain tips and hints, letterheads, and boiler-plate. For example, if you frequently design how-to articles about electrical installations, you could prepare a frame that contains a standard warning to take great care with high-voltage lines, save the warning, and insert it wherever it's appropriate.

You can link information in frames using DDE and OLE through Windows. (DDE and OLE are described in Chapter 6.) That way, charts imported from Excel, for example, will be updated each time the information in Excel is updated.

If you are using NewWave, Hewlett-Packard's Windows enhancement package, you have even more powerful links available. You can turn a frame over to another NewWave-aware program so it will place its display right in the Ami Pro text. Ami Pro was the leader in embracing NewWave, but unfortunately, it hasn't been followed by a huge crowd of other programs.

ADDING FRAMES TO A PAGE

There are two ways to create a new frame. The quickest method is to use the frame icon on the icon palette. In Chapter 2, you created a sample document and added a frame with the frame icon, which looks like a picture frame. To create a new frame quickly, click on the frame icon, place the mouse pointer where you want the upper-left corner of the frame to appear, and drag the mouse pointer. A rectangle follows the mouse pointer to show the shape of the frame you are creating. Release the mouse button when it is sized as you want.

Alternatively, you can use the Create Frame option on the Frame menu to add a frame. We will use this method now to create two new frames.

1. Pull down the Frame menu and select Create Frame. You will see the dialog box shown in Figure 7.1.

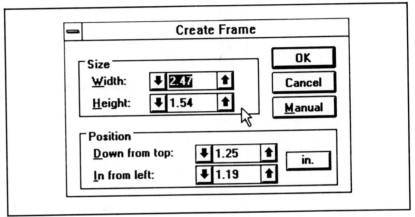

Figure 7.1: Create Frame dialog box

In the Size section of the Create Frame dialog box, you can specify the width and height of the frame. The options in the Position section set the frame's distance from the top of the page and the left margin. You can change the values or accept the ones that are already in the text boxes. Clicking on the button marked Manual has the same effect as clicking on the frame icon in the icon palette.

2. Click on OK.

A new frame appears on the page. The frame wil have the dimensions currently set in the Create Frame dialog box. Now let's add the other frame manually.

3. Pull down the Frame menu and select Create Frame.

4. Click on Manual. The mouse pointer will turn into a frame.

5. Drag a frame that is partially on top of the frame you just created, as shown in Figure 7.2.

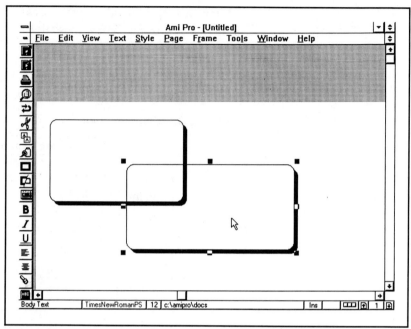

Figure 7.2: Overlapping frames

MANIPULATING FRAMES

Frames can be manipulated in many of the same ways as text. You can cut, copy, and paste them as if they were text. You can select a frame by clicking on it or by, and then change its position or size or delete it.

Resizing a Frame   To resize a frame, place the mouse pointer on a corner handle (one of the tiny black rectangles at the upper-left, lower-left, upper-right, or lower-right corner of the frame), press the mouse button, and drag the frame into the new shape. Using this technique, you can stretch and shrink the frame in any way, changing the position of the edge of the frame.

If you want to constrain the resizing to only one dimension, place the mouse pointer on one of the center handles on the sides of the frame, and then drag the frame to its new size.

The corner handles will adjust the size of the frame in two dimensions. The side handles will adjust the frame size only in one dimension.

Moving a Frame   To move a frame, place the mouse pointer within the selected frame and press the mouse pointer. Drag the mouse, and the frame will follow the mouse movement.

If you drag the frame past the bottom of the page, the frame will move to the next page. Ami Pro will create new pages for you as you move.

Deleting a Frame   If the frame is surrounded by eight tiny black rectangles, it is selected. All you have to do to remove it is press the Del key. If the frame is not surrounded by rectangles, click anywhere within it, and then press Del.

MODIFYING FRAMES

The Columns and Tabs page of the Modify Frame Layout dialog box is very similar to the Columns and Tabs page of the Modify Style dialog box (described in Chapter 5).

The default frame is a rounded rectangle with a drop shadow. Through the Modify Frame Layout dialog box, you can change the frame's type, size, and position, and lines and shadows. You can also set columns and tabs for the text inside the frame.

There are two ways to access the Modify Frame Layout dialog box:

- Click on one of the frames to select it, and then click on the modify frame layout icon in the icon palette (the one next to the frame icon in the default arrangement).
- Pull down the Frame menu and select Modify Frame Layout.

The Modify Frame Layout dialog box, shown in Figure 7.3, is set up in the same format as the Modify Style and Modify Page Layout dialog boxes, which we explored in Chapter 5.

If you click on the Make Default button, in the bottom-left corner of the dialog box, the modifications you make will be applied automatically to all the frames you create.

CHOOSING FRAME TYPE OPTIONS

The first page of the Modify Frame Layout dialog box has options for the way that the text wraps around the frame, the frame's display, and the frame's placement on the page.

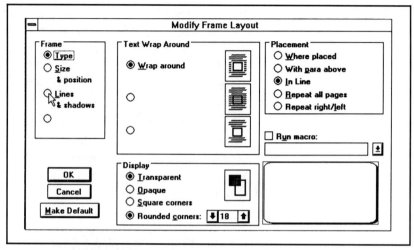

Figure 7.3: Modify Frame Layout dialog box

Changing the Text Wrap   The Text Wrap Around section includes three options along with illustrations of their effects:

- Wrap Around: Flows the text around all four sides of the frame.

- No Wrap Around: Flows the text through the frame. If the frame is transparent, the text is visible beneath it. If the frame is opaque, it will cover the text.

- No Wrap Beside: Flows the text above and under the frame, dividing the text horizontally. The text stops above the frame and continues below it.

You will see how these settings affect the page later in the chapter.

Changing the Text Placement   You can select from five placement choices:

- Where Placed: Attaches the frame to the page where it is created. It will not move with text when text is moved around and there is only one frame (it will not be repeated on subsequent pages like repeating frames).

If you want to keep the frame with the paragraph regardless of page breaks, select the Keep With Next Paragraph option in the Modify Style dialog box. You might want to create a special style for this, similar to Body Text but connected to the next paragraph.

When you select Facing Pages from the View menu, you will be able to see which pages Ami Pro considers to be on the right and on the left. Also, right-hand pages usually have odd numbers.

- With Para Above: Attaches the frame to the paragraph it follows, which is useful for frames for captions. Note that if the text is moved around so that the frame is moved to the next page, the paragraph to which it is attached will not be moved to the next page.

- Flow With Text: Attaches the frame to its position in the text. This is useful for keeping illustrations near the reference in text, for example. Note that the movement of a frame attached to text will be severely restricted. The frame must always overlap the text line where it is anchored.

- Repeat All Pages: Places the frame in the same position on each page.

- Repeat Right/Left: Places a frame that is on a right-hand page on each right-hand page throughout the document, or a frame on a left-hand page on every left-hand page in the document. If you are creating a document that will be printed on both sides of the page and want the frame on the outside edge of right and left pages, create matching frames on consecutive pages in the positions where you want them and select this placement.

Changing the Display   The Display section of the Modify Frame Layout dialog box contains options that affect the frame's corners and fill. You can choose Transparent to make the frame see-through, or Opaque, so that it becomes an object that covers whatever is beneath it. Sometimes you will want your frames to be transparent, but usually, you will want a frame to be opaque.

You can choose square or rounded corners for your frame. If you select rounded corners, you can adjust their degree of roundness by setting a value in the box beside the option.

SPECIFYING THE FRAME SIZE AND POSITION

Rather than using the mouse pointer to drag a frame into another size or position, you can make these adjustments through the Size & Position page of the Modify Frame Layout dialog box. Click on the Size & Position button in the Frame box to see the options shown in Figure 7.4.

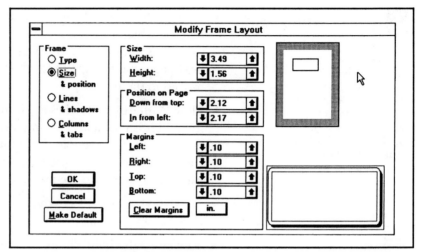

Figure 7.4: Size & Position page of Modify Frame Layout dialog box

Using the options on this page, you can specify the position and size of the selected frame to the hundredth of an inch. The frame's position is illustrated in the top-left corner of the dialog box. You can also set the margins of the frame by setting values in the boxes in the Margins section.

SELECTING FRAME LINES AND SHADOWS

Click on Lines & Shadows in the Frame box at the left side of the Modify Frame Layout dialog box to see the choices shown in Figure 7.5.

The Lines section of the box sets which lines your changes will affect. You can choose a line type from the Style box and change its color by choosing from the palette beneath the Lines section.

In the Shadow section, you can choose None to remove the shadow. The other options set the shadow's depth and style. The color choices for shadows are beneath those for lines.

The Background palette sets the color of the interior of the frame.

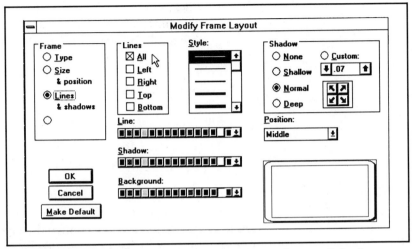

Figure 7.5: Lines & Shadows page of Modify Frame Layout dialog box

WORKING WITH MULTIPLE FRAMES ▬

You cannot use the Modify Frame Layout dialog box to change several frames at one time. You must work with each frame separately.

Ami Pro provides several features for manipulating the frames in your documents. You can rearrange their layering on the page and group frames to link them together.

CHANGING FRAME LAYERING

When you are using more than one frame on a page, the layering of those frames will affect the appearance of the page. Let's begin by getting a clearer view of the two frames you created in this chapter:

1. Pull down the Frame menu and select Modify Frame Layout to display the Modify Frame Layout dialog box.

2. Click on Opaque in the Display box, make sure Where Placed is selected, and then click on OK.

3. Hold down the Shift key and click on the other frame.

Both frames are now selected. Note that each has its own handles.

4. Click on the modify frame layout icon in the icon palette (the one that looks like a frame with a thick border on one side a thin border on the other) to return to the Modify Frame Layout dialog box.

You can't do it, can you? You can only modify one frame at a time.

5. Click on the frame that is not yet opaque.

6. Open the Modify Frame Layout dialog box, click on Opaque, and click on OK.

Now you can clearly see that one frame is in front of the other. The order in which you created the frames determines which ones appear in front of others. You can change the layering by using the Bring to Front and Send to Back commands on the Frame menu.

7. Click on the frame that appears to be in the background to select it.

8. Pull down the Frame menu and select Bring to Front.

The frame that was behind now appears in front of the other frame.

You cannot place a new frame on top of frame that is anchored to the text. If you attempt to do so, both frames will be adjusted so they will not overlap.

You can't select multiple frames if the frame you are trying to select is anchored to the text (for example, with the With Para Above or Flow with Text options in the Modify Frame Layout dialog box). The position of the frame depends on the location of the text to which it is anchored.

GROUPING FRAMES

By using the Group command on the Frame menu, you can group frames so that Ami Pro treats them as a single unit. Grouping frames is useful when you want to build individual frames into larger units. For example, you might group frames that contain an illustration and a caption or a collection of related illustrations.

To group frames, select all the frames you want to group by holding down the Shift key as you click on each one. Then pull down the Frame menu and click on Group.

After you group frames, you cannot modify or size them. If you select the frames and drag one of their handles, all the frames in the group will follow your mouse pointer, moving rather than expanding or shrinking.

You can tell when two or more frames are grouped by clicking on one of them. If it belongs to a group, all the other frames in the group will also be selected. If the frame you select is a member of a group that includes frames that are not currently visible (on another page or a remote area of the current page), pull down the Frame menu and look at the Group option. If the frame is a member of a group, there will be a check mark next to Group.

If you want to ungroup frames so that you can work with them individually, select the grouped frames, and then click on Group on the Frame menu to remove the check mark.

WORKING WITH FRAMES AND TEXT

If you are searching with Find & Replace, you must specify Include Other Text Streams in the Find & Replace Options dialog box to search through both body text and frame text.

In Ami Pro, the text inside a frame and body text are different text streams. Through the options in the Modify Frame Layout dialog box, you can define the relationship of the frame and its text to the body text on the page. You can place a frame at a specific place in text and it will always be connected to that text, as if the frame were a letter in the text. You can flow text around the frame or make a break in the text so that the frame never has normal text beside it on the page. Or you can link the frame to the page so it will always be in the same place, even when the text on the page moves around as it is edited.

The default setting is to have the text wrap around the frame. Unless the text on the page is in columns, placing a frame on the page will cause the text to form two columns in the vicinity of the frame. If this is not what you want, you can change the format using one of the following methods:

- Place the frame so close to the edge of the page that there will be no space for a second column.

- Make the text two columns so it will flow around the frame smoothly.

- Select No Wrap Around or No Wrap Beside in the Modify Frame Layout dialog box.

To see the effects of the text wrap settings, follow these steps:

1. Click on the icon that looks like a floppy disk with an arrow leading away from it to display the Open dialog box.

2. Click on SWEET.SAM, and then click on the button marked Insert to add the document to the window with your frames.

As shown in Figure 7.6, Ami Pro placed the text around the frames, dividing the sentences so that they are difficult to read.

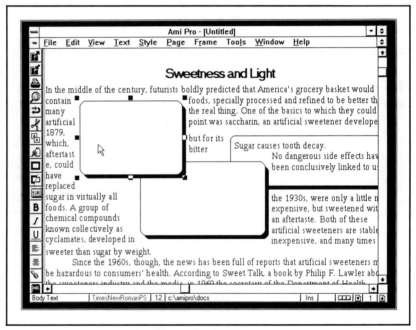

Figure 7.6: Text wrapped around frames

3. Click on the top frame and select Modify Frame Layout from the Frame menu.

4. Click on No Wrap Around in the Text Wrap Around area of the Modify Frame Layout dialog box, and then click on OK.

Now the text has disappeared because it is covered by the opaque frame, as shown in Figure 7.7.

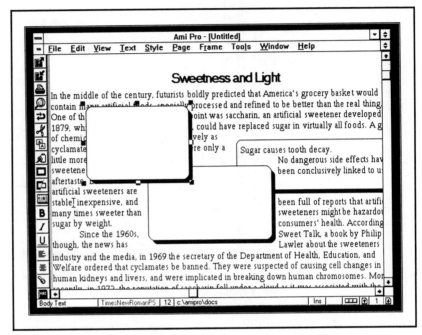

Figure 7.7: Opaque frame completely obscures the text

5. Return to the Modify Frame Layout dialog box, select No Wrap Beside, and click on OK.

Now the text is divided horizontally. The result is that the entire text is shoved downward, as shown in Figure 7.8.

WORKING WITH FRAMES AND GRAPHICS

You can adjust the appearance of a graphic within a frame by using the Graphics Scaling option on the Frame menu. This displays the dialog box shown in Figure 7.9.

You cannot adjust the size of the graphic by adjusting the size of the frame. The frame can be sized as big as the sheet of paper, but the graphic will remain the same size.

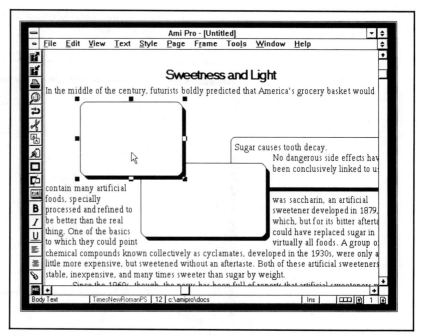

Figure 7.8: Text with no wrap beside frames

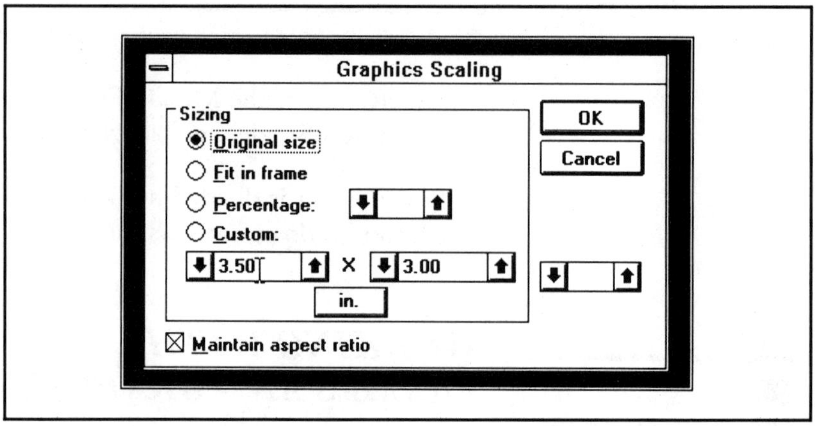

Figure 7.9: Graphics Scaling dialog box

The options in this dialog box allow you to stretch or shrink graphics along with the frame. When Original Size is selected, the graphic will remain the same size, no matter how you size the frame.

Choosing the Fit in Frame option causes the graphic to be sized to fit within the frame. You can also choose a percentage to make the graphic bigger or smaller or specify a width and height for it.

Checking the Maintain Aspect Ratio option causes the height and width of the graphic to be scaled together so they will always be proportional. For representational art, such as a picture of a face or a puppy, you will want to maintain the aspect ratio to prevent a funhouse mirror effect. If the graphic is an abstract image, such as one made up of blocks, you may not be concerned with this type of distortion.

The Rotate option allows you to change the angle of the graphic within the frame. You can specify the amount of degrees to slant the image, or even turn it upside down.

DESIGNING WITH FRAMES

In the following steps, we will use the techniques described in this chapter to create a design that includes a frame, chart, and graphic.

1. Clear the screen by selecting Close until there is no document in the Ami Pro window.

2. Select New from the File menu and accept ˜DEFAULT-.STY as the style sheet.

3. Click on the frame icon in the icon palette and create a small frame.

4. Double-click on the frame and type **Sales of machine guns have actually increased in recent years.**

5. Press Esc until the frame is not selected anymore. The handles will disappear, and the text cursor will return to the page.

6. Pull down the Tools menu and select Charting.

Since the Clipboard does not contain any data, you will see a dialog box with the message

The clipboard contains no text data. Do you wish to enter the data now?

While you are typing, the handles around the frame turn gray. This means that the frame is selected, but because you are using it for text entry, you cannot size or move the frame. Before you can adjust the frame, you must deselect to remove the text cursor from it (by pressing Esc), and then select it again.

7. Click on OK, and the Charting Data dialog box will appear.

8. Enter the following figures: **12591**, **15291**, and **19521**.

9. Click on OK, and then click on OK in the Charting dialog box. Your chart should look like the one shown in Figure 7.10.

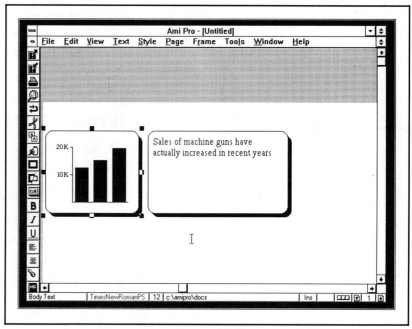

Figure 7.10: Two frames, including one containing text (right) and the other containing a chart (left)

Next, we'll create a frame that will serve as a design element.

10. Pull down the Frame menu, click on Modify Frame Layout, select Where Placed, and then click on OK.

11. Create a larger frame overlapping the bottom of the frame with text in it, as shown in Figure 7.11.

12. Display the Modify Frame Layout dialog box and select No Wrap Beside.

13. Select Lines & Shadows in the Frame section of the Modify Frame Layout box.

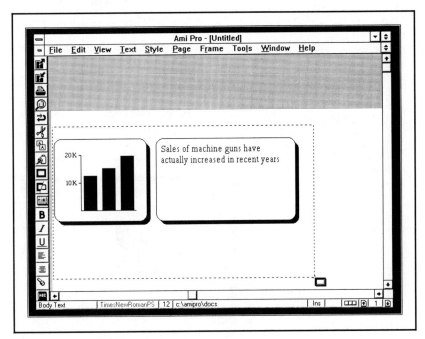

Figure 7.11: Third frame on page

14. Select red as both the line color and the background color and keep the shadow color black. Click on OK to close the dialog box.

15. Click on the frame containing the chart and return to the Modify Frame Layout dialog box. If Transparent is not checked, click on this option.

16. Click on Lines & Shadows. Click on All in the Lines area to turn off the lines around the frame and click on None in the Shadow area to eliminate the shadow. Then click on OK.

17. Click on the frame containing the text and return to the Modify Frame Layout dialog box. If Transparent is not checked, click on this option.

When the chart and text frames are transparent, the red background will show through when the frames are layered.

18. Click on Lines & Shadows. Click on All in the Lines area to turn off the lines around the frame and click on None in the Shadow area to eliminate the shadow.

19. Click on Type.

20. Adjust the size of the text frame so that it's only slightly larger than the text. If it is too small, some of the text will disappear. If that happens, make the frame slightly larger.

At this point, your screen should look like the one shown in Figure 7.12.

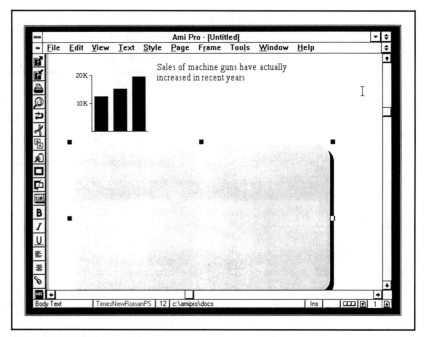

Figure 7.12: Unlayered frames

21. Drag the text so that it is in the top area within the red frame, ending near the right border (so there is room for the chart on the left).

The frame is no longer visible because it is behind the red frame, which was created before this frame. The first step in bringing the text to

The simplest solution would be to select the frame on top and use the Send to Back option on the Frame menu. We are taking the more difficult approach here so you will better understand how to manipulate frames in your own documents.

the front is to select the frame. Although it is already selected because you just moved it, we are going to deselect it first so you can experience some of the problems you may encounter in your own work.

22. Click away from the frame or press Esc so no frame is selected.

Now you are faced with the prospect of selecting a frame you can't see.

23. Position the mouse pointer on top of the area where you know the text frame is beneath the red frame. Hold down the Ctrl key and click twice.

The first time you clicked, the red frame was selected. The next time you clicked, the text frame, though hidden, was selected. You can see its handles through the red frame. However, you can't do anything with the selected frame because anytime you click within the red frame, you will select the red frame.

24. With the text frame selected, pull down the Frame menu and select Bring to Front. The text will appear in front of the red frame.

25. Click on the chart and select Bring to Front from the Frame menu.

Nothing seems to happen because the frame is not layered yet, but when you place the chart on the red frame, it will already be in front.

26. Drag the chart into the left area within the red frame.

Your screen should now look like the one shown in Figure 7.13. As you can see, the chart is too small to be read easily. Now we will enlarge the chart.

27. With the chart frame selected, pull down the Frame menu and select Graphics Scaling to display the Graphics Scaling dialog box. Click on Fit in Frame, and then click on OK.

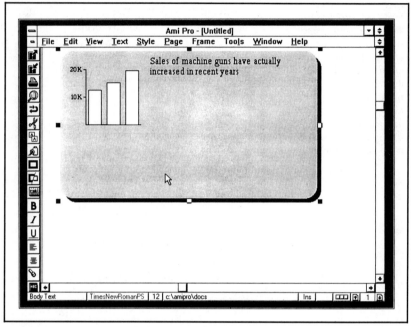

Figure 7.13: Individual items brought together

28. Adjust the frame so the chart is wider, as shown in Figure 7.14.

We will add one more element to this page to complete the design: a picture of a man firing a machine gun, which is one of the images supplied in Ami Pro's symbol files.

You could add the picture by selecting the Import Picture option on the File menu and AmiDraw as the file format.

29. Pull down the Tools menu and select Drawing. A new frame will appear.

30. Pull down the File menu and select Import Drawing. You will see the dialog box shown in Figure 7.15.

The AIMFIRE.SDW file is selected. This is the drawing of a man with an automatic rifle, as shown in the preview box in the lower-right corner of the dialog box. If there is no list of drawings in the dialog box, or if AIMFIRE.SDW isn't one of them, you are probably in the wrong directory. Use the Disk and Directory boxes to change to the DRAW-SYM subdirectory of the AMIPRO directory.

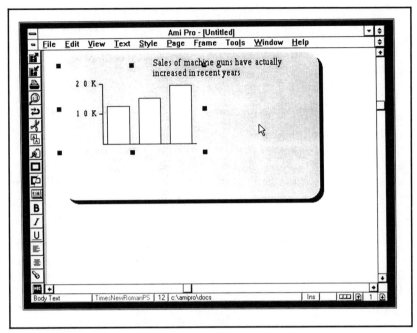

Figure 7.14: Enlarged chart

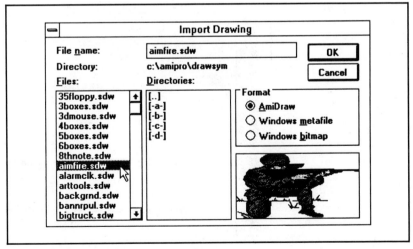

Figure 7.15: Import Drawing dialog box

31. With AIMFIRE.SDW selected, click on OK. The rifleman will appear in its own frame. Click away from the frame to exit drawing mode.

32. Click on the frame again and resize it by dragging the handles until it is barely larger than the drawing.

33. Display the Modify Frame Layout dialog box and select Where Placed, Transparent, and No Wrap Around. Go to the Lines & Shadows page and click on All in the Lines section and None in the Shadow section to remove the outline and shadow. Then click on OK.

34. Move the frame of the picture so that it overlaps the red frame.

35. Pull down the Frame menu and select Graphics Scaling. Select Fit in Frame and click on the check box marked Maintain Aspect Ratio. Then click on OK.

36. Adjust the frame of the picture until the image appears balanced, as shown in Figure 7.16.

Figure 7.16: Completed design

37. Click away from the frames, and then hold down the Shift key and click on each of the frames in turn (there are four now) so that all of them are selected.

38. Pull down the Frame menu and select Group to group the frames so the composition can't be changed.

39. Save the document under the name **MACHNGUN.SAM**.

Since frames are associated with charts and pictures, we have worked with graphics in this chapter. In the next chapter, you will learn more about creating graphics with Ami Pro.

CHAPTER 8

Creating Graphics

IN THE PREVIOUS CHAPTER, YOU LEARNED HOW TO work with one of Ami Pro's main graphic elements: the frame. But Ami Pro offers far more graphic capabilities than simple boxes. You can use its plethora of drawing tools to create your own graphics, ranging from simple squares and circles to freehand drawings. You can also use the program's charting feature to create charts of all types.

DRAWING WITH AMI PRO

To access Ami Pro's drawing features, choose the Drawing option on the Tools menu. A frame will appear on the screen, and you will be presented with a new set of menus and tools, as shown in Figure 8.1.

Under the menu bar are 23 icons representing the tools you can use to create and modify objects. Table 8.1 summarizes the functions of the drawing tools.

Using the drawing tools, you can create and modify objects within the frame on the drawing screen. To leave drawing mode, click outside the drawing frame. Reenter drawing mode by double-clicking inside the drawing frame.

The size of the frame is determined by the current settings in the Create Frame dialog box, which is described in Chapter 7.

CREATING SHAPES

The Ami Pro drawing tools are useful for creating simple drawings that consist of various shapes. In the following steps, we will create a logo using the snap-to, rounded square, circle, and text tools. Refer to Table 8.1 for the icons that represent the tools.

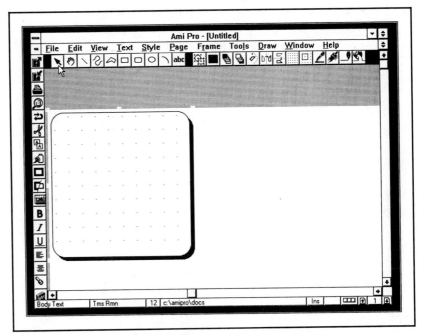

Figure 8.1: Ami Pro drawing screen

Table 8.1: Ami Pro Drawing Tools

Icon	Name	Function
↖	Selection arrow	Selects and sizes objects.
✋	Hand tool	Moves the drawing screen behind the drawing frame, bringing new sections of the drawing screen into view.
╲	Line tool	Draws a straight line from one point to another. To restrain the line to 45-degree angles (0, 45, 90, 135, 180, 225, 270, or 315 degrees), hold down the Shift key while drawing.

Table 8.1: Ami Pro Drawing Tools (Continued)

Icon	Name	Function
〜	Polyline tool	Draws lines where you click the mouse button. Double-click to stop drawing. For freehand drawing, hold down the Shift key while dragging.
△	Polygon tool	Draws closed polygon shapes. Drag to draw lines. Double-click to close the shape. For freehand drawing, hold down the Shift key while dragging.
□	Square tool	Draws rectangles. To create a perfect square, hold down the Shift key while drawing.
▢	Rounded square tool	Draws rectangles with rounded corners. To create a perfect rounded-corner square, hold down the Shift key while drawing.
○	Circle tool	Draws ellipses. To create a perfect circle, hold down the Shift key while drawing.
⌐	Arc tool	Draws a quarter of an ellipse. This is a parabolic arc.
abc	Text tool	Adds text. Click the I-beam mouse cursor and type the characters you want to include in the drawing.
⊕	Select all tool	Selects everything in the drawing frame.
◧	Group/ungroup tool	Groups selected objects into a single unit. If the objects are grouped, this tool ungroups them.
◩	Bring to front tool	Brings the selected object or objects to the front, on top of everything else in the drawing frame.

Table 8.1: Ami Pro Drawing Tools (Continued)

Icon	Name	Function
	Send to back tool	Places the selected object or objects in the back, behind the other objects in the drawing frame.
	Rotate tool	Rotates the selected object in 10-degree increments. Set the amount of rotation with the Rotate option on the Draw menu.
	Flip horizontally tool	Flips the selected object from left to right.
	Flip vertically tool	Flips the selected object from top to bottom.
	Show/hide grid tool	Toggles the grid on (visible) and off (invisible).
	Snap-to tool	When turned on (the square in the tool is not aligned with the grid), snaps objects on grid points.
	Extract line and fill tool	Stores the line and fill styles of the selected object in memory temporarily so that you can copy the same styles to another object.
	Apply line and fill tool	Applies the styles stored in memory by the extract line and fill tool to an object. Click on the object to which you want to apply the styles and select this tool.
	Line style tool	Displays the Line Styles dialog box, which is used to specify line thickness, color, and line endings for the selected object.
	Fill pattern tool	Displays the Fill Pattern dialog box, which is used to specify a pattern and color for the selected object.

You might want to take the time to click on each of the drawing tools just to see what they do before creating the logo. When you are finished experimenting, click on the select all tool and press Del to clear the drawing frame.

1. Pull down the Tools menu and click on Drawing to enter drawing mode.

2. Make sure the snap-to tool is turned on (in the icon, the tiny square is not aligned to the grid; on a monochrome screen, the icon may not be visible when snap-to is turned on).

3. If tiny dots, called the grid, are not visible in the drawing frame, click on the show/hide grid tool to display the grid.

With the grid visible and snap-to turned on, we are ready to create a shape with the rounded square tool. We will constrain the drawing to a perfect square by holding down the Shift key while using the tool.

4. Click on the rounded square tool and press the Shift key. Press the mouse button and drag the mouse diagonally within the drawing frame. Release the mouse button when the rounded square is the size shown in Figure 8.2.

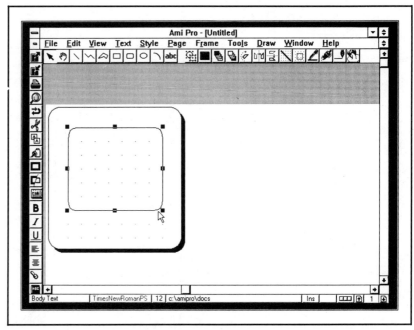

Figure 8.2: Rounded-corner square snapped to grid in drawing frame

Note that the square "snaps" to the grid because the snap-to tool was turned on. Using the snap-to feature ensures that your objects will be of a regular size and can be moved only along the points of the grid. You can turn off snap-to for more flexible object placement, or adjust the size of the space between the dots in the grid by using the Grid Settings option on the Draw menu.

The other shape in our logo will be an oval, or ellipse, created with the circle tool. Since we do not want to draw a perfect circle, use the tool alone, without the Shift key.

5. Click on the circle tool and place the mouse pointer near the middle of the left side of the rounded-corner square. Press and hold down the mouse button, drag to the lower-right corner of the square, and release the mouse button.

6. Click on the text tool and click the I-beam on the left end of the ellipse. Type **sun.**

7. Click on the selection arrow and place the arrow on the text. Press the mouse button and drag the text to the right until it's approximately centered in the ellipse.

You have now created an ellipse in front of a rounded-corner rectangle. Next, we want to make the objects look solid.

SELECTING COLORS AND PATTERNS

You can fill the shapes you create with patterns and colors. Now we will fill the square in the logo with blue and the ellipse with yellow. Then we will choose a color for the text.

1. Click on the rounded-corner square to select it and click on the fill pattern tool. You will see the dialog box shown in Figure 8.3.

The pattern at the far left end of the Pattern section of the Fill Pattern dialog represents no pattern, or no fill for the selected object.

In the Fill Pattern dialog box, you can select from dozens of colors and eight patterns (including solid fill and no fill). You can also create a custom color, as described later in the chapter.

2. Select a dark indigo (blue) color in the Fill Pattern dialog box.

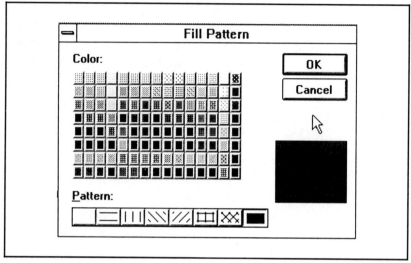

Figure 8.3: Fill Pattern dialog box

3. Click on the pattern at the far right end of the Pattern area, which fills the square with a solid color.

4. Click on OK.

Since the ellipse is transparent, all you see now is a blue square. In order to give the ellipse a fill, you must first select it.

5. Click on the ellipse. If you accidentally select the square, press the Ctrl key and try again.

6. Click on the fill pattern tool and select a bright yellow from the Fill Pattern dialog box. Click on OK.

7. Click on the line style tool to display the Line Styles dialog box, shown in Figure 8.4.

The Line Styles dialog box contains a list box of line styles, ten different endings selections, and a palette of color choices.

8. Select yellow for the line color and click on OK.

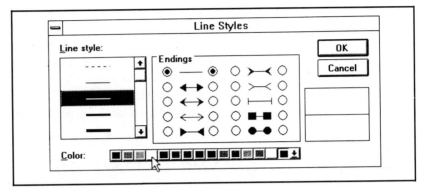

Figure 8.4: Line Styles dialog box

The yellow ellipse appears in front of the dark blue rounded-corner square because it was drawn more recently. The text appears in front of the ellipse for the same reason. Let's make the text the same color as the square beneath the ellipse.

9. Click on the text, pull down the Text menu in the main menu bar, and select Font.

10. In the Font dialog box, click on the downward-pointing arrow at the right end of the palette. You will see a palette similar to the one in the Fill Pattern dialog box.

11. Click on a dark indigo color again, and then click on OK in the Font dialog box.

We have completed the sample logo, which consists of two shapes and text, each filled with a color.

12. Save the document as **SUN.SAM**.

The logo may look a little jagged in the illustration in this book, but that is because the drawing is reproduced at screen resolution—below the 300 dot per inch (dpi) pitch of a laser printer, and far, far below the high quality you will obtain if you route this text through a typesetter. Ami Pro can generate PostScript output through Windows. The quality of the output depends on the capabilities of the printer, not the computer screen resolution. If you have a laser printer, you might want to pause right now to print the current page.

In some cases, your on-screen drawings will look smoother than your printed reproductions. For example, if your computer is equipped with antialiasing hardware (such as a graphics board with the Edsun chip), the objects will look smooth and perfectly contoured on your screen. When you print the drawing on a 9-pin dot-matrix printer at or near screen resolution, the lines look jagged. This same drawing printed on a laser printer will look very smooth.

MANIPULATING OBJECTS

You can import AmiDraw or Windows metafile graphics into Ami Pro, as described in Chapter 6, and use Ami Pro's drawing tools to modify them. (Imported bit-map images can only be resized in draw mode.)

After you have created objects in Ami Pro, you can modify them by using drawing tools, such as the rotate and flip horizontally tools. You can also move, copy, resize, and reshape objects and create custom colors, as described in the following sections.

SELECTING OBJECTS

As when you change text, you must first select an object before you can modify it. Use the following techniques to select objects in a drawing frame:

- To select an object, click on the selection arrow and then click within the object you want to select.

- To select an object within a stack of objects, click on the selection arrow, click within one of the objects in the stack, hold down the Ctrl key, and keep clicking until the object you want is selected.

- To select multiple objects, hold down the Shift key and click on each of the objects in turn.

- To deselect an object, click away from it, or hold down the Shift key and click on it.

Selected objects appear with handles, which you can use to size the shapes in the drawing frame.

MOVING, COPYING, SIZING, AND SHAPING OBJECTS

After an object (or objects) is selected, you can modify it by using one of the following methods:

- To move an object, place the selection arrow within it and drag.

- To copy an object, place the selection arrow within it, press the Shift key, and drag.

- To size an object, drag one of the square, black handles that appear around its perimeter. Side handles adjust the size in one direction. Corner handles adjust the size in two directions.

- To change the shape of an object, double-click within the selected object. You can change the control points that make up the object, alter the position of the center of rotation, or rotate the object.

- To delete an object, press Del.

You can also use the Cut, Copy, and Paste commands on the Edit menu or their keyboard equivalents to modify your drawings.

Now we'll draw some other types of shapes and modify them using the techniques described above.

1. Pull down the File menu and select New. When the new window appears, click on its Maximize box to make it fill the Ami Pro window.

2. Select Drawing from the Tools menu.

3. Make sure the snap-to tool is turned on, and then click on the polyline tool.

4. Click 20 or 25 times on random points in the drawing frame, and then double-click to stop drawing.

5. Double-click anywhere within the polyline shape.

To rotate an object
smoothly, don't use
the rotate tool. Instead,
double-click inside the
selected object to see the
center of rotation (a large
black spot), the control
points that make up the
object, and rotation
arrows. Drag a rotation
arrow in the direction you
want to rotate the object.

As shown in the example in Figure 8.5, the shape now has features you can use to change it. The small black rectangles are the control points of the shape, the large black dot in the center is the center of rotation, and the four arrows around the outside are rotation handles. If you drag a rotation handle, you will rotate the whole shape. You can drag the center of rotation to a new location, and the polyline will rotate around it. When you drag a control point, you alter one of the angles.

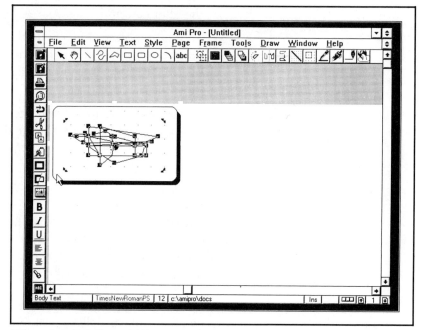

Figure 8.5: Polyline with its control points, rotation handles, and center of rotation visible

6. Place the mouse pointer on one of the small black rectangles that appear at the bends in the polyline, press the mouse button, and drag the rectangle.

The lines that make up the angle that runs through that control point will move to follow the control point, changing the angle. You can also delete control points to change the shape.

7. Double-click on the control point you just dragged.

The control point disappears, and the line that used to be bent now runs straight between the other two control points that make up the angle. If you double-click on an endpoint, the last segment on that end will disappear.

8. Drag the rotation handles of the shape.

9. Drag the center of rotation to one side and drag the rotation handles again.

10. Click on the select all tool and press Del to remove all the objects from the drawing frame.

11. Turn off the snap-to tool.

12. Click on the polygon tool, click about 10 times around the drawing frame, and then double-click. The polygon shape will close automatically.

13. Click on the fill pattern tool and choose a pink color from the Fill Pattern dialog box.

Your polygon may look similar to the one shown in Figure 8.6. When a polygon's outline crosses itself, the colors cancel each other out.

14. Double-click within the polygon to see its control points and center of rotation.

15. Drag some of the control points. Try to make parts of the polygon cross itself.

16. Double-click in the center of a side (*not* on a control point).

It looks as if one of the control points has disappeared. But actually, you have just created a new control point.

17. Place the mouse pointer on the location where the control point should be. Press the mouse button and drag. The new control point will move away, creating a new side.

18. Click on the select all tool and press Del to clear the drawing frame.

19. Click on the square tool and draw a rectangle in the drawing frame.

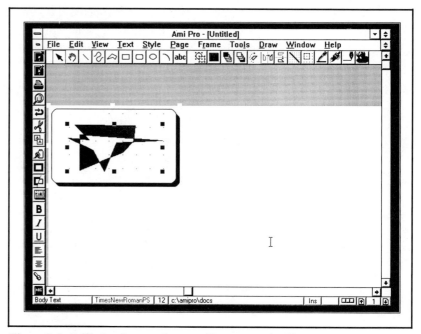

Figure 8.6: A filled polygon whose outline crosses itself

20. Click on the circle tool and draw an ellipse. Drag the ellipse so that it's close to the center of the rectangle.

21. With the ellipse selected, hold down the Shift key and click on the rectangle.

Both objects should be selected, and you should see two sets of handles on the screen.

22. Click on the group tool, and only one set of control handles will be visible.

23. Double-click within the grouped object. All you will be able to see is the center of rotation and the rotation handles.

You have grouped the two objects into a single object. Unfortunately, in the process of grouping, you have lost access to some useful tools, such as the control points.

24. Click on the group tool again to ungroup the two objects.

25. Click away from the two objects so they are no longer selected.

26. Click on the ellipse to select it.

Your screen should look similar to the one shown in Figure 8.7. Now we're going to move the objects off-center and make the ellipse more irregular. Then we will flip the object.

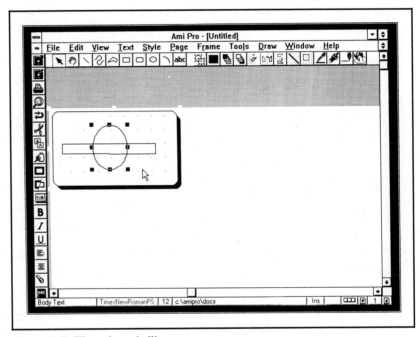

Figure 8.7: The selected ellipse

27. Double-click inside the ellipse to see its control points. Then drag a couple of the control points to distort the ellipse.

You can move a shape when its control points are visible by positioning the mouse pointer away from a control point and dragging.

28. Place the mouse pointer on the outline of the ellipse and drag it off the center of the rectangle.

29. Click on the flip horizontally tool, and the ellipse will face in the opposite direction.

30. Click on the flip vertically tool, and the ellipse will turn upside down.

31. Clear the drawing frame by clicking on the select all tool and pressing Del.

32. Click on the line tool and draw a line from the center of the drawing frame to the lower-right corner.

33. Click on the selection arrow and click on the line to select it.

34. With the line selected, click on the line styles tool.

35. In the Endings section of the Line Styles dialog box, click on the fourth arrowhead in the left column and the second style in the right column, as shown in Figure 8.8. Then click on OK.

36. Click on the circle tool, hold down the Shift key, and draw a circle with its center at the arrowhead.

37. Click on the selection arrow and click on the circle to select it.

38. Click on the fill pattern tool and fill the circle with a yellow color.

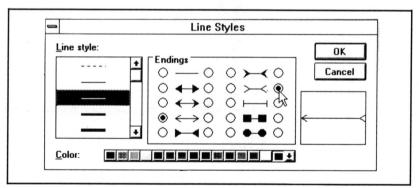

Figure 8.8: The endings selections made in the Line Styles dialog box

Now the arrowhead has disappeared behind the newer circle.

39. With the circle selected, click on the send to back tool to place the circle behind the arrowhead.

Leave these objects in the drawing frame. We will use them shortly.

CUSTOMIZING COLORS

If you cannot find the colors you want to use for your graphics in Ami Pro's palettes, you can mix your own custom colors. Double-click on any of the colors in the palette in the Fill Pattern dialog box (or the Modify Frame Layout dialog box) to see the Custom Colors dialog box, shown in Figure 8.9.

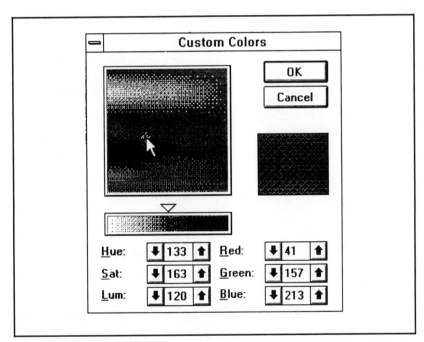

Figure 8.9: Custom Colors dialog box

To mix a new color, drag the mouse pointer over the colored area in the top-left corner until the color you want is in the box in the middle of the right side of the dialog box. If you want to mix a color by entering values, you can enter the hue, saturation (Sat), and luminance (Lum) values in the text boxes at the bottom left of the dialog box, and the red, green, blue percentages in the text boxes on the right side. You can also change the luminance value by dragging through the box above the hue, saturation, and luminance text boxes.

CREATING A LETTERHEAD: A GRAPHICS PROJECT

Now that you have had some practice using Ami Pro's drawing tools, you can put them to use for practical projects. In this section, we will work on the typical business project of creating a letterhead.

Let's suppose that we have been contracted by a company that makes DOS utilities to create a letterhead for its correspondence. The company is called DIR Straits. By coincidence, we created their logo in our last exercise: the circle with an arrow through its center.

If you skipped the last exercise but want to follow this one, go back to the previous section and complete steps 31 through 39.

1. Click outside the drawing frame created in the last exercise to leave drawing mode.

2. Click once on the drawing frame, and then click on the modify frame icon in the icon palette to display the Modify Frame Layout dialog box.

3. Click on the arrow at the right end of the Background palette and click on the pale yellow color in the top row.

4. Click the Lines Shadows in the Frame section. In the Shadow section, click on None to eliminate the drop shadow beneath the drawing frame.

5. Click on Type in the Frame section, and then click on Square Corners in the Display section.

6. Select Where Placed in the Placement section.

7. Click on No Wrap Beside in the Text Wrap Around section.

8. Click on OK to make the changes and leave the Modify Frame Layout dialog box.

The Modify Frame Layout dialog box settings produce a frame with no shadow containing the logo of the DIR Straits company. Now we need another frame for the text of the letterhead.

9. Click on the frame icon in the icon palette. Drag a frame that takes up the rest of the top part of the page, as shown in Figure 8.10.

10. Click on the modify frame layout icon in the icon palette and set the options to make the new frame similar to the drawing frame: yellow, squared corners, and no shadow.

11. Double-click within the new frame and type **DIR Straits**.

12. Use the mouse to drag through the text and select it.

13. Pull down the Text menu and select Font.

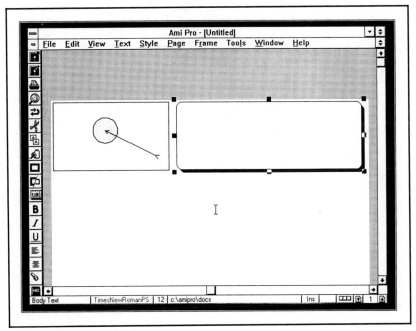

Figure 8.10: Logo and frames for the letterhead

If only DIR appears in the new frame, your text is too large or your frame is too small. Return to the Fonts dialog box and make the text slightly smaller. Keep adjusting it until the text is as large as possible and yet fits completely in the frame.

14. Make the text Tms Rmn or Roman with a size of 55 points, and then click on OK.

15. Pull down the Text menu, select Alignment, and click on Center to center the text in the frame.

16. Move the text cursor to the end of *DIR Straits* and press ◄┘ to create a new line. You may need to adjust the size of text to make the text cursor visible.

17. Type **DOS Utilities and Design Consultants**.

18. Press ← again and type **81 Thomas Mann Expressway**.

19. Press the spacebar twice and type **Euphrates, California**.

20. If the text is not centered, drag through it and select Center from the Alignment dialog box.

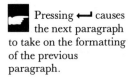
Pressing ← causes the next paragraph to take on the formatting of the previous paragraph.

Your completed letterhead should look like the one shown in Figure 8.11.

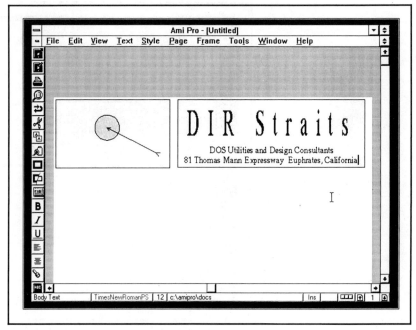

Figure 8.11: Completed letterhead

21. Save the letterhead as **DIRSTRTS.SAM**.

CREATING CHARTS

In Chapters 2 and 7, you have used the Charting option on the Tools menu to create simple bar charts. When you select this option, Ami Pro assumes that the data for the chart is in the Clipboard.

One way to get data into the Clipboard is by copying it from a spreadsheet. You could also enter values in an Ami Pro document and copy them to the Clipboard.

When you click on the OK button in the Charting dialog box, a chart in the type you selected will appear in a frame on the page. You can return to the Charting dialog box by simply double-clicking on the frame.

SELECTING A CHART TYPE

The types of charts you can create with Ami Pro appear in the Charting dialog box. Each type of chart is useful for a different kind of data. Select from the following chart types:

- Column chart: Used to show discrete values, similar to a line chart.

- Stacked-column chart: Used to show how parts make up a whole, similar to a pie chart. The height of the column represents the total of the component parts.

- Bar chart: Similar to a column chart, but oriented horizontally rather than vertically.

- Stacked-bar chart: Similar to the stacked-column chart, but turned 90 degrees.

- Line chart: Used to track changes over time.

- Area chart: Used to track changes in relative proportions over time. When area charts are used to represent absolute values, the height of the top of the area represents the total of the component areas.

- Line-and-picture: Similar to a line chart. Choose from two variations: a chart in which a single line marker is used for each series of elements, or one in which a different line marker is used for each horizontal tick mark (so that different line markers are used along each individual series of elements).

- Pie chart: Used to show how component parts contribute to the whole. The circumference of the circle represents 100 percent. A pie chart presents relative data rather than absolute data. You can select from a regular pie chart or an exploded pie chart.

- Picture chart: Like a bar chart, except that it uses vertically distorted line markers.

- Stacked-picture chart: Like a stacked-bar chart, except that it uses enlarged line marker shapes instead of bars.

The appearance of the chart in the type you select depends on the data you are graphing. To see which type is best suited for your data, click on each of these options in the Charting dialog box.

CHOOSING CHARTING OPTIONS

In the Options section of the Charting dialog box, you can select to give your chart a legend or grid, or make it three-dimensional. A legend explains what the pattern or color in a chart represents.

Axes are used to illustrate the ranges involved in a chart. The horizontal axis (also called the x-axis or the mantissa) runs along the bottom of a chart and usually represents time. The vertical axis (also called the y-axis or the ordinate) runs up the left of most charts, and it usually represents quantities.

You may want to select a grid for charts with axes. Tick marks are marks placed at regular intervals on the axes. A grid is an extended set of tick marks, with lines running through the chart. A grid makes a chart easier to interpret, but it also makes the chart more cluttered.

The 3D option makes a chart three-dimensional rather than two-dimensional. For example, the bars in a bar chart look like rectangular solid shapes. If you choose 3D, the Perspective option becomes available. Use this option to set the depth of the chart shapes and make them appear in perspective (with "closer" parts larger and "more distant" parts smaller).

By default, Ami Pro automatically adjusts the minimum, maximum, and increment values on the axes of your chart. If you would prefer to use different values, click on Automatic in the Axis section of the Charting dialog box and enter the new settings.

To edit the values that are used in the chart, click on the button marked Data. Your values will appear in a large text box.

When you have selected a type of chart that uses line markers (a line-and-picture, picture, or stacked-picture chart), the Pictures button in the Charting dialog box becomes available. Click on the Picture button to see the shapes you can use in your charts. The

Charting Pictures dialog box and the dialog box for importing your own AmiDraw picture are shown in Figure 8.12.

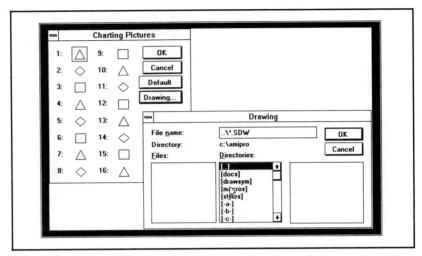

Figure 8.12: Selecting pictures

The Flip Data check box changes the arrangement of the series of data. It switches the data from the horizontal and vertical axes.

You can also choose colors for your charts, as explained in the next section.

SETTING UP A COLOR CHART

In the following steps, we will create a color bar chart. While setting up the chart, we will use some of the options described in the previous section.

1. Open a new document and type the following information into it, pressing Tab between columns of text and ← at the end of each line.

Maintenance	200	100
Materials	150	110
Manpower	800	650

This information represents expenditures for maintenance, materials, and manpower in two different years.

2. Drag through the text and select Cut from the Edit menu.

3. Select Charting from the Tools menu. You will see the dialog box shown in Figure 8.13.

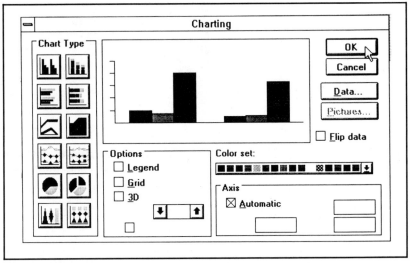

Figure 8.13: Charting dialog box with values for sample chart

Because of how the values were entered, the chart shows how the expenditures for maintenance, materials, and manpower compare with each other during the two years represented. But suppose that we want to show how each set of expenditures compared with the same set in each year, such as how manpower in one year compares with manpower in the other year. This is where the Flip Data option comes in handy.

4. Click on the Flip Data check box. This exchanges series of information, as shown in Figure 8.14.

5. Click on Legend to add a legend to the chart.

6. Click on Grid, 3D, and Perspective.

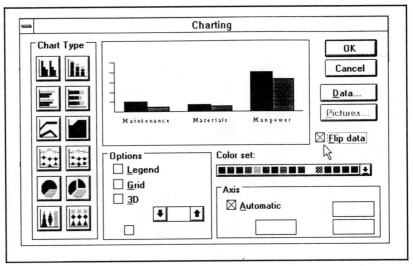

Figure 8.14: Chart with flipped data

The Depth text box allows you to specify a third dimension for the chart. You can experiment by adjusting the depth values to see what effect they have on the chart. When you are finished, return the value to 50.

7. Click on the downward-pointing arrow at the right end of the color palette.

You will see a larger palette. Instead of selecting single colors on this palette, you will select a series of colors represented by the color bar in a row. However, you are not limited to the colors you see in the color palette.

8. Double-click on one of the colors in one of the color bars.

You will see the familiar Fill Pattern dialog box. This allows you to specify a pattern as well as a color for this particular part of the range.

9. In the Fill Pattern dialog box, click on a pattern with diagonal stripes.

10. Click on OK to place the chart in the document.

Use the Custom Colors dialog box (double-click on one of the colors in the Fill Patterns dialog box) to mix your own colors for your charts. For example, do charts in your company colors, or put your series in your color and your competitor's series in mud brown.

Your completed chart should look like the one shown in Figure 8.15.

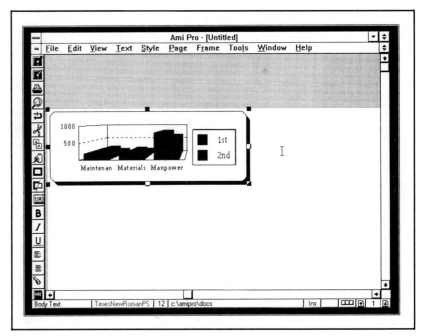

Figure 8.15: Completed three-dimensional chart

After you create a chart, you can enhance it by adding frames to it and grouping the frames to make them one unit, as explained in Chapter 7. However, you should be careful not to add too much to a chart. Make sure that the chart remains clear and simple enough to be read at a glance. A chart that takes several seconds to figure out might as well be replaced by text.

PART 4

Working with
Power Features

CHAPTER 9

Merging
Documents

IF YOU NEED TO PRODUCE FORM LETTERS FOR business or personal use, you will appreciate Ami Pro's merge feature. You can use this feature to create all types of documents, from contracts to invitations. You can generate personalized advertising for all of your best customers, produce mailing labels, or print requests for information.

PRODUCING FORM DOCUMENTS

Merging is a way to insert specific pieces of information, called variable information because it is different for each document, into a document as it is being printed. The variable information comes from a data file, which can be created with a database program or in Ami Pro. The document that the information will be merged into is a normal text file with special coding to mark where the variable information should be inserted.

STRUCTURING DATA FILES

The data file for a merge operation consists of three parts: the delimiters, which are the symbols that are used to separate information in the file; the field names, which are the names in the merge document that will be replaced by the variable information; and the actual data to be merged in each copy of the document.

You establish which symbols are used as delimiters in the first line of your data file. Generally, the hyphen (-) separates fields, and the vertical bar (¦) separates records. Other valid symbols that can be used as delimiters are $ (dollar sign), # (number sign), ! (exclamation point), % (percent sign), ((open parenthesis),) (close parenthesis), and ~ (tilde). These symbols can be used either as field delimiters or record delimiters, depending on how they appear in the first line of the file.

The next section of the file (the next line) establishes the list of field names. Typical field names for an address, for example, are First Name, Last Name, Street, City, State, and Zip. You can use up to 79 characters, with any combination of letters and numbers, for a field name.

The next section of the data file contains the variable information. For an address merge, this would include each name, street, city, state, and zip code for the documents. This section could consist of a few pieces of information or thousands.

Let's create a brief data file:

You can type field names in uppercase or lowercase letters. Ami Pro will automatically display them in all uppercase letters.

Be careful to enter the variable information in the correct fields, or the wrong data will appear in the merged documents. When you use a database program to create the data file, the fields are clearly marked and may even be restricted. However, when you create a data file with Ami Pro, there are no safeguards to prevent you from making such errors.

1. Start Ami Pro and open a new document.

2. Type the following information:

   -¦

   HAIR-EYES-NAME¦

   red-blue-Charly¦

   black-green-Beth¦

3. Save the data file as **DESCRIP.SAM**.

We will use this data file with the merge document, which we will create in the next section.

CREATING MERGE DOCUMENTS

The keys to the merging process are the merge fields that you insert in the merge document. Merge fields mark where the variable information in the data file is to be placed during printing. In the merge document, the field names are enclosed in angle braces (< >).

To insert a merge field, place the text cursor where the variable information should go, and then select Insert from the Edit menu. From the Insert menu, select Merge Field to display the Insert Merge Field dialog box. Click on the Data File button and select the data file that contains the information for the merge document from the list of files. After you select a data file, the names of the fields appear in the Insert Merge Field dialog box. Choose the field name that represents the data to be inserted at the current cursor position, and then click on Insert to place the field name in the document.

Now we will use this procedure to create a short merge document with the field names from our sample data file.

1. Open a new file and type the following text:

   The subject's name is . The subject has   hair and   eyes.

Be sure to leave a space before the first period and two spaces before *hair* and *eyes*. If you don't enter the spaces, the variable information will be merged without them, so that the words and sentences aren't separated.

2. Place the text cursor just before the first period, pull down the Edit menu, and select Insert.

3. From the Insert menu, select Merge Field.

4. In the Insert Merge Field dialog box, click on the Data File button. You will see the dialog box shown in Figure 9.1.

5. Scroll through the list of files until you locate the data file from which you want to insert information: DESCRIP.SAM. Double-click on its name.

The field names in the data file will appear in the Field Names list box in the Insert Merge Field dialog box.

6. In the Insert Merge Field dialog box, click on NAME in the Field Names list box, and then click on Insert.

When you click on Insert in the Insert Merge Field dialog box, the field name <NAME> will be inserted at the cursor location in your merge document. The dialog box remains on the screen.

7. Click on the middle of the space before *hair* in the merge document. There should be a space before and a space after the text cursor. If not, use the cursor keys to adjust the position of the cursor.

8. In the Insert Merge Field dialog box, click on HAIR, then the Insert button to insert <HAIR> into the document.

If the Insert Merge Field dialog box is in the way, drag it by its title bar to another location. Note that this dialog box has many features normally associated with a window: a Control menu (close box), a title bar, and persistence—it doesn't go away after you use it.

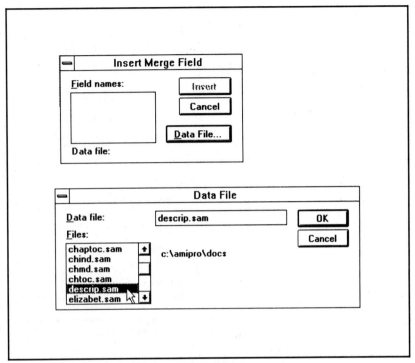

Figure 9.1: Data File and Insert Merge Field dialog boxes

9. Click in the middle of the space before *eyes* in the document. Again, adjust the position of the text cursor so that there is a space before and after it.

10. Click on EYES, then Insert in the Insert Merge Field dialog box to add <EYES> to the document.

11. Double-click on the close box in the Insert Merge Field dialog box.

12. Save the file as **SUBJTLST.SAM**.

With the data file and merge document set up properly, you are ready to produce your form documents.

PRINTING THE DOCUMENTS

The actual merging takes place when you print your documents. Everything up to this point is preparation for the merge.

When you are ready to produce your documents, select Merge from the File menu. You can select merge options, or just click on OK to accept the option for merging and printing the documents.

Follow these steps to merge and print your sample documents:

1. Pull down the File menu and select Merge. You will see the dialog box in Figure 9.2.

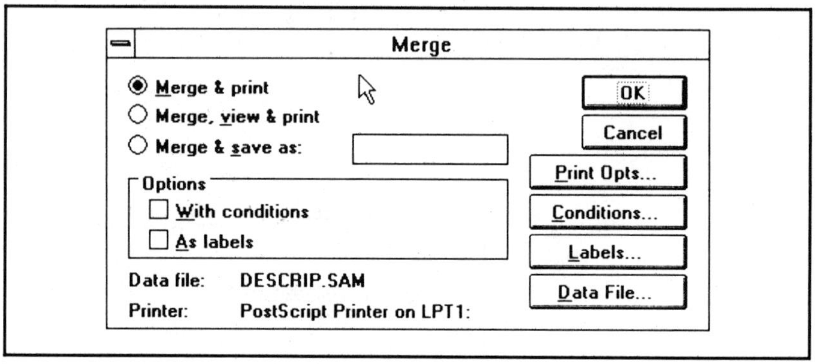

Figure 9.2: Merge dialog box

Instead of just printing your documents, you can choose Merge, View & Print to view the merged documents on your screen before printing them. Alternatively, you can choose Merge & Save As to save the merged documents as a single file that can be printed at another time. The other merging options are described later in the chapter.

2. Make sure that the printer listed at the bottom of the dialog box is the one that is currently connected to your computer, and that your printer is turned on and on-line. Then click on OK.

Ami Pro will generate two pages—one for each record in the data file.

If the Merge dialog box lists the wrong printer, click on the Print Opts button, click on the Setup button in the Print dialog box, and change to the correct printer.

CONDITIONAL MERGING

A more advanced merge operation is based on conditions that you specify. A condition tells Ami Pro to do the merge if some situation exists; otherwise, do not merge the information. Think of a condition as a test. Each database record is compared to the conditions. If it passes the test, it is included; if it fails the test, it is excluded.

To create conditions, choose File from the Merge menu, click on With Conditions in the Merge dialog box, and then click on the Conditions button. In the Merge Conditions dialog box, click on the first check box next to If to turn on this condition, and then click on the name of the field to which you want to apply the condition. Place the cursor in the list in the Operator box and choose one of the following operators:

=	Equal to
<	Less than
>	Greater than
! =	Not equal to
< =	Less than or equal to
> =	Greater than or equal to

Next, type the value to be used with the operator. For example, if you wanted to include only products that cost less than $100, you would choose the < operator and type 100 in the Value box.

You can define up to three conditions for a merge operation. Continue to turn on conditions and specify operators and values for each one.

When you specify more than one condition, you can define them as And or Or conditions. Or is inclusive. With Or conditions, the field must fail both tests to be excluded. By contrast, if you use And, the field is excluded if it fails either of the tests.

To see how conditions work, we will modify our data file and merge document, and then specify a condition based on the new fields we added.

1. Open the DESCRIP.SAM file and click the mouse pointer between NAME and the vertical bar.

2. Type **-AGE-INCOME**.

3. Click between *Charly* and the vertical bar and type **-25-50000**.

4. Click between *Beth* and the vertical bar and type **-32-75000**.

5. Click on the line beneath *Beth*, type **blonde-gray-Hobart-45-25000¦**, and press ⬅.

6. Type **brown-hazel-Zora-39-35000¦**.

7. Press Ctrl-S to save the file.

Now we have some quantifiable fields in our records. Next, we will add the fields to the merge document.

8. Open the SUBJTLST.SAM file, click after the end of the text, and press ⬅.

9. Type **Subject's age is   and income is** .

Be sure to leave two spaces after the first *is* and a space between the second *is* and the period.

10. Click on the center of the space between *is* and *and*.

11. Pull down the Edit menu, select Insert, and then choose Merge Field.

12. In the list of fields, click on AGE, then Insert.

13. Click just ahead of the period in the document, then on INCOME, then on Insert.

14. Pull down the File menu and select Merge.

15. In the Merge dialog box, click on With Conditions.

16. The Merge Conditions dialog box appears. Click on the Conditions button to bring up the list of the available fields in the Field Name box.

17. Click on the check box beside the first If. Place the cursor in the first Field Name box and then click on AGE in the Field Name list to place it in the box.

As shown in Figure 9.3, the Field Name list box is joined by the Operator box.

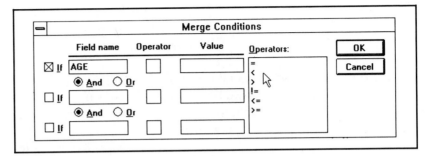

Figure 9.3: Merge Conditions dialog box

18. Move the cursor to the Operator box and click on the less-than sign (<).

19. The cursor automatically moves to the first Value box. Type **40**.

This condition specifies people who are under 40 years of age. People who are 40 will be left out, along with anyone who is 41, 42, and so on.

20. Click on the check box next to the second If. Place the cursor in the second Field Name box and then click on INCOME in the Field Name list box.

21. Click on the greater-than sign (>).

22. The cursor moves automatically to the second Value box. Type **25000**.

This condition excludes anyone whose income is $25,000 or lower.

23. Click on OK.

24. In the Merge dialog box, make sure that Merge & Print is selected and click on OK.

Three pages are printed: Charly, age 25, with an income of $50,000; Beth, age 32, with an income of $75,000; and Zora, age 39, with an income of $35,000.

25. Return to the Merge Conditions dialog box and delete all the conditions by clicking on the check box next to each If to remove the check marks.

In this example, we left And as the setting between the conditions. If we had selected Or, our list would have included anyone who is younger than 40 *or* whose income is greater than $25,000.

Another strategy is to use the same field in two conditions to limit the merge. In our example, choosing the AGE field and specifying > 25 for one condition, selecting And, and then selecting AGE again and entering < 40, would result in a merge that included only people who are above 25 (Beth, Hobart, and Zora) and below 40 (Charly, Beth, and Zora). When And is used, only records that pass both tests would be included (Beth and Zora), and so only their records would be used in the merge.

MERGING MAILING LABELS

Printing mailing labels is another major application of the merge function. If you have a large mailing list, you can merge it to create labels.

To merge your address data file to print labels, set up the data file and merge document with the appropriate fields, as described earlier in this chapter. When you are ready to print the labels, choose Merge from the File menu, and in the Merge dialog box, click on the As Labels check box in the Options section, then on the Labels button.

Print sample labels to see if the Merge Labels dialog box settings are appropriate.

The Merge Labels dialog box that appears contains settings for the number of labels across and down the page, indents for positioning the address of the labels, and the number of copies of each label. The default settings are for printing sheet labels.

Now we will revise our sample data file, create a new merge document for labels, and merge them.

1. Return to the DESCRIP.SAM file by clicking on its window or pulling down the Window menu and selecting it.

2. Pull down the File menu, select Save As, and change the name of the data file to **XMASLIST.SAM**. The new name will appear in the window's title bar.

3. In the second line of the data file, drag through *HAIR-EYES-NAME* and type **LASTNAME-FIRSTNAME**.

4. Drag through *AGE-INCOME* and type **ADDRESS-CITY-STATE-ZIP**.

5. In the third line, drag through *red-blue* and type **Bluestein**. Click after *25* and type **51 Augment Lane-Chicago-Illinois**.

6. In the fourth line, drag through *black-green* and type **Black**. Click after *32* and type **23 Berryville Road-New Era-Michigan**.

7. In the fifth line, drag through *blonde-gray* and type **Barbour**. Click after *45* and type **1 Harrison Avenue-Peoria-Illinois**.

8. In the sixth line, drag through *brown-hazel* and type **Hazelton**. Click after *39* and type **A Pillsbury Terrace-Verona-Iowa**.

9. Press Ctrl-S to save the file.

Your modified data file should look like the one shown in Figure 9.4. Now we are ready to create the merge document for the labels. This is easy because Ami Pro provides the ˜ LABEL.STY style sheet, which is designed specifically for mailing labels.

10. Pull down the File menu, select New, click on ˜ LABEL.STY in the New dialog box, and click on OK.

11. Select Insert from the Edit menu and click on Merge Field.

12. Click on the Data File button and double-click on the name XMASLIST.SAM in the list box.

13. Click on FIRSTNAME and click on Insert.

14. Click in the mailing label document after the <FIRSTNAME> field, press the spacebar, click on LASTNAME, and click on Insert.

15. Click in the label after <LASTNAME> and press ⏎ to complete the first line of the mailing label document.

16. Click on ADDRESS, click on Insert, click in the mailing label after <ADDRESS>, and press ⏎.

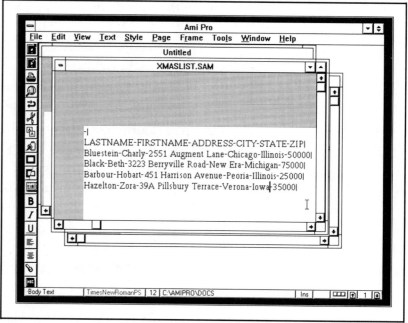

Figure 9.4: Completed data file

17. Click on CITY, click on Insert, and then click after
    <CITY> in the mailing label.

18. Type a comma and a space in the label. Then click on
    STATE and click on Insert.

19. Click in the mailing label after <STATE> and press the
    spacebar. Click on ZIP, then on Insert.

The mailing label merge document now has all the fields it needs
for printing.

20. Double-click on the Insert Merge Field dialog box
    close box.

21. Pull down the File menu and select Merge.

22. In the Merge dialog box, click on the As Labels check box,
    then on the Labels button.

The Merge Labels dialog box, shown in Figure 9.5, will take care of nearly all the work for you. You can accept the default settings for sheet labels or make the necessary changes.

23. When the settings in the Merge Labels dialog box are correct for your labels and printer, click on OK.

24. Put your sheets of labels in your sheet feeder and click on OK in the Merge dialog box.

Ami Pro will print the four labels using the addresses in the data file. If the addresses are not positioned correctly on the labels, adjust the settings in the Merge Labels dialog box and try again, or make changes to the ~ LABEL.STY style sheet.

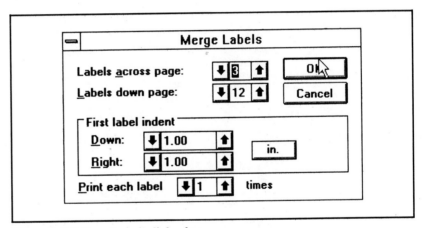

Figure 9.5: Merge Labels dialog box

CHAPTER 10

Structuring Your Documents with the Outliner

ALMOST ALL GOOD WORD PROCESSING PROGRAMS offer an outlining feature. An outline helps you organize your document, making it easier to write, edit, and read. A well-organized document imparts information in a way that it easily digested, and the information will be retained longer and more reliably.

Ami Pro has made it easy to create and use an outline. Its outlining feature will recognize up to nine levels of styles and will use them in the organization of the outline. This way, you can have your headings and subheadings in place before writing. You can also *contract*, or collapse, lower level headings under higher level headings so that all that appears are the upper level heads. This is an organizational aid because you can see at a glance whether your headings are comprehensive and logically arranged.

WORKING WITH THE OUTLINER

If you open an existing document and then choose Outline Mode from the View menu, Ami Pro will put that document in outline form.

To access Ami Pro's outlining tools, pull down the View menu and select Outline Mode. Figure 10.1 shows a sample outline in outline mode.

In outline mode, the headings are indented to match their levels. Next to each heading there is either a small plus or minus sign. A plus sign indicates that the heading has at least one subordinate heading. A minus sign shows that no subordinate levels exist below the heading.

USING THE OUTLINING TOOLS

The tools appear in the outline bar just beneath the menu bar. The numbers 1 through 9 in the outline bar represent levels of contraction. Click on the number that corresponds to the levels you want to see, and all the lower levels will disappear from view. For example, if you clicked on the 1 on the left end of the outline bar shown in Figure 10.1, you would see the screen shown in Figure 10.2.

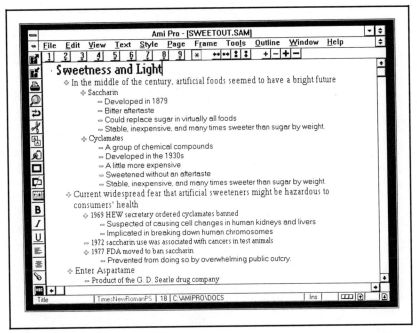

Figure 10.1: Sample outline in outline mode

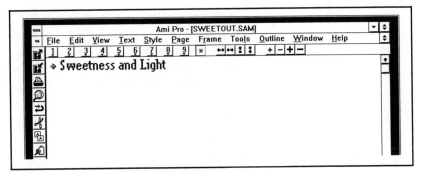

Figure 10.2: Outline contracted to its highest level

When you contract a heading, the plus sign to the left of it will appear in a different color (cyan on some monitors). This is an indication that the heading has subordinate levels that are not visible.

The asterisk, next to the 9 on the outline bar, reverses any contraction. Click on it to make all the text in the outline visible.

Following the asterisk are four icons with arrows pointing in different directions. These work as follows:

- The left-pointing arrow (immediately to the right of the asterisk on the outline bar) *promotes*, or raises, the selected heading one level. You can get the same effect by pressing Alt-← or by selecting Promote from the Outline menu.

- The right-pointing arrow *demotes*, or lowers, the level of the selected heading. You can also demote a heading by pressing Alt-→ or by selecting Demote from the Outline menu.

- The up-pointing arrow moves the selected heading up in the outline (the heading will trade places with the heading or text preceding it). Using the keyboard, press Alt-↑ to move a heading up.

- The down-pointing arrow moves the selected heading down one level in the outline (the heading will trade places with the heading or text that follows it). You can also press Alt-↓ to move a heading down.

The icons with pluses and minuses on the right end of the outline bar also control expanding and contracting headings. The big minus at the extreme right end of the outline bar contracts the whole outline under the main heading. The small minus contracts the outline one level at a time. Similarly, the big plus expands everything at the level of the head the cursor is on or below, and the small plus expands the outline incrementally, one level at a time.

Most of the controls in outline mode concern expanding and contracting, adjusting levels of heads, and moving heads and the subheads and text beneath them from place to place. Ami Pro provides several ways to accomplish the same tasks, as summarized in Table 10.1.

REARRANGING AN OUTLINE

In outline mode, you can easily rearrange your information, moving headings and their subordinate headings in one step. When you

Table 10.1: Outline Controls

FUNCTION	METHODS
Expand globally	Click on the asterisk.
	Click on the highest heading and click on the large plus in the outline bar.
	Click on the highest heading and select Expand from the Outline menu.
	Click on the highest level heading and press Alt-PgDn.
Expand incrementally	Click on the number in the outline bar corresponding to the level of expansion you want to see.
	Double-click on a plus sign that is in a different color (cyan on some monitors).
	Click on the heading you want to expand and select Expand from the Outline menu.
	Click on the heading you want to expand and press Alt-PgDn.
Contract globally	Click on the asterisk.
	Click on the highest heading and click on the large minus in the outline bar.
	Click on the highest heading and select Contract from the Outline menu.
	Click on the highest heading and press Alt-PgUp.
Contract incrementally	Click on the number in the outline bar corresponding to the level you want to see.

Table 10.1: Outline Controls (continued)

FUNCTION	METHODS
	Double-click on a white plus sign.
	Click on the heading you want to contract and select Contract from the Outline menu.
	Click on the heading you want to contract and press Alt-PgUp.
Promote a heading and everything subordinate to that heading	Drag the plus sign at the left of that heading to the left.
	Click on the plus sign at the left of that heading and click on the left-pointing arrow in the outline bar.
	Click on the plus sign at the left of that heading and press Alt-←.
	Click on the plus sign at the left of that heading and select Promote from the Outline menu.
Promote only the heading and nothing that follows it	Click in the heading and click on the left-pointing arrow in the outline bar.
	Click in the heading and select Promote from the Outline menu.
	Click in the heading and press Alt-←.
Demote a heading and everything subordinate to that heading	Drag the plus sign at the left of that heading to the right.

Table 10.1: Outline Controls (continued)

FUNCTION	METHODS
Demote only the heading and nothing that follows it	Click on the plus sign at the left of that heading and click on the right-pointing arrow in the outline bar.
	Click on the plus sign at the left of that heading and press Alt-→.
	Click on the plus sign at the left of that heading and select Demote from the Outline menu.
	Click in the heading and click on the right-pointing arrow in the outline bar.
	Click in the heading and select Demote from the Outline menu.
	Click in the heading and press Alt-→.
Move a subheading up without affecting its subordinate headings and text	Click on the heading and click on the up-pointing arrow in the outline bar.
	Click on the heading and press Alt-↑.
	Click on the heading and select Move Up in the Outline menu.
Move a subheading up along with its subordinate headings and text	Click on the plus sign at the left of the heading and click on the up-pointing arrow in the outline bar.
	Click on the plus sign at the left of the heading and press Alt-↑.

Table 10.1: Outline Controls (continued)

FUNCTION	METHODS
Move a subheading down without affecting its subordinate headings and text	Click on the plus sign at the left of the heading and select Move Up in the Outline menu.
	Click on the heading and click on the down-pointing arrow in the outline bar.
	Click on the heading and press Alt-↓.
	Click on the heading and select Move Down in the Outline menu.
Move a subheading down along with its subordinate headings and text	Click on the plus sign at the left of the heading and click on the down-pointing arrow in the outline bar.
	Click on the plus sign at the left of the heading and press Alt-↓.
	Click on the plus sign at the left of the heading and select Move Down in the Outline menu.

Note: In this table, clicking on a plus sign at the left of a heading means to press the mouse button and drag a tiny fraction of an inch to the right or left. This has the effect of selecting the heading and all the subordinate headings and text.

drag a heading to a new location in outline mode, all the subordinate levels of text that go with it will move, too.

To move a section of an outline, place the mouse pointer on the plus sign at the left side of the main heading, press the mouse button, and drag upward or downward. A bar (or line) will accompany your mouse pointer. When you release the mouse button, the heading and all its subordinate text will appear in the new

PRINTING AN OUTLINE

You print an outline just as you would print any other document. Pull down the File menu, select Print, and then make the necessary adjustments in the Print dialog box. Click on OK, and Ami Pro will print the outline.

The levels that appear in the printout are the same as those that appear on the screen. The outline is printed at its current level of contraction or expansion.

CREATING AN OUTLINE: A STRUCTURING PROJECT

As an example of using the outliner to begin a writing project, we will create a brief outline on schizophrenia. We will type headings at several levels, and then rearrange them for a better structure.

ADDING HEADINGS

To add headings in outline view, move the text cursor to the appropriate level and type the text. Follow these steps to begin our sample outline:

1. Pull down the File menu, select New, and accept ~DEFAULT.STY as the style sheet.

2. Pull down the View menu and click on Outline Mode.

You will see the outline bar, with the text cursor to the left of a single minus sign at the top of the screen. The location of the minus sign indicates the level of the text you will enter.

3. Drag the minus sign, which appears under the 2 in the outline bar, one space to the left, so that it is under the 1.

Beginning at the lowest level of indentation makes our first outline entry a major heading.

When you press ↵, the text cursor remains at the major head level. At this level, you place topics of an equal level.

4. Type **Schizophrenia** and press ↵.

The minus sign next to the heading changes to a plus sign to indicate that the major heading now has a subordinate heading.

5. Drag the minus sign for the next heading one space to the right, so it is under the 2 in the icon bar.

6. Type **Medical Treatment of Schizophrenia** and press ←.

7. At the same level as the second heading, type **Social Adjustment of Schizophrenics** and press ← again.

At this point, your screen should look like the one shown in Figure 10.3. We have typed our outline headings in initial capitals so that they can easily be converted to headings and subheadings in the document. By the time you are finished with the outline, your headings and subheadings will be in place, and you can fill in the transitions and supporting text.

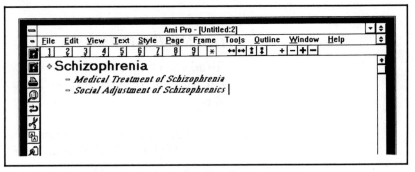

Figure 10.3: Outline with two levels of headings

8. Click after the first second-level heading, *Medical Treatment of Schizophrenia*, and press ← to add another line.

9. Press Alt-→ to demote the heading. Then type the following subheadings for medical treatment, pressing ← after each one but the last.

Antipsychotic Medications

Psychological Counseling

Institutional Milieu

Experimental Treatments

10. Click after *Antipsychotic Medications*, press ←⏎, and then press Alt-→.

11. Type **The History of Antipsychotic Medication**, press ←⏎, and then press Alt-→.

12. Type **Essentially no medical treatment for psychosis until the 1950s** and press ←⏎.

13. Type **Early treatment with morphine**, press ←⏎, and then press Alt-→.

14. Type **Zelda Fitzgerald**.

Here, you could insert a paragraph from the biography of Zelda Fitzgerald to tell about her treatment in Europe by the doctor who coined the word *schizophrenia*. The outline so far looks like the one shown in Figure 10.4.

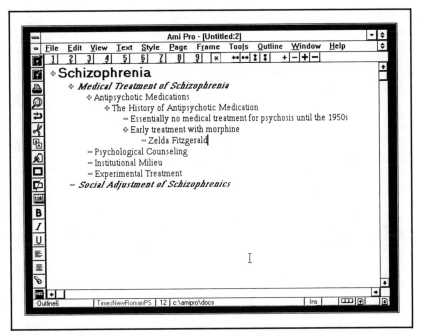

Figure 10.4: Outline with several levels of headings

15. Click after *Social Adjustment of Schizophrenics*, press ⬅, and then press Alt-➔.

16. Type **Effect of Psychotic Symptoms on Socialization** and press ⬅.

17. Type **Effect of Side Effects of Antipsychotic Medications on Socialization** and press ⬅.

You now have an outline with six levels of headings. Next, we'll see how this structure can be improved.

IMPROVING THE OUTLINE

By looking your outline over carefully and critically, you can see if the information it contains is well organized. Usually, you will type topics as you think of them to record all your ideas. Then you can use Ami Pro's outlining tools to reorganize the information into a logical flow.

In our sample outline, the first topic is *Medical Treatment of Schizophrenia*. However, this is not a good way to begin because we should define *schizophrenia* before describing its treatment. We will improve the outline by adding another section for the definition.

1. Click after the first heading (*Schizophrenia*), press ⬅, and then press Alt-➔.

2. Type **What Is Schizophrenia?**, press ⬅, and then Alt-➔.

3. Type **Diagnosis**, press ⬅, and type **Incidence**.

We also want to add a section about social adjustment of schizophrenics as part of the definition section. We already entered this topic as the second second-level heading. Rather than retype the text, we will move the heading up.

When you start to drag, the heading and all its subordinate headings are automatically selected, and you can see a horizontal bar. This bar shows where the heading will be placed when you release the mouse button.

4. Place your mouse pointer on the minus sign to the left of *Social Adjustment of Schizophrenics* and press the mouse button.

5. Drag the mouse pointer upward. When the horizontal bar is between *Incidence* and *Medical Treatment of Schizophrenia*, release the mouse button.

The heading and all its subordinate headings are now in the new location, at the same levels as they were in their original position. Now we need to adjust their levels so this section is subordinate to *What Is Schizophrenia?*.

6. Place the mouse cursor on the plus sign next to *Social Adjustment of Schizophrenics* and drag the heading to the right one space. When you begin dragging, a vertical bar appears to indicate where the heading is going. Drag the vertical bar from the 2 in the outline bar to the 3.

The revised outline is shown in Figure 10.5. You could continue editing the outline using the techniques described in the preceding sections. You may have noticed that we created and edited the sample outline without going through a menu or clicking on a tool in the outline bar.

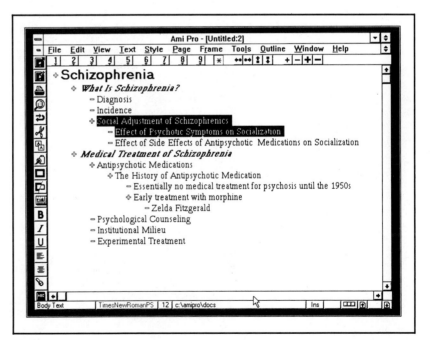

Figure 10.5: Revised outline

USING OUTLINE STYLES

When you are creating an outline solely for your own use, you probably will not care about its styles. However, if you are preparing an outline for review by someone else, such as a teacher, boss, or literary agent, you may want to specify outline styles.

APPLYING TEXT STYLES

In order for any changes you make in the Outline Styles dialog box (described in the next section) to take effect, the Use Outline Styles option in the Outline menu must be turned off (without a check mark).

One way to change the appearance of your outline is to use different text styles for the different level headings. Pull down the Outline menu and select Use Outline Styles. Ami Pro will automatically apply outline styles to your text.

Figure 10.6 shows our sample outline after choosing Use Outline Styles on the Outline menu. As shown in the figure, the different fonts further distinguish the various levels.

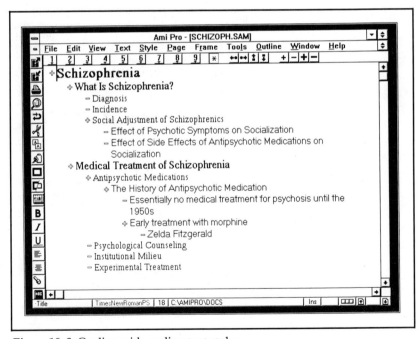

Figure 10.6: Outline with outline text styles

FORMATTING OUTLINES

To format your outline in a special style, use the Outline Styles option on the Style menu. This displays a dialog box with a variety of formatting options. For example, you can add the roman numerals, letters, and numbers commonly associated with outlines. You can also change the indentation spacing used for each outline level.

As an example, we will add the traditional heading labeling scheme to our sample outline.

1. Pull down the Style menu and select Outline Styles to display the Outline Styles dialog box, shown in Figure 10.7.

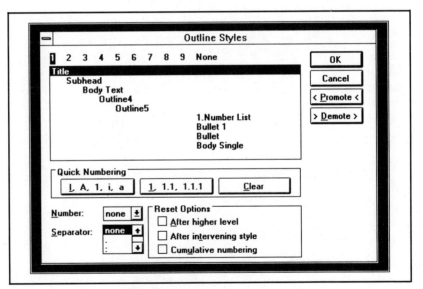

Figure 10.7: Outline Styles dialog box

The example box at the top of the dialog box shows the format currently set for the outline. You can change the indentation level of a heading by clicking on the level in this box and dragging it to its new indentation level, or by clicking on the level and then clicking on the Promote or Demote button on the right side of the dialog box.

2. Click on Title in the example box at the top of the dialog box.

3. Click on the downward-pointing arrow next to the Number text box at the bottom of the dialog box. You will see the options None, 1, I, i, A, and a.

4. Click on I to select it.

Look at the example box, and you will see that the format is now ITitle, which is not quite what we wanted. We need to add a period between the roman numeral and heading.

5. Click on the downward-pointing arrow next to the Separator list box (below the Number text box) to see the options: None, ., :, -,),], ( ), .) and (.).

6. Scroll to the period and click on it.

Unfortunately, Ami Pro does not allow for placing a space between the period and the heading.

The entry now says I. Title. We could repeat the procedure to format the other levels, but there is a quicker way.

7. Click on the leftmost option in the Quick Numbering section of the dialog box (below the example box).

Ami Pro will instantly reformat the outline in the example box with the numbering style you selected.

8. Click on OK.

9. Pull down the Outline menu and look at the Use Outline Styles option. It must be turned off if you want to apply your new format to the outline. If a check mark appears next to it, click on it to remove it.

The actual outline will be formatted according to the new settings in the Outline Styles dialog box. Your screen should look like the one shown in Figure 10.8.

Figure 10.8: Formatted outline

You cannot select and change the numbers and letters at the left of the outline items. They are embedded in the formatting.

USING THE OUTLINER TO CREATE A STUDY AID OR TEST

The outliner as study aid was invented by a friend of mine, Denny Atkin, published by Heidi Aycock, another friend, and reprinted in the *New York Times*.

Another, less obvious use of Ami Pro's outliner is as a study aid. An outliner is ideally suited for this application because of its contraction and expansion capabilities, which serve as a means for hiding and revealing information.

For your study sheet, write the questions in one level and the answers in a lower level. When you contract the levels with answers, only the questions will be visible. This allows you to reveal the answer when you are ready to verify that yours was correct, and see just one answer at a time.

This same technique could be used to create a test for students. You could print and duplicate the outline with contracted levels as test sheets to be distributed to the class. For grading, print a copy of the outline with all the levels expanded.

Let's set up a study sheet. This will be a vocabulary drill.

1. Select New from the File menu and ˜ DEFAULT.STY from the New dialog box. Click on the Maximize box in the document window.

2. Pull down the View menu and select Outline Mode. Drag the minus sign that appears two spaces to the left.

3. Type the list of vocabulary words, pressing ⟵ after each word: **pulque, radiosymmetrical, schatchen,** and **theomachy**.

4. Click next to *pulque*, press ⟵, and then press Alt-→.

5. Type **A fermented drink from Mexico, made from the juice of the maguey.**

6. Click next to *radiosymmetrical*, press ⟵, and press Alt-→.

7. Type **Radially symmetrical.**

8. Click next to *schatchen*, press ⟵, and press Alt-→.

9. Type **A marriage broker.**

10. Click next to *theomachy*, press ⟵, and press Alt-→.

11. Type **A battle among or against the gods.**

Your outline should look like the one shown in Figure 10.9.

12. Click on the 1 in the outline bar to collapse the second-level entries into the first-level entries.

Each of the plus signs changes color to indicate text is compressed beneath the headings.

13. Double-click on the plus sign next to a word to see what it means. Double-click again on the white plus sign to hide the answer.

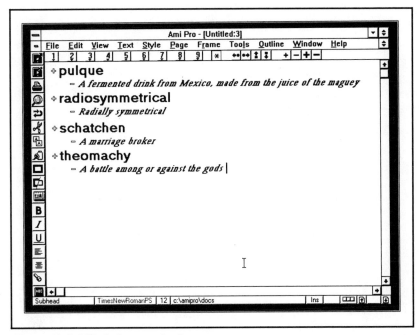

Figure 10.9: Vocabulary study sheet

This exercise shows the versatility of the outliner. Using your own ideas, you can adapt many of Ami Pro's features to special functions.

CHAPTER 11

Automating Your Work with Macros

A MACRO IS A COMPUTER PROGRAM THAT PERFORMS tasks for you automatically. Anyone can write a macro. You don't need to know a macro programming language, or have any computer programming experience at all to create useful macros. All you have to do is remember to turn the macro recorder on before you perform an action and to turn the recorder off when you are finished. Then you will have a macro that will perform the action for you.

In the course of your work with Ami Pro, you will have to perform some type of routine action repeatedly, perhaps once for each page or once for each document. Such actions are good candidates for macros. For example, if you frequently open the same file, you can create a macro to do it for you. Macros can be as simple as a single menu selection or complex routines that set up headers and footers, create frames, apply styles, and even call other macros.

After you create a macro, the list of commands necessary to accomplish the task is saved in memory. You can run the macro to have it automatically perform the actions by pressing a key combination, making a menu selection, or by clicking on your macro icon in the icon palette.

RECORDING AND RUNNING MACROS

When you are about to begin performing some task that you know you will have to do again, consider recording it as a macro. You can save your macro to a file so that you can use it as many times as you like, or record a quick macro for use in a single session.

CREATING A KEY-COMBINATION MACRO

To record a macro to be played back with a key combination, before you start the task you want the macro to perform, select Macros from the Tools menu, and then choose Record. In the

Record Macro dialog box, specify the key combination you want to use to run the macro and a name for the macro file. Then go through the actions you want to record. When you are finished, choose Macros from the Tools menu and select End Record.

If you would like to see a description of your macro when you work with macro files, use the Doc Info option on the File menu. Type a detailed description of the macro's purpose in the Description section of the Doc Info dialog box. The description will appear in the Record, Play, and Edit Macro dialog boxes. You should try to use descriptive names for your macro files, but as with other file names, they cannot exceed eight characters. If you will be creating many macros, use the Doc Info dialog box to provide descriptions.

You can use both keyboard and mouse commands while you are recording a macro. If you use a mouse, the commands entered with the mouse will be recorded, but the mouse movements will not.

As an example, we will create a macro to open SWEET.SAM, the document you created in Chapter 2. Then, you will be able to simply press a key combination to bring the file into Ami Pro. When you're finished with this book, you can delete the file from the disk to get rid of the macro.

1. Pull down the Tools menu and select Macros. You will see the submenu shown in Figure 11.1.

2. Select Record to display the Record Macro dialog box, shown in Figure 11.2.

3. Click on the text box beneath Playback Shortcut Keys.

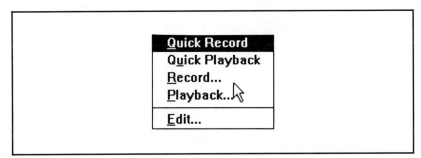

Figure 11.1: Macros submenu

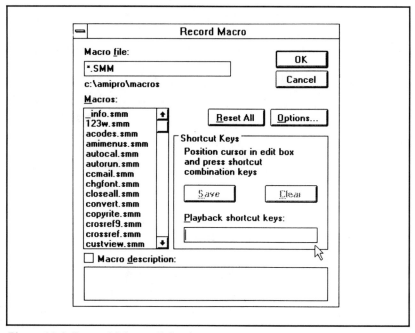

Figure 11.2: Record Macro dialog box

4. Press Shift-Ctrl-Z. This is the key combination you will press to load SWEET.SAM.

5. Double-click on the Macro File text box at the top of the dialog box and type **SWEET.SMM**.

6. Click on OK.

SMM is the extension that tells Ami Pro that the file contains a macro.

You should now see the words

Recording Macro

in red in the status bar. This indicates that Ami Pro is ready to record your keypresses. The next step is to go through the procedure you want the macro to perform.

7. Pull down the File menu and select Open.

8. In the File Name text box, type **SWEET.SAM**, and then click on OK.

The next important step is to stop recording the macro.

A quick way to stop recording a macro is to click with the mouse on the Recording Macro indicator in the status bar.

9. Pull down the Tools menu, select Macros, and click on End Record.

The macro is complete. Now let's see how it works.

10. Pull down the File menu and select Close.

11. Press Shift-Ctrl-Z. In an instant, the SWEET.SAM document will open.

Another way to run a recorded macro is to select Playback from the Macros submenu. Then choose the macro file name from the list. You might need to select from the list if you forget the keystrokes for the macro or are not sure what it does. The Play Macro dialog box shows the key combination for the selected macro and its description (if you entered one).

RECORDING QUICK MACROS

Quick macros are designed for use during only one session. They are stored in memory for as long as Ami Pro is running. The procedure is quicker than recording a regular macro. You simply select Quick Record from the Macro submenu, and then immediately record your keystrokes. To run the quick macro, select Quick Playback from the Macros submenu.

Suppose that some of the work that you are going to do in the current session requires that you open a new document and enter your return address and the date. Let's record a quick macro to accomplish this:

The Recording Macro indicator will appear in the status bar.

1. Pull down the Tools menu, select Macros, and then choose Quick Record from the Macros submenu.

2. Pull down the File menu, select New, Click on OK in the New dialog box.

3. Type your address and press ⏎ twice after the last line.

4. Pull down the Edit menu and select Insert, choose Date/Time from the submenu, and then select Today's Date.

5. Click on the Recording Macro indicator in the status bar.

That's it. You have recorded a quick macro. Now let's see how it works.

6. Pull down the Tools menu, select Macros, and click on Quick Playback.

Each time you select Quick Playback, you will open a new document, with your return address and today's date already entered.

Saving a Quick Macro   After you create a quick macro, you may decide that it is too useful to lose after you leave Ami Pro. Quick macros are saved to disk, but always under the same name, so each time you create a new quick macro, you overwrite the old macro. The quick macro is saved under the name UNTITLED.SMM. If you want to save it under another name, use the File Management item on the File menu.

Follow these steps to rename our sample quick macro:

1. Pull down the File menu and select File Management.

2. Pull down the View menu and select *.S?M Files.

3. Pull down the File menu and select Change Directory.

4. In the dialog box, type **C:\AMIPRO\MACROS** and click on OK.

5. Pull down the File menu and select Rename to display the Rename dialog box.

6. Type **UNTITLED.SMM** in the Rename text box.

7. Click on the To text box and type in another file name: **MYMACRO.SMM**.

8. Click on OK.

Now the macro is available for use in future sessions. You can run it by selecting it from the Play Macro dialog box.

RUNNING STARTUP AND EXIT MACROS

You might have a macro that you want to run immediately each time you start up Ami Pro. For example, you may always open the same document at the beginning of a session. You might also have a macro that you would like to execute each time you leave Ami Pro, such as one that resets a default or copies your work to another directory.

Through the User Setup dialog box, you can specify startup and exit macros. Pull down the Tools menu and select User Setup. The Run Macros section is at the bottom of the User Setup dialog box. In the Program Load text box, you can designate a macro to run as the program is loaded. Use the Program Exit text box to choose a macro to run when the program is shut down. Click on the downward-pointing arrow at the right end of either text box to see the list of macro file names.

EDITING MACRO FILES

After you have created a macro, you can edit it to correct errors and make improvements. You can either open the macro file as a regular document or display it in a macro-editing window.

OPENING A MACRO FILE

You can open a macro file as a regular text file by using the Open command on the File menu. Let's open our SWEET.SMM macro file to see how it is written.

1. Pull down the File menu and select Open.

2. Click on the downward-pointing arrow at the right end of the File Type text box and select Ami Pro Macro. The Files list box will fill with files that have the SMM extension.

3. Find SWEET.SMM and double-click on it.

The macro text appears in a separate window, as shown in Figure 11.3. Even if you are not familiar with a programming language, you can probably figure out what the commands mean. We are just taking a look at the SWEET.SMM macro, so we will close it without making any changes.

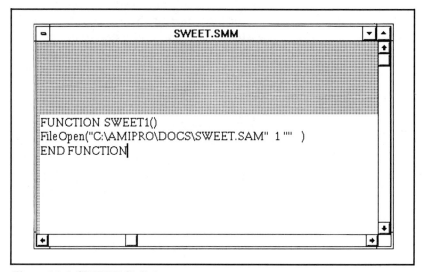

```
FUNCTION SWEET1()
FileOpen("C:\AMIPRO\DOCS\SWEET.SAM" 1 ""   )
END FUNCTION
```

Figure 11.3: SWEET.SMM macro

4. Close the SWEET.SMM window by double-clicking on its close box.

You can edit the macro file in a text window as you would edit a regular document: by changing, adding, and deleting characters. However, the macro commands must be spelled correctly and use the proper syntax, or the macro won't work. You will learn how to get help with your macros shortly.

The *syntax* of a programming command is its structure, including its coding and format for any parameters the command uses. *Parameters* are the parts of a command that define how it will function.

USING A MACRO-EDITING WINDOW

Rather than editing a macro by opening it as a document, you can display it in a macro editing window. Pull down the Tools menu, select Macros, and then choose Edit from the Macros submenu. You will see the Edit Macro dialog box, which looks like the Record

Macro dialog box (Figure 11.2). Click on the name of the macro file you want to edit, and then click on OK to open the file.

A window containing the text of the macro will appear. You can edit your macro in the same way that you edit a regular text file. To close the macro-editing window, double-click on its close box.

WRITING YOUR OWN MACROS

You can write your own macros by editing ones that you have recorded or by typing in all the macro commands yourself. Ami Pro's macro language is similar to BASIC and other programming languages, allowing for branching and conditional statements.

The following sections provide a brief introduction to the use of the macro language. If you are interested in writing macros, select Macro Doc from the Help menu to view the macro documentation, which describes the commands and rules for using the program's macro language.

GETTING MACRO HELP

Ami Pro devotes a whole section of its Help facility to macros. The Macro Doc topic on the Help menu gives you access to a list of macro functions, as well as explanations of how each function works. To see what type of information Ami Pro's Help facility can provide, follow these steps:

1. Click on Help and select Macro Doc.

2. In the Help window, scroll down to Macro Functions A–C and click on it.

Clicking on any green text in a Help window opens a window containing more information about the subject.

You will see the window shown in Figure 11.4, listing macro functions alphabetically. To find out more about a function, click on its name.

3. Click on About.

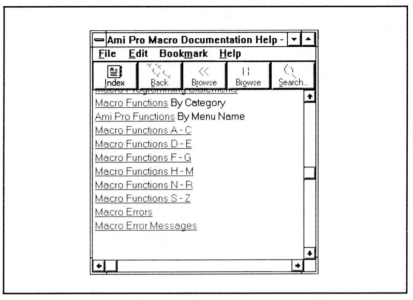

Figure 11.4: Beginning of the list of macro functions

You can print the Help information displayed on your screen by selecting Print Topic from the File menu in the Help window.

You will see a window similar to the one shown in Figure 11.5. The Help information includes the description, syntax, and value returned by the function. As explained in the Description section, About causes the About box to be displayed, as if you selected About Ami Pro from the Help menu.

4. Close the Help window by double-clicking on its close box.

When you are editing or writing a macro, you can refer to the Macro Doc section of Help for the correct spelling and syntax of functions.

ADDING A MENU

You can write individual macros that are very simple and chain them together to create more complex macros.

One of the ways you can use Ami Pro's macro language it to create custom menus. Your menu macros can call other macros to execute the selections on your custom menus.

1. Open a new file and accept ˜DEFAULT.STY as the style sheet.

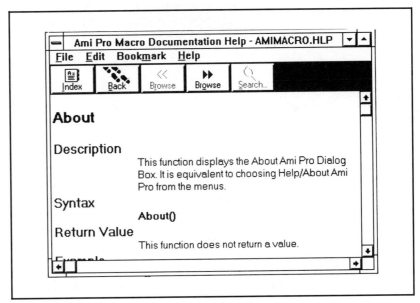

Figure 11.5: Help information on the About function

2. Type the following macro text.

FUNCTION menuitem1( )

AddMenu(1, "&Document")

AddMenuItem(1, "&Document", "sweet", "c: \amipro\macros\sweet.sm m")

END FUNCTION

Your screen should look like the one shown in Figure 11.6.

3. Pull down the File menu and click on Save.

4. In the Save As dialog box, click on the downward-pointing arrow at the right end of the File Type text box. From the list that appears, select Ami Pro Macro.

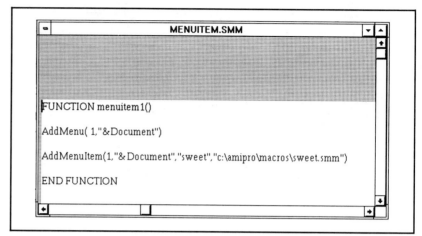

Figure 11.6: Sample macro

5. Double-click on the File Name text box and type
   MAKEMENU.SMM. Then click on OK.

If you typed the macro in correctly, the file will be saved as a
macro. However, if you made any typing errors, Ami Pro may refuse
to save the file until you correct them. This is because Ami Pro checks
the macro file as part of its saving procedure, rather than waiting, as
some programs will, until you have saved and run the macro to
detect the error (and then, like as not, crashing the program).

Now let's run the macro to see the menu we created. Since this
macro does not have a key combination assigned to it, you must use
the Play Macro dialog box to run it.

6. Pull down the Tools menu, select Macros, and click on
   Playback.

Like the Record Macros and Edit Macros dialog boxes, the Play
Macro dialog contains a list box with the names of all the macro files.

7. Locate MAKEMENU.SMM and double-click on it.

You should see something new on the menu bar. At the extreme right end is Document, with the *D* underlined.

8. Press Alt-D to pull down the new Document menu.

Since we specified only one menu item in our macro, the Document menu has a single option: sweet.

9. Click on sweet in the Document menu to run the SWEET.SMM macro and open the SWEET.SAM document.

Our Document menu appears on the Ami Pro menu bar because, in the AddMenu command, we specified 1 as the menu bar identification. It says Document because that is the text we put within quotation marks in the command. The ampersand before Document caused the letter following it, the *D*, to be underlined.

In the AddMenuItem command, we specified the menu bar (1) and the name of the menu on which to add the option. The menu name must match the name of the pull-down menu exactly, including any ampersand (&) characters. The menu name is followed by the text to appear as the menu option (sweet). You can place an ampersand (&) in front of a character to underline it in the menu and make it the shortcut key for selecting the option.

The last part of the Add Menu Item command in our example is the path and name of the macro to run if this menu item is selected. If no path is given, the default document and macro paths will be searched. You can also specify the function within the macro file to call and any parameters that function may require. If you want to run an Ami Pro function, type its name without quotation marks or parentheses.

Look up the macro commands for making menus in the Mac Doc Help windows.

DELETING A MENU

You can easily remove a menu you added by using the Delete-Menu command. Now we will edit the MAKEMENU.SMM macro file so that it deletes our new menu.

1. Close SWEET.SAM and return to MAKEMENU.SMM.

2. In the MAKEMENU.SMM text, drag through AddMenu with the mouse pointer.

3. Type **DeleteMenu**. Then drag through the line that contains the AddMenuItem command and press Del.

4. Pull down the File menu and select Save As.

5. If Ami Pro Macro does not appear in the File Type text box, scroll through the list box and select it.

6. In the File Name text box, type **DELEMENU.SMM** as the new file name.

7. Click on OK.

Next, we have to run the macro to get rid of the Document menu.

8. Select Macros from the Tools menu, choose Playback, and double-click on DELEMENU.SMM.

The menu should disappear from the menu bar.

CUSTOMIZING THE ICON PALETTE

For maximum accessibility, your macros can be added to the icon palette. You can also change the current palette so that it includes other Ami Pro standard functions.

ADDING A MACRO ICON

Through the Customize SmartIcons dialog box, you can choose an icon to represent your macro and place the icon wherever you want on the palette. As an example, we'll add the SWEET.SMM macro to the icon palette.

1. Pull down the Tools menu and select SmartIcons.

2. In the SmartIcons dialog box, click on the Customize button. You will see the Customize SmartIcons dialog box, shown in Figure 11.7.

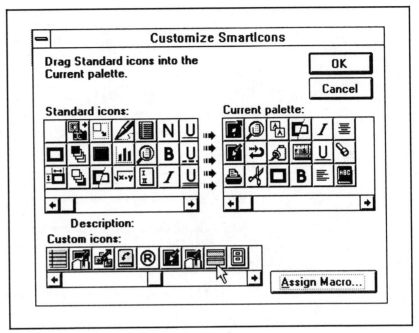

Figure 11.7: Customize SmartIcons dialog box

The Customize SmartIcons dialog box shows the standard icons, the icons that are currently on the palette, and the custom icons. When you click on a custom icon, the words

Macro Button

appear just above the Custom Icons section. In the figure, a custom icon is about to be selected. It's the second from the last icon.

3. Click on the icon of your choice.

4. Drag the icon to the right palette box, the one with the heading Current Palette. Place the icon in the white area to the right of the existing icons.

5. Click on Assign Macro to display the Assign Macro dialog box, as shown in Figure 11.8.

6. Click on Next Icon until you see the icon you have selected in the Selected Icon box.

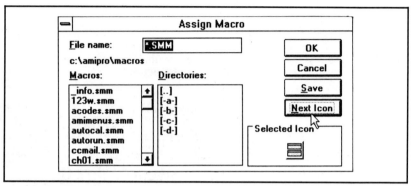

Figure 11.8: Assign Macro dialog box

7. Scroll through the Macros list box until you see SWEET-.SMM, and then click on it to select it.

8. Click on Save to associate the macro with the icon.

9. Click on OK to close the dialog box.

At this point, you could just drag the new icon into the last position in the Current Palette section, and the icon that was in that position would move over (and long longer appear on the screen). However, we will do some rearranging so you can get an idea of how the Customize SmartIcons dialog box works.

When you click on the flashlight icon, Find & Replace appears in the Description area of the dialog box. That's because the flashlight icon calls up Find & Replace.

10. In the Customize SmartIcons dialog box, drag the flashlight icon from the Current Palette section to the Standard Icons section on the left.

11. Click on OK in the Customize SmartIcons dialog box to close it.

12. Click on OK in the SmartIcons dialog box.

Your new icon should now appear in the icon palette.

13. Click on the icon to make sure it works.

Now let's return the Find & Replace icon, which you may find very useful in your own work, to the icon palette.

14. Pull down the Tools menu, select SmartIcons, and click on Customize in the SmartIcons dialog box.

15. In the Customize SmartIcons dialog box, click on the right arrow of the scroll bar associated with the Standard Icons section until the flashlight icon comes into view.

16. Place your mouse pointer on the icon and press and hold down the mouse button. Drag the icon to the Current Palette section.

17. Place the mouse pointer on the SWEET icon and press the mouse button. Drag the icon to the Custom Icons section at the bottom of the dialog box. When you release the mouse button, the icon will be removed from the Current Palette box.

18. Click on OK in the Customize SmartIcons dialog box and the SmartIcons dialog box.

Simply dragging the SWEET icon away from the Current Palette selection box will remove it from the box. You don't have to return it "to the shelf."

USING AMI PRO'S STANDARD ICONS

Rather than adding your macro to the icon palette, you can make an icon for one of Ami Pro's standard functions appear in your icon palette. The current palette icons can be replaced with standard icons. When you click on an icon in the Current Palette section of the Customize SmartIcons dialog box, its function appears in the Description area, above the Custom Icons section. Table 11.1 summarizes the functions of the current palette icons, in the order that they appear in the icon palette.

Table 11.1: Current Palette Icons

Icon	Function
	Open
	Save
	Print

Table 11.1: Current Palette Icons (Continued)

Icon	Function
	Full Page/Current View Toggle
	Undo
	Cut
	Copy
	Paste
	Add a Frame
	Modify Frame Layout
	Show/Hide Tab Ruler Toggle
B	Bold Text
I	Italic Text
U	Underline Text
	Left Align Text
	Center Text
	Find & Replace
	Spelling

See Appendix C for a list of standard icons and their functions.

Click on the icons in the Standard Icons section of the Customize SmartIcons dialog box to see descriptions of the functions they represent. The last few have to do with macros. Later, you might want to return to this dialog box and replace some of the less frequently used icons with macro record and play icons. These can save you several steps in creating and using macros.

CHAPTER 12

Using Design Features

AMI PRO PROVIDES MANY FEATURES FOR DESIGNING the pages of your document. You can use different styles for your text to format its appearance and create or import many types of graphics. The placement of these elements form the layout of the page. A pleasing layout can entice people to read the page; an unbalanced layout will have the opposite effect. This chapter provides information about designing page layout with Ami Pro.

PLANNING PAGE LAYOUT

The purpose of a document is to convey information. This information may be explicit, as in a set of directions telling what to do in case of an emergency, or it may be implicit, as in a short story about a young boy's last day with his grandfather.

The purpose of the document's design, or layout, is to direct the reader's eye to the information that is important. Too many elements in the layout can confuse and distract the reader. On the other hand, if there is no attention paid to layout, the page will look so boring that it won't attract or direct the eye. Why bother printing a document that will not be read?

The contents of your document and its intended audience will dictate its layout. For example, if you are preparing a list of steps to take in case of emergency, you may want to have the numbers for the steps oversized so the reader won't become confused and accidentally skip steps or perform the same steps more than once. The steps need to be as brief, understandable, and in as large a typeface as possible. You will probably want to have graphics that clearly illustrate the things that need to be done. You might want to put in lines that help to keep the steps separated. Warnings might be in italic, or perhaps printed in a different color.

Laying out a short story for review by an editor requires a different approach. You might use an attractive typeface, perhaps in a slightly

You should be thinking about the layout all the time, but don't concern yourself with setting it up while you are writing. Wait until after your text is completed to work with the page layout.

larger size for the title and your name and address on the cover page. Editors like to see lots of white space on the first page (for notes) and wide margins throughout. You might include a header on the second page and all subsequent pages, giving your name and address and the title of the story (in a shortened form, if it's a long title), and a footer on each page giving the page number. You probably will not want to use any rules or lines, pictures, or colors.

To get ideas about how to design a particular document, study similar documents. By looking over the design work done by others, you will discover elements that are successful and elements that don't work.

Your page layout may consist of the following elements:

- Text, including the document itself, headers and footers, footnotes, titles, subheads, and margin notes

- Lines, boxes, white space, arrows, and shaded and colored areas

- Graphic elements including icons, drawings, charts, formulas, and photographs

- Page elements, including frames, margins, and orientation

The following sections describe how to use Ami Pro's tools to add these elements and provide some suggestions to help you make your design choices.

USING TYPE

A good book about designing with type is *Looking Good in Print,* by Roger C. Parker (Ventana Press). Microsoft Press also has a pair of books called *Desktop Publishing by Design,* one of which concentrates on Ventura Publisher and the other on PageMaker (you can ignore the sections that are software specific).

If you are lucky enough to have a wide selection of typefaces available to you, choosing the right ones will require some experimenting. Although a good guideline is to use a sans serif face for the headings and a serif typeface for the body text, this rule isn't cast in stone. Try other typefaces. The way Ami Pro uses styles makes it easy to specify different typefaces and apply them throughout the document with a single dialog box selection.

Look at samples of other documents in the typefaces you are considering to see if they reflect the image you have in mind and if they are readable enough for your purposes. Refer to books devoted to type and design.

FORMATTING WITH THE RULER

Ami Pro's ruler establishes the tabs and margins for the page. The ruler isn't always visible. If you don't see anything ruler-like immediately beneath the menu bar, pull down the View menu and select Show Ruler.

As you learned in Chapter 5, you can set tabs for a style using the Modify Style dialog box, or set them for just the current paragraph using the text ruler that appears on your screen when you select Show Ruler.

Click on the ruler to display the tab and margin controls, as shown in Figure 12.1. Using these controls, you can select the type of tabs and the number of columns to set for the current paragraph.

The settings you make in the ruler affect only the selected paragraph (the paragraph where the text cursor is located). To affect the whole page, use the Modify Page Layout option on the Page menu.

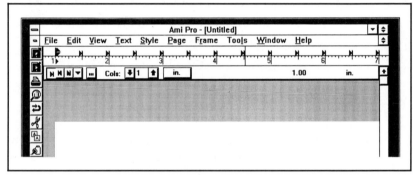

Figure 12.1: Ruler with tab and margin controls

This ruler is useful because it doesn't affect the entire page or everything with the current style, as do the rulers in the Modify Style and Modify Page Layout dialog boxes. It affects only the paragraphs that are currently selected.

To remove the ruler, pull down the View menu and select Hide Ruler.

ADDING HEADERS AND FOOTERS

Headers and footers are text that appears at the top and bottom, respectively, of each page. You can enter them directly in the document window, as we have done in some of the exercises in this book.

The margins of pages are marked by a shaded grid, so you will know when you have reached the top or bottom.

To enter a header, scroll to the very top of the page, click in the shaded area, and type the text. Similarly, to enter a footer, scroll to the very bottom of the page, click in the shaded area, and type the footer text.

MODIFYING HEADERS AND FOOTERS

The Header and Footer pages of the Modify Page Layout dialog box are shown in Chapter 5.

If you aren't satisfied with the appearance of the header or footer, you can use the Modify Page Layout dialog box to change it. As described in Chapter 5, access the Modify Page Layout dialog box by selecting Modify Page Layout from the Page menu, and then click on the Header or Footer button in the Modify list.

Use the settings on the Header or Footer page to change the tabs, margins, indents, number of columns, and column balance. You can select the Begin on Second Page option to prevent the header or footer from appearing on the first page of the document. This is useful for papers or reports that have a cover sheet or first page that should not have a header or footer.

If you want to use one header or footer for right pages and another one for left pages, select the corresponding option in the Pages section of the Header or Footer page. Right and left headers and footers are frequently used in documents printed on two sides of the page, which contain spreads of facing pages.

SETTING UP FLOATING HEADERS AND FOOTERS

The header or footer you type outside the margins in the document window will be repeated on every page (except the first, if you chose the Begin on Second Page in the Modify Page Layout dialog box). If you want to use different headers and footers within a document, perhaps to identify the chapters or other divisions of a long document, you can set up floating headers and footers.

To create a floating header or footer, click where the new header or footer should begin, pull down the Page menu, and select Floating Header/Footer. You will see the dialog box shown in Figure 12.2.

Click on OK to enter a mark on the page to which your floating header or footer is connected. Then type the header or footer in the margin as you would enter a regular header or footer. If the mark is

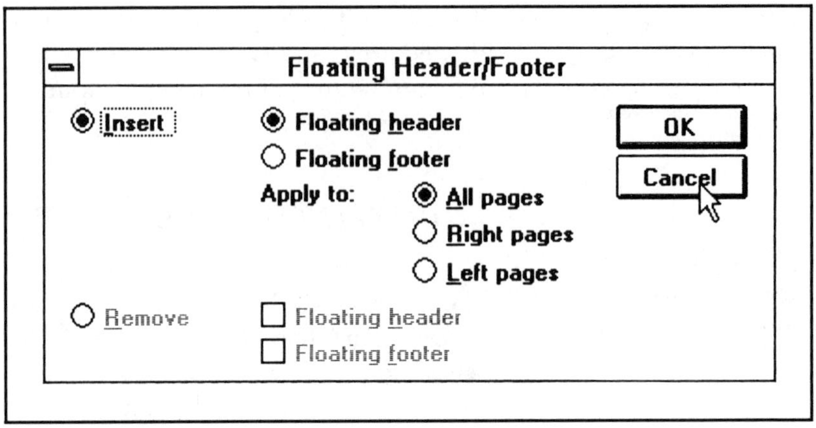

Figure 12.2: Floating Header/Footer dialog box

The floating header or footer mark will not be visible unless Marks is selected in the View Preferences dialog box (accessing by Preferences from the Veiw menu).

on the first line of the page, place the header or footer on the current page. If it is on any line other than the first line, enter the header or footer on the next page. The header or footer will "float" with the text by following the mark in the text.

PLACING PICTURES IN DOCUMENTS

Laying out a page with graphics requires attention to the details. For example, if you have a photograph of a person in profile, you must be careful of the space between that person's nose and the text. Jamming a person's nose into the text will make the reader feel uncomfortable. When cropping this photograph, you should leave a wider space between the person's face and the text than between the text and the back of the person's head. The following sections describe some of the factors to consider when using pictures.

FOLLOWING THE DIRECTION OF THE PICTURE

Pictures often have a direction. If there are people in a picture, they are probably looking in one direction. If there is a car in the picture, it's headed in one direction, whether it's moving or not.

The reader will naturally look in the direction of the picture. If the text is on the right and the picture that accompanies it is on the left, with a leftward direction, the reader is going to look at whatever is to the left of the picture instead of the story about the picture. If the picture is of a race car moving to the left and the story is about the Queen of England, the reader is going to experience some dissonance, perhaps thinking for a brief moment that the queen has been run over by a race car or that she has taken up racing. In short, you must consider the direction of a picture in deciding how to place it on the page. If possible, make the pictures point to the stories that talk about them.

HANDLING BLACK-AND-WHITE PICTURES

One problem with computer graphics is that they are usually printed in black and white. Black-and-white pictures are generally not as quickly understood as color pictures. Furthermore, there are severe restrictions on the levels of gray available in a laser printer printout. You may have only 20 or so gray scales in the final printout, even if there are 256 gray scales in the graphic on the computer screen.

The information that the eye and brain of the reader receives from a printed black-and-white picture corresponds to the clarity of the picture. When you are designing with black-and-white images, try to eliminate any ambiguity about the content of the pictures.

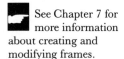 See Chapter 7 for more information about creating and modifying frames.

One way to clarify a picture is by giving it a caption. Captions can be entered in frames, which can then be grouped with the frames containing pictures so they will always be connected. Use the Create Frame option on the Frame menu or the icon in the icon palette to draw frames, and then set their characteristics in the Modify Frame Layout dialog box. Use the Group option on the Frame menu to group the caption and picture frames.

USING COLOR

Ami Pro provides options for using colors for your text and graphics. However, adding colors on your computer screen is not the same as putting the colors on paper. The least expensive way to produce color documents is with an ink-jet or a dot-matrix printer. Corel Systems has recommended using a color dot-matrix printer (such as the Star Rainbow) for prepress proofing. The output of color thermal printers is higher quality, but such printers are very expensive.

A color printer will do a fair job of reproducing the colors that will appear in the final printout. But is it good enough to call a final printout? Should you place it in a client's hands? Take the time to make the decision for yourself. If you want the highest possible quality, set up your document for production by a commercial printer.

SETTING PAGE ORIENTATION AND SIZE

The page *orientation* refers to how the text is printed across the page. Your choices are portrait orientation or landscape orientation. Portrait orientation is often called Tall. It's the normal way to view the page: 11 inches high and 8^1/$_2$ inches wide. Landscape, or Wide, is the alternate way to hold the page: 11 inches wide and 8^1/$_2$ inches tall. You set the orientation in Ami Pro through the Page Settings page of the Modify Page Layout dialog box.

If you plan to print your document on paper that is not 8^1/$_2$ by 11 inches, set up your page layout accordingly. Select the page size in the Page Settings page of the Modify Page Layout dialog box. The Page Size section provides options for legal, letter, and four other standard sizes:

- A4: 8.27 by 11.69 inches
- A3: 11.69 by 16.53 inches
- A5: 5.83 by 8.27 inches
- B5: 6.93 by 9.84 inches

You can also set any custom size. The page on the Ami Pro screen will automatically take on the dimensions you specify here.

SETTING UP FOR POSTSCRIPT PRINTING

Generally, you will set up your printer when you set up Windows, and you will not change this setup until you purchase another printer. However, if you're using a PostScript printer and you haven't set your timeouts, you should take the time to do so.

PostScript printers can take a long time to interpret the information sent to them. Here's how to prevent your computer from giving up too soon:

1. In Ami Pro, pull down the Control menu and select Control Panel. You will see the dialog box shown in Figure 12.3.

2. Double-click on the Printers icon to display the Printers dialog box, shown in Figure 12.4.

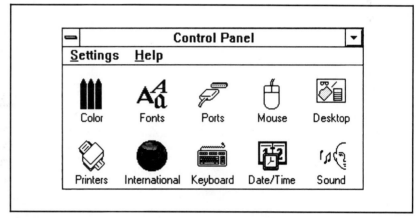

Figure 12.3: Control Panel accessed from Ami Pro

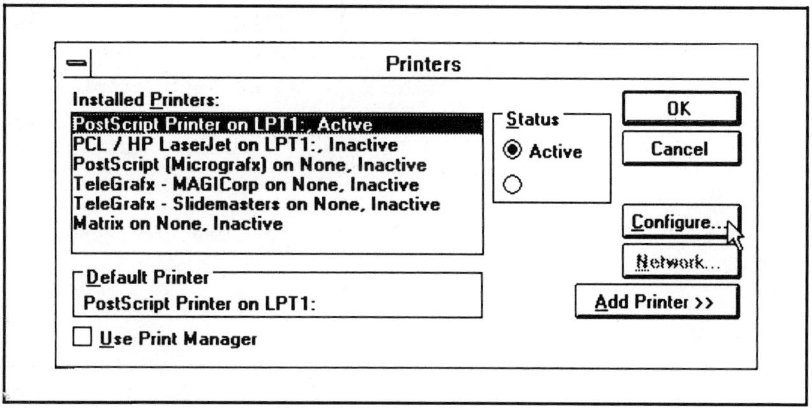

Figure 12.4: Printers dialog box

If the printer spooler is turned off, you can't do anything while the printout is being sent to the printer. The problem with the printer spooler may be resolved in the new version of Windows, so try it out if you have the latest version.

Note that Use Print Manager is not selected in the Printers dialog box. Windows provides a printer spooler that allows printouts to be sent to the printer "in the background" so you can continue writing or performing other tasks while the computer takes care of printing. This works well when the printout is mostly text, but when it comes time to send PostScript graphics to the printer, the spooler seems to have problems. Since Ami Pro has its own printer spooler, there is no need to use the Print Manager spooler with Ami Pro.

3. Click on Configure, and set the Transmission Retry option (at the bottom of the Printers - Configure dialog box) to 999, as shown in Figure 12.5.

The maximum value for the Transmission Retry option is 999. This setting causes Windows to wait several minutes before giving up on the printer.

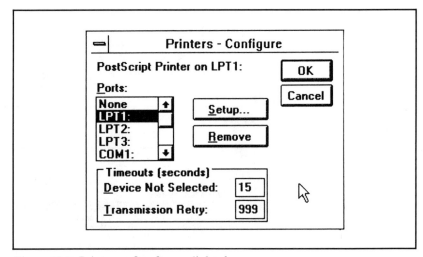

Figure 12.5: Printers - Configure dialog box

CHAPTER 13

Using Advanced Features

AMI PRO IS PACKED WITH ADVANCED, POWERFUL features. These features make it easy to perform sophisticated tasks:

- Create tables, complete with rules and footnotes
- Use formulas in your tables
- Sort items to arrange them alphanumerically or numerically
- Mark and review revisions made to documents
- Create equations as graphics by choosing their formats, symbols, and commands
- Insert power fields that function like miniprograms

This chapter describes how to use these features in your own documents.

WORKING WITH TABLES

You can create columns of tabular data by setting tabs in your document. This is not difficult for simple tables, but if you are constructing a table with many columns, lengthy entries, or special formatting, adjusting the columns and data can be a nightmare. Fortunately, Ami Pro has a powerful table generator, which can format your tables for you.

The table generator is also useful for creating columns of text that you don't consider a table. It will neatly format the columns, adjusting the heights of the entries to match the amount of text you enter. For example, you can make an orderly table of questions and answers in a two-column format. Type the questions in one column and the answers in the other.

CREATING TABLES

The Create Table dialog box also contains a Layout button, which displays the Modify Table Layout dialog box. Modifying the table layout is described later in the chapter.

You access the table generator through the Tables option on the Tools menu. This option displays the Create Table dialog box, in which you enter the number of columns and rows in the table. When you click on OK, Ami Pro creates the empty table. All you have to do is type in the information, pressing the Tab key to move from column to column.

You can enter a table in a frame or on the page. Tables on the page can stretch from page to page. Tables in frames are limited to a single page. To place a table in a frame, create the frame, select it, and then choose Tables from the Tools menu. The empty table will appear inside the frame.

As an example, we will create a short table.

1. Pull down the Tools menu and select Tables. You will see the dialog box shown in Figure 13.1.

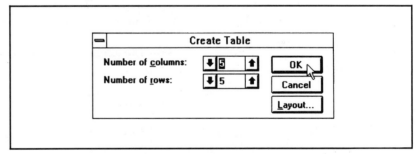

Figure 13.1: Create Table dialog box

The lines between the columns and rows do not appear in the printed table. However, you can add lines to the printout by using the Lines/Shades option on the Table menu.

2. Set the number of columns to 3 and the number of rows to 9. Then click on OK to create a table.

The blank table appears on the screen, along with a new Table menu on the menu bar, as shown in Figure 13.2. The table is divided into individual cells to hold each entry.

You can click anywhere within a cell to begin entering data into the cell.

3. If the text cursor isn't already in the top-left cell, click on that cell.

4. Type **Mercury** and press Tab.

5. Type **3000** (Mercury's diameter) and press Tab.

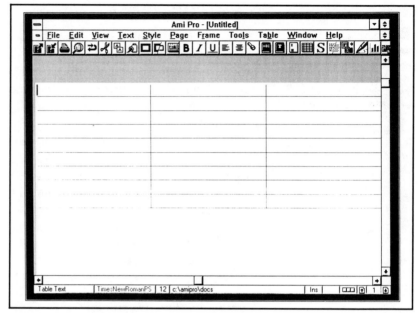

Figure 13.2: The new table

When you press Tab after typing a number, the number moves to the right end of the cell. Nonnumeric entries remain left aligned in the cell.

   6. Type **58.6** (Mercury's period of axial rotation) and press Tab.

You have filled in the first row of a table that will contain data about the planets.

   7. Fill in the remaining rows of the table with the following data:

Venus	**7700**	**224.7**
Earth	**7927**	**365**
Mars	**4200**	**687**
Jupiter	**88700**	**4328**
Saturn	**75100**	**10752.9**
Uranus	**29200**	**30663.652**

Neptune	27700	60152
Pluto	unknown	90410.5

Your completed table should look like the one shown in Figure 13.3. Notice that Ami Pro automatically added commas as thousand separators in the numbers. It also rounded the number with three decimal places, 30663.652, to two decimal places.

Ami Pro - [PLANETS.SAM]

File Edit View Text Style Page Frame Tools Table Window Help

Mercury	3,000	58.60
Venus	7,700	224.70
Earth	7,927	365.00
Mars	4,200	687.00
Jupiter	88,700	4,328.00
Saturn	75,100	10,752.90
Uranus	29,200	30,663.65
Neptune	27,700	60,152.00
Pluto	unknown	90,410.50

Figure 13.3: Table with data entered

MOVING AND SELECTING CELLS IN TABLES

Ami Pro provides a variety of ways to move the cursor within a table. You can use one of the following methods to move from cell to cell.

- Click with the mouse on a cell to move the cursor to that cell.
- Press Tab or Ctrl-→ to move the cursor to the next cell to the right.
- Press Shift-Tab or Ctrl-← to move the cursor to the next cell to the left.

If you press the → or ← key alone, you will move through words and figures one character at a time.

- Press Ctrl-↑ or Ctrl-↓ to move the cursor to the next row upward or downward, respectively.

- Press Home to move the cursor to the first character space within a cell. Home, Home moves the cursor to the first character space in the first cell in a row.

- Press End to move the cursor to the last character space within a cell. End, End moves the cursor to the first character space in the last cell in a row.

- Press ←, →, ↑, or ↓ to move the cursor in the indicated direction within a cell.

You can select cells, rows, and columns by dragging with the mouse. To select cells using the keyboard, use a Shift-Ctrl-arrow key combination. Shift-Ctrl-↑ or ↓ selects the current cell and the cell above or the cell below. Continue pressing this key combination to select as much of the column as you want. Shift-Ctrl-→ or ← selects the current cell and the cell to the right or left. Continue pressing the combination to select as much of the row as you want.

To select the entire table, move the cursor beyond the last character space in the table. The text cursor will appear as tall as the entire table. Press Shift-←, and the table will be selected. You can also drag through the whole table and then press Shift-← to select it.

CREATING TABLE STYLES

To format a cell of a table differently from the rest, you must create a new style. There is a special page of the Modify Style dialog box devoted to table styles.

In our sample table, the numbers in the third column represent days. We will create a style to format those cells to have two decimal places.

> By dragging with the mouse, you can select an entire column, without selecting adjacent columns.

1. Place the mouse cursor in the third cell in the first row, press the mouse button, and drag down and to the right. (The last column should be selected.)

2. Pull down the Style menu and select Create Style.

3. Type **Dectable** in the text box, make sure that Table Text is selected as the style on which to base it, and then click on Modify.

4. Click on the Table Format button in the Modify section of the Modify Style dialog box to see the Table Format page, shown in Figure 13.4.

Using the options on this page of the Modify Style dialog box, you can set the format of cells, numbers, and negative values. When you choose Currency in the Cell Format list, you can select the symbol and have it appear before (Leading) or after (Trailing) the number. The example box at the bottom of the dialog box shows the selected format.

5. Click on Fixed Decimal. If the No. Decimal Places box does not show 2, double-click on it and type **2**. Then click on OK.

6. If the last column of the table is not still selected, drag through it again.

7. Click on the text style indicator in the status bar and select Dectable as the style.

All the numbers will be formatted with two decimal places.

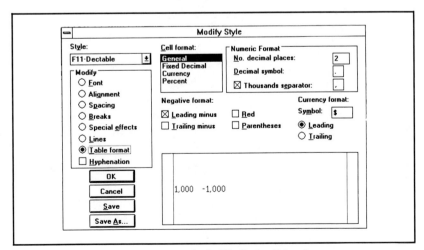

Figure 13.4: Table Format page of Modify Style dialog box

ADDING LINES AND SHADING

The lines that you see around the table cells on the screen do not print. You can add lines to the printed version through the Lines/ Shades dialog box. Let's put an outline around our sample table.

1. Drag the mouse cursor through the whole table, from the top-left cell to the bottom-right cell, and the text cursor will be as tall as all nine rows.

2. Pull down the Table menu and select Lines/Shades to see the dialog box shown in Figure 13.5.

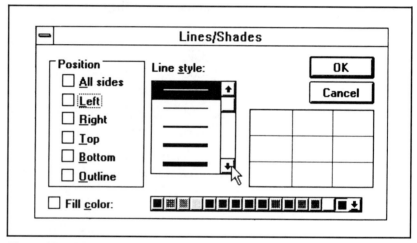

Figure 13.5: Lines/Shades dialog box

This dialog box contains options for the position of lines and the line style, as well as a Fill Color palette for adding shading to cells. The options you choose will affect only the selected cell or cells in the table.

The position choices specify where the lines appear in relation to the selected cell or cells. You can scroll through the Line Style box to see more choices. If you want to fill a cell or cells with color, select one from the palette at the bottom of the dialog box. Click on the downward-pointing arrow on the right side of the palette to see more choices. You can also double-click on any color to access custom colors.

Use shading to highlight information, such as totals or goals.

3. Click on the Outline check box in the Position section of the dialog box to place an outline around the table.

4. Click on the third line in the Line Style list box.

5. Click on OK to leave the dialog box.

ADDING FOOTNOTES

Some tables need footnotes to show the source of the data or to provide other information about the data. To add a footnote, use the Footnote option on the Tools menu.

Let's create a footnote for our sample table:

1. Click on the first cell in the top row of the table.

2. Pull down the Tools menu and select Footnotes.

3. Make sure Insert Footnote is selected and click on OK.

4. Type **Closest planet to the sun**.

Your table should now look like the one shown in Figure 13.6. The footnote reference number, a superscript 1, appears next to the entry in the first column, and the footnote appears at the bottom of the table. You might want to print the sample table now to see how it looks on the page before continuing. Figure 13.7 shows the printed table.

EDITING TABLES

The Paste Link command is covered in Chapter 6.

You can use the Cut, Copy, Paste, and Paste Link commands on the Edit menu to edit your table and to link it with other applications. Use the standard Ami Pro text-editing methods to make changes to the entries within individual cells.

To delete a footnote, drag through the superscript footnote reference number in the table to select it, and then press the Del key. When the reference number is deleted, the footnote text is also removed.

If there are multiple lines within a cell, you may need to see where the carriage returns are in order to edit the cell. You can have Ami Pro show where the ◄┘ was pressed by selecting Preferences from the View menu and clicking on the check box next to Tabs & Returns. Then the carriage returns will appear as paragraph symbols (¶).

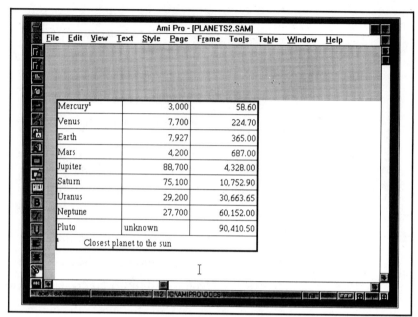

Figure 13.6: Footnote added to table

Mercury[1]	3,000	58.60
Venus	7,700	224.70
Earth	7,927	365.00
Mars	4,200	687.00
Jupiter	88,700	4,328.00
Saturn	75,100	10,752.90
Uranus	29,200	30,663.65
Neptune	27,700	60,152.00
Pluto	unknown	90,410.50

[1] Closest planet to the sun

Figure 13.7: The printed table

FORMATTING TABLES

You can modify the format of the table through the Modify Table Layout dialog box, shown in Figure 13.8. Click inside the table, pull down the Table menu, and select Modify Table Layout to access this dialog box.

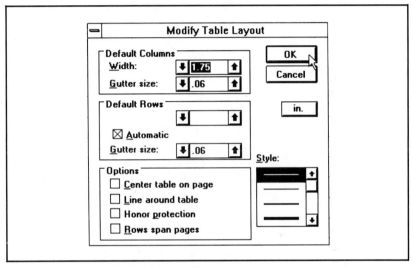

Figure 13.8: Modify Table Layout dialog box

When Automatic is selected in the Default Rows section of the Modify Table Layout dialog box, the height of the cell will be adjusted to match the number of lines it contains. You can prevent this adjustment by turning off Automatic.

In the Default Columns section, set the width of the columns and the size of the gutter (space between columns). You can also set the height of the rows by turning off the automatic sizing. Click on the Automatic check box in the Default Rows area to remove the X, and then set the row height and gutter (space between rows).

The Options section of the dialog box contains selections for centering the table on the page, placing a line around the table, protecting cells, and having the rows span pages (useful for spreads on facing pages). If you choose Line Around Table, select a line style from the Style list box. Like the Outline option in the Lines/Shades dialog box, Line Around Table generates lines around the whole table, but the lines are a bit further from the table text.

PROTECTING TABLE CELLS

In order to protect cells (lock them from editing) you must select Protect from the Table menu, as well as Honor Protection from the Modify Table Layout dialog box. Use the following general procedure to protect cells in a table:

1. Drag through the cells you do not want to be changed.

2. Pull down the Table menu and select Protect.

3. Select Modify Table Layout from the Table menu.

4. In the dialog box, select Honor Protection, and then click on OK.

After you protect cells, you will not be able to move the text cursor into them. To remove the protection so that the cells can be edited, turn off Honor Protection in the Modify Table Layout dialog box, select the cells, and then turn off Protect on the Table menu.

USING OTHER TABLE FORMATTING OPTIONS

The other formatting options on the Table menu allow you to work with your tables as follows:

If there isn't room to insert a column, the Columns button under Insert will be dimmed.

- Insert Column/Row: Click on the column to the right of the where you want to add a new column, or on the row above which you want to insert a new row, and then choose this option. Select Columns or Rows under Insert in the Insert Column/Row dialog box. To add a column the left of the currently selected column, or to add a row below the currrently selected row, select the After button. You can also insert more than one column or row at a time by changing the entry in the Number to Insert box.

Use headings for tables that are longer than one page.

- Headings: Drag through the row of information you want to use as a heading that appears at the top of each page of the table and select this option.

- Leaders: Click on the cell or select the area you want filled with leaders (leaders will appear wherever there would ordinarily be empty space) and select this option. Then choose from the list of leader styles: periods, dashes, line, or none.

USING FORMULAS IN TABLES

You can use your Ami Pro table as a minispreadsheet, complete with formulas to total columns or perform other mathematical functions.

IDENTIFYING COLUMNS AND ROWS

As in a spreadsheet, an Ami Pro table can have column and row designators that are used for identifying cells. Follow these steps to display the column and row designators for our sample table:

1. Pull down the View menu and select Preferences.
2. Click on the check box next to Table Row/Column Headings and then click on OK.

Figure 13.9 shows our table with column and row designators. The rows are numbered, and the columns have letters. Cells are identified by their letter and number. For example, the first cell in the first row is cell A1.

USING QUICK ADD

Since the most common mathematical operation performed in a table is to sum columns or rows, Ami Pro provides the Quick Add option on the Table menu. It will sum the contents of the row or column you specify and place the results in the selected cell.

Now we will add a blank column to the sample table and use Quick Add to sum and insert a total.

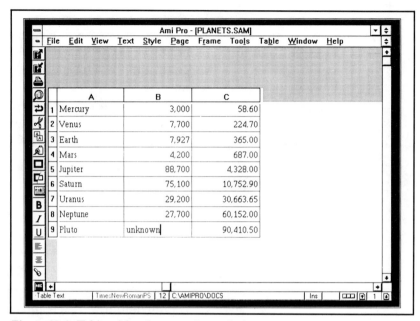

Figure 13.9: Table with column and row designators

1. Click on the third column, select Insert Column/Row from the Table menu, and then choose Columns in the Insert section of the dialog box.

2. Click on cell C1, pull down the Table menu, and select Quick Add.

You see a tiny menu with two options: Row or Column. Ami Pro will automatically generate the formula for summing the cells in a column or row.

3. Click on Row.

Ami Pro calculates the sum of the columns to the left (3,000) and places it in cell C1.

> If the fourth column goes off the screen, choose the Modify Table Layout option from the Table menu and make the columns narrower.

ENTERING FORMULAS

By using formulas, you can add, subtract, multiply, and divide cells. You enter a formula into a table cell by selecting Edit Formulas from the

Table menu and typing the formula in the Edit Formula dialog box. Ami Pro uses the same basic structure for formulas as spreadsheet programs do.

As an example, we will enter a formula to divide the diameter of Venus by its period of rotation.

1. Click on the cell C2, pull down the Table menu, and select Edit Formulas. You will see the dialog box shown in Figure 13.10.

2. In the Formula text box, type **B2/D2**, and then click on OK.

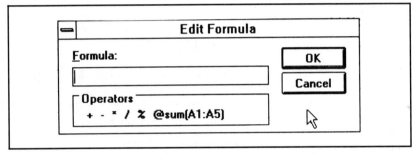

Figure 13.10: Edit Formula dialog box

Cell C2 now contains 34.27, which is the result of dividing the value in cell B2 by the value in cell D2. Suppose that you want to place the same value in cell C5. Let's try copying it.

3. Click on cell C2, pull down the Edit menu, and select Copy.

4. Click on cell C5 and select Paste from the Edit menu.

Instead of copying 34.27, Ami Pro has placed 20.49 in cell C5. You can see what happened by examining the formula copied into the cell.

5. With cell C5 still selected, pull down the Table menu and select Edit Formula.

The Formula box contains B5/D5. When you copied the formula B2/D2 from cell C2 to cell C5, Ami Pro assumed that you wanted the value for that row's cells. The cell references are *relative*. You can make the references *absolute,* so that they do not change, by preceding the designators with a dollar sign.

6. Select cell C5 if it isn't already selected, and then press Del to clear the formula.

7. Double-click on cell C2, and the Edit Formula dialog box will open automatically because this cell contains a formula.

8. Edit the entry to read $B$2/$D$2 and click on OK.

9. Select Copy from the Edit menu.

10. Click on cell C5 and select Paste from the Edit menu.

The value should be the same as the one in cell C2. Now let's see what happens when you enter a value that Ami Pro cannot interpret.

> Each time you move the cursor out of a cell, the table formulas are recalculated.

11. Select cell B2, enter **$200**, and press Tab.

The spreadsheet is recalculated, and REF appears in cells C2 and C5. This indicates that Ami Pro couldn't make sense of the value you just typed. Notice that the new value remains at the left end of the cell it occupies, which means that Ami Pro considers this a text entry in a cell formatted for a number. The problem is caused by the dollar sign you entered.

> When a cell is formatted as currency, Ami Pro adds the dollar sign automatically.

12. Drag through the entry, press Del, reenter **7700**, and press Tab.

Now let's make the formula more complex by adding another operation and using parentheses to order it.

13. Click on cell C9 and select Edit Formula from the Table menu.

14. In the Edit Formula dialog box, edit the formula to read **(C2-SUM(D1:D9))**.

The value in cell C9 will be 197,608.08, the result of the sum of cells D1 through D9 subtracted from the value in cell C2.

SORTING TO ORGANIZE INFORMATION

Chapter 10 describes how to create a data file in Ami Pro.

Sorting alphabetically or numerically is an efficient way to organize data. By using the Sort option on the Tools menu, you can sort regular text in documents, as well as entries in data files and tables.

Follow these steps to see how Ami Pro's sorting function works:

1. Clear the screen by closing any currently open files.

2. Open a new window.

3. Type the following information, pressing Tab between the columns:

Gabby	10	48858
William	32	33030
Prestor	18	27421
Akkim	21	95128

4. Drag through all the text in the list.

5. Pull down the Tools menu and select Sort. You will see the dialog box shown in Figure 13.11.

6. Click on OK to sort the list in alphanumeric, ascending order.

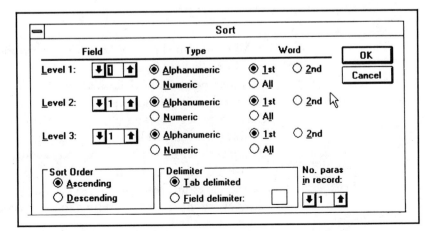

Figure 13.11: Sort dialog box

CHOOSING THE SORT ORDER

You can choose to sort the list alphanumerically or numerically. A numeric sort will arrange the entries according to their numeric values. An alphanumeric sort will put the entries in order by their ASCII values.

You also have a choice of an ascending or descending sort. An ascending sort organizes values from the least to the greatest. Descending sorts organize values from the greatest to the least.

ASCII stands for American Standard Codes International Institute. It assigns a numeric value to every chartacter that appears on the screen. For example, the ASCII value for the numeral 1 is 49; for capital A, it is 65; and for lowercase a, it is 97.

SORTING BY FIELDS AND PARAGRAPHS

A *field* is a value between tabs or between a tab and a carriage return (paragraph break). In our sample list, Gabby, 10, and 48858 are fields. Together they make up a *record,* which is delimited by a paragraph return.

In the Sort dialog box, the numbers in the text boxes under Field represent the field number. Levels 1, 2, and 3 represent the precedence of that field. For example, if you sorted our list on the second field by changing the number 1 for Level 1 under Field to 2, it would be reordered like this:

Gabby	10	48858
Prestor	18	27421
Akkim	21	95128
William	32	33030

You can also choose to base the sort on the second word or all the words in the field instead of the first.

A field need not be delimited by a tab. You can specify any character as a delimiter. Click on the Field Delimiter button at the bottom of the Sort dialog box and type a new delimiter in the text box.

You can even sort lists composed of paragraphs of text. In the Sort dialog box, enter a value in the text box under No. Paras in Record, or use the up and down arrows to adjust the existing value. For example, setting No. Paras in Record to 3 will cause Ami Pro to consider every third carriage return to be a record delimiter.

REDLINING TO IDENTIFY CHANGES IN TEXT

Identifying where changes have been made to a document is useful when you are working on a project with others. For example, lawyers use special marks to indicate new text entered into contracts and agreements so that the other signatories will know where changes were made. Editors mark revisions on drafts for authors to review.

With Ami Pro's revision-marking feature, you can easily mark insertions and deletions and then review each one. The default marking for new text is blue and italic, and deleted text is red with a line through it. When you are reviewing the changes, you can choose to selectively accept and cancel each one.

When a document with revision marks is printed, newly inserted text is printed in the revision-marking style, with a bar in the left margin.

MARKING CHANGES

You turn on revision marking by clicking on the typing mode indicator in the status bar. As an example, we will open SWEET.SAM, turn on revision marking, and make a change:

If you saved the SWEET.SMM macro (created in Chapter 11), you can quickly load SWEET.SAM by pressing Ctrl-Shift-Z.

1. Load SWEET.SAM.

2. Click on the typing mode indicator in the status bar (which shows Ins because you are in Insert mode) until it changes to Rev.

3. Click in the text before *1960s* in the first line of the second paragraph and type **late**.

The new text should be blue italics. While you are in Revision Marking mode, all your additions will be shown like this, and the deleted characters will be red with a line through them. You can turn off revision marking by clicking on the typing mode indicator until you are in Insert or Typeover mode.

REVIEWING REVISION MARKS

To review the revisions, select Revision Marking from the Tools menu. This displays the Revision Marking dialog box, which allows you to review the changes individually or accept or cancel all of them. Follow these steps to review the marks in SWEET.SAM:

1. Pull down the Tools menu and select Revision Marking. You will see the dialog box shown in Figure 13.12.

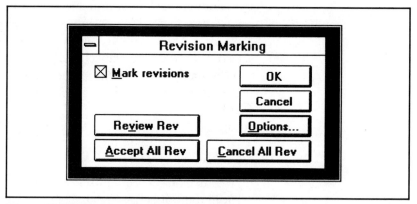

Figure 13.12: Revision Marking dialog box

The Mark Revisions box in the Revision Marking dialog box is checked when you change from Insert or Typeover mode to Revision Marking mode. You can click on Accept All Rev to remove the text marked as deletions and make the inserted text look like normal paragraph text. Choose Cancel All Rev to eliminate the insertions and keep the deleted text. Click on Review Rev to decide on a case-by-case basis. The Options button displays a dialog box with choices for the way text is marked, as explained in the next section.

2. Click on Review Rev. Ami Pro will highlight the first change and display the dialog box shown in Figure 13.13.

3. Click on Cancel This Insertion.

The highlighted text will disappear. Since this is the only revision mark in the document, the review process ends. If there were more

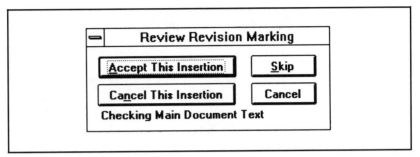

Figure 13.13: Review Revision Marking dialog box

revision marks, Ami Pro would highlight the next change and wait for your selection in the Review Revision Marking dialog box.

CHANGING THE DISPLAY OF REVISION MARKS

You can place the revision marks in the margin of the document and choose different styles and colors for insertion and deletion marks through the Revision Marking Options dialog box, shown in Figure 13.14. To display this dialog box, choose Revision Marking from the Tools menu, and then click on the Options button in the Revision Marking dialog box.

In the Mark Insertions As section of the dialog box, you can set the insertions to appear as plain (No Attribute) or boldfaced text, or with

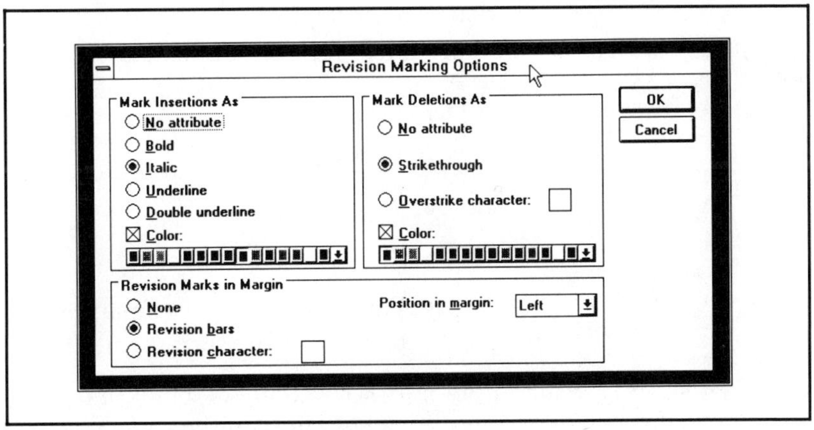

Figure 13.14: Revision Marking Options dialog box

a single or double underline. In the Mark Deletions As section, you can change deletions to plain text or type in a different character to strike through the text. You also can change the color of both insertions and deletions.

To show revision marks in the margin, make sure Revision Bars is selected in the Revision Marks in Margin section at the bottom of the dialog box, as shown in Figure 13.14. You can use the Position in Margin list box to put the revision bars in the left, right, or both margins.

CREATING EQUATIONS

With many word processing programs, entering an equation in a document is a frustrating experience with unsatisfactory results. But Ami Pro has special tools that make it easy to format and type even complex equations.

USING THE EQUATION TOOLS

To access the equation tools, pull down the Tools menu and select Equations. Now there is an Equation menu on the menu bar, and two rows of icons appear under the menu bar, as shown in Figure 13.15. One portion of the equation bar contains templates for formatting equations, and the other part has symbols and characters commonly used in equations. Using these tools, you create an equation as a graphic.

From left to right, the templates format the equation as follows:

To leave equation mode, click outside the equation frame. Double-click inside the equation frame to return to equation mode.

- Fraction

- Radical

- Superscript

- Subscript

- Parentheses (creates a pair of parentheses and places the text cursor between them)

- Brackets (creates a pair of brackets and places the text cursor between them)

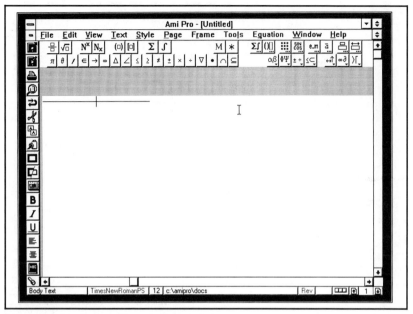

Figure 13.15: Screen for creating equations

- Sum operator
- Integral operator

The next two icons are toggles. Click on the capital M to change from math mode to text mode when you want to insert some ordinary text. The asterisk icon turns on and off the display of invisible elements, such as the small frame that appears between inserted parentheses, which helps you format your equations.

The next eight icons are for choosing the components of your equation:

- Operator: Displays a dialog box that contains a choice of operators and allows you to control their position and size, as shown in Figure 13.16.

- Brackets: Displays a dialog box with different bracket styles, as shown in Figure 13.17.

- Create Matrix: Displays a dialog box you can use to format a matrix, as shown in Figure 13.18.

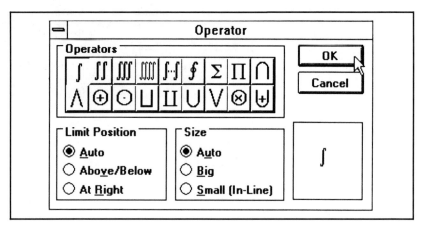

Figure 13.16: Operator dialog box

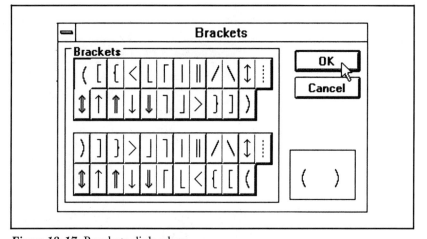

Figure 13.17: Brackets dialog box

- Function: Displays a dialog box with a functions list box, as shown in Figure 13.19. You can also create your own function.

- Space: Displays a dialog box that contains a choice of types of spaces, as shown in Figure 13.20.

- Revise Character: Displays a dialog box for changing the appearance of the selected equation character, as shown in Figure 13.21.

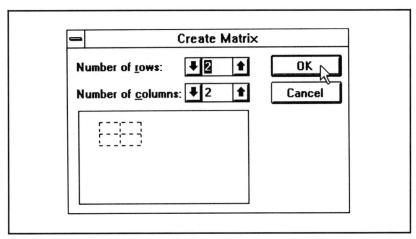

Figure 13.18: Create Matrix dialog box

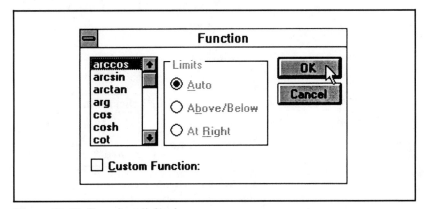

Figure 13.19: Function dialog box

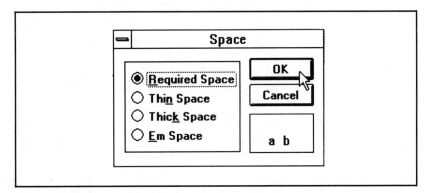

Figure 13.20: Space dialog box

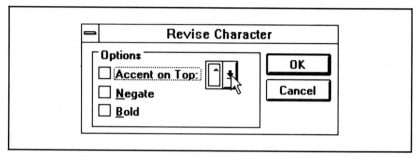

Figure 13.21: Revise dialog box

- Label: Displays a dialog box for selecting the placement of labels, as shown in Figure 13.22.

- Over/Under: Displays a dialog box for choosing a symbol to appear above or below the whole equation, as shown in Figure 13.23.

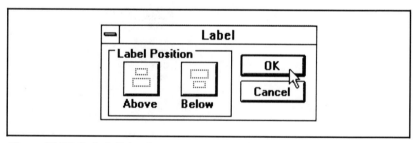

Figure 13.22: Label dialog box

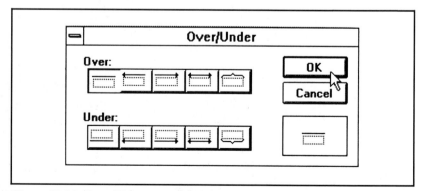

Figure 13.23: Over/Under dialog box

The second row of icons begins at the left with a series of characters frequently used for formulas: pi, theta, and so on. At the right end is a series of pull-down menus with more complete collections of symbols:

- Lowercase Greek characters

- Uppercase Greek characters

- Binary operators

- Binary relations

- Arrows

- Miscellaneous

- Delimiters

To enter a character, either click on one of the symbols on the left end of the second row in the equation bar, or pull down one of the menus on the right side and click on one of the symbols. The character will be entered in the current cursor location.

ENTERING EQUATIONS

Another way to enter equation mode is by using the frame icon to drag a frame, and while the frame is selected, clicking on Equations on the Tools menu.

Like other Ami Pro graphics, equations are created within frames. When you select Equation from the Tools menu, Ami Pro places an equation frame on the screen.

In the following steps, we will create two equations:

1. Pull down the Tools menu and select Equations. You will see the equation bar and menu.

2. Click on the first icon in the top row of icons, which is the fraction icon.

Ami Pro now displays the format for a fraction inside the frame. You see a short horizontal bar with a block above and below. The text cursor is blinking on the top block, ready for you to enter a value or a symbol.

3. Type **1**, click on the block at the bottom of the fraction, and type **2**.

You have entered a simple fraction, but you cannot see it very well. To get a better view, you need to adjust the size of the frame that contains the equation.

4. Click on the Modify Frame icon.

5. In the Modify Frame Layout dialog box, click on Size & Position in the Frame box.

6. Click on the arrows at the right end of the Size text boxes until the frame is 1 inch in width and height.

7. Click on Lines & Shadows, and then click on All in the Lines box.

Now you have a border that lets you know how much space you have. After you are finished creating the equation, you can remove the border. Now let's try something a little more complicated.

8. Click on the numerator to the right of the 1 and press Backspace to delete the 1.

9. To add a minus sign, press the hyphen key.

10. Click on the insert math/text icon (the red M) so it has a T for Text, and type **b**.

11. Click on the ± icon in the second row of icons (seventh from the right).

12. Click on the radical sign (second from left in the first row of icons).

13. Click on the insert math/text icon (which should have changed back to M when you added a math symbol) to change to text mode and type **b**.

You could also add another minus sign by dragging through the first minus sign, copying it to the Clipboard, and then pasting it into position.

14. Click on the superscript icon (third from the left in the top row of icons) and type **2**.

15. Select Symbol Keyboard from the Equation menu, and then press the hyphen key to insert another minus sign.

16. If the insert math/text icon is an M again, click on it, and then type **4ac**.

17. Click after the 2 in the denominator. Make sure the insert math/text icon is set to text and type **a**.

Your finished equation should look like the one shown in Figure 13.24. You could have created it using the options on the Equation menu, which perform the same functions as the icons on the equation bar. The Equation menu also gives you access to a unique dialog box, as described in the next section.

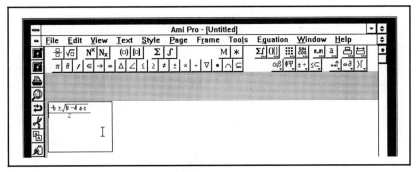

Figure 13.24: The completed equation

ENTERING EQUATIONS AS TEX COMMANDS

Another way to create equations is as TeX commands. TeX is a type-setting language, like PostScript, but designed specifically for mathematical formulas. You can use TeX commands instead of using the equation bar's icons and menus.

Select Insert from the Equation menu, and then choose TeX Command from the Insert submenu. This displays the dialog box shown in Figure 13.25. Select the command you want to insert in the equation and click on OK to place the function or symbol in the equation frame at the cursor position. You can save the file as a TeX format file and load TeX files for printing with Ami Pro, or for inserting elsewhere in the document or another document.

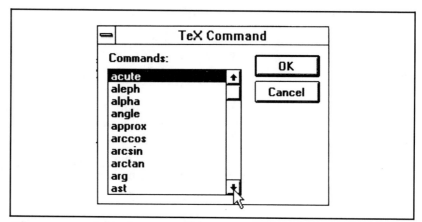

Figure 13.25: TeX Command dialog box

USING POWER FIELDS

Power fields are a special feature of Ami Pro. You can use them to gather information or perform calculations or other operations at specific points in the text. Power fields allow you to embed tiny programs right into the text.

Here are some examples of what power fields can do:

- Maintain a reference to an item. For example, the reference *See chart, page 22* can be controlled by a power field so that the page number will be updated if the text moves.

- Prompt you for information and place it at a specified location in the document.

- Display hypertext messages that tell you where to turn for additional help.

To insert a power field, pull down the Edit menu, select Power Fields, and then choose Insert. This displays a dialog box that contains a list of predefined fields, which include functions and commands, as well as a text box for creating your own fields.

INSERTING A PREDEFINED POWER FIELD

As an example, we will insert a power field that will always show the last date the current text was saved.

1. Save your equation document and open a new document.

2. Type **This text was last saved on.**

3. Place the cursor just ahead of the period. If you are not already in Insert mode, click on the typing mode indicator in the status bar until it shows Ins.

4. Select Power Fields from the Edit menu and then select Insert from the submenu. You will see the dialog box shown in Figure 13.26.

5. Scroll through the Fields list box until you see EditDate and click on it. In the Options list box (next to the Fields list box), you will see a list of date formats.

6. Click on the format that shows the day of the week, the month, date, and four-digit year.

7. Click on OK to insert the power field.

The text on the screen should now be similar to *This text was last saved on Thursday, May 18, 1992.*

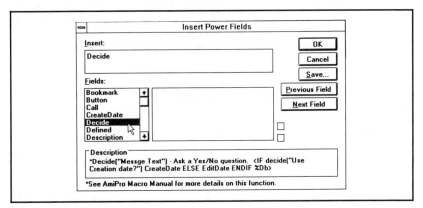

Figure 13.26: Insert Power Fields dialog box

CREATING A COMPLEX POWER FIELD

A power field has two parts: instructions and results. In our example above, the date was the result and the code that generated the date was the instruction. Instructions can contain bookmarks, variables, macros, merge fields, numbers, math operators (+ , − , *, /), text, and other power fields.

Let's create another, slightly more complex power field to illustrate some of these points.

1. Close any open documents and open a new document

2. Pull down the Edit menu, select Power Fields, and select Insert.

3. Scroll down the Fields list box and select Decide.

At the bottom of the dialog box, you see an explanation of the selected function and an example. Decide creates a dialog box that contains two buttons: Yes and No. If you select Yes, the first action will be carried out. If you select No, the command after ELSE will be carried out.

4. Click ahead of Decide in the text box under Insert, type **IF**, and press the spacebar.

5. Click after Decide in the text box at the top and type the following:

("Enter filesize here?") FileSize ENDIF

6. Click on OK.

Ami Pro will test the power field by displaying the dialog box shown in Figure 13.27.

7. Click on No.

8. Click on Save, and you will be prompted for a name and a description of your power field.

9. Type **TextSize** as the name and **Power field to show file size in K** as the description. Then click OK.

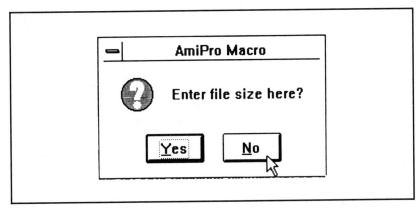

Figure 13.27: Dialog box for testing power field

Now TextSize will always appear as one of the defined power fields in the Fields list box.

10. Double-click on the close box of the Insert Power Fields dialog box.

11. To see your power field, pull down the View menu and select Show Power Fields. It should look like Figure 13.28.

12. To hide the power field, select Hide Power Fields from the View menu.

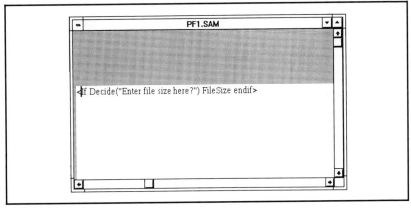

Figure 13.28: The power field revealed

In order for this power field to do its job, you must update it. The Update command is on the Power Fields submenu of the Edit menu.

13. Pull down the Edit menu, select Power Fields, and then choose Update.

14. When you see the dialog box asking whether to display the file size, click on Yes.

The file size in kilobytes should appear on your screen.

Power fields and the other advanced features described in this chapter make Ami Pro more than just a word processor. As you gain more experience with these features, you will be able to take full advantage of this powerful program.

APPENDIX A

Installing
Ami Pro

IT IS VERY EASY TO INSTALL AMI PRO. ALL YOU HAVE to do is insert the disks when prompted to do so and provide some information about your system. But before you begin installing Ami Pro, make sure that you have the right equipment to run it.

HARDWARE AND SOFTWARE REQUIREMENTS

The following are the minimum requirements for running Ami Pro:

- IBM AT compatible computer, with an 80286 or higher central processing unit (CPU)
- Windows-compatible EGA, VGA, or Hercules graphics card and monitor
- 1 megabyte (MB) of random access memory (RAM)
- 6.5MB to 10.5MB of hard-disk space
- DOS 3.0 or higher
- Windows 3.0 or higher
- A mouse

See Appendix B for more information about NewWave.

The optimum system is an IBM-compatible computer with an 80386 microprocessor and at least 2MB of RAM. DOS 5.0 or higher is recommended. If you have NewWave, Hewlett-Packard's Windows enhancement package, you can run Ami Pro under it.

STEP-BY-STEP INSTALLATION

To install Ami Pro to run under Windows, follow these steps:

1. Run Windows by typing **WIN** at the DOS command prompt.

2. Double-click on the Main program group.

3. Place the first Ami Pro installation disk in the floppy disk drive.

4. Double-click on the File Manager option in the Main program group.

5. When the File Manager is running, click on the icon that stands for the drive that contains the Ami Pro installation disk.

6. Double-click on the folder that appears in the Directory Tree window (this represents opening the disk).

You can easily list the file names in alphabetical order by pulling down the View menu and selecting By Name as the listing option.

You will see a list containing all the file names in the root directory of the disk. The files are probably listed alphabetically.

7. Find INSTALL.EXE in the list of the file names and double-click on it.

8. When you are asked for your name and the name of your company, type in this information.

Use the Tab key to move the text cursor from one text box to the next, or click the mouse on the box where you want to type. Ami Pro won't proceed unless you enter your name and company information.

If you have enough disk space, you should install Ami Pro with options. However, if you do install just the defaults, you can install the options later by using the Install Ami Pro Options Only selection.

9. When the Main menu appears, select to install Ami Pro with Options, Ami Pro with Defaults, or Ami Pro Options Only.

If you select Install Ami Pro with Options, you will be able to select from a list of options: Ami Pro (a rather important option, weighing in at just over 5MB), Drawing, Charting, Equation Editor, Thesaurus, Macro Documentation, Dialog Editor, and Sample Documents.

The list shows the amount of disk space necessary for each option. If you select Ami Pro with Defaults, you will install Ami Pro, Drawing, Charting, Thesaurus, and Macro Documentation.

10. If you selected to install Ami Pro with Options, you will see the Specifying Options and Directories window. Click on the options that you think you will need.

At the bottom of the window, you will see the total space needed to load all the options, along with the total amount of disk space available on the disk.

11. Click on OK when you are finished selecting options.

12. When you are asked whether you will be running Ami Pro under Windows or NewWave. Select the environment you will be using.

If you don't have enough disk space to accommodate all the options you selected, the installation program will pause to ask whether it should proceed. You can opt to continue and risk the possibility that the installation program will fail, return to the Main menu and make alternate selections to use less space for Ami Pro, or cancel the installation so that you can remove enough files and directories to install the program.

⊙ You won't be able to run two different Ami Pro programs from Windows; you will have to run one or the other. Therefore, you probably should overwrite the directories. To have two different versions of the program on disk is a waste of disk space.

If you already have a previous version of Ami Pro, the installation program will pause to ask whether to overwrite the directories you have. If you want to completely replace the existing directories, click on OK. If not, click on the text boxes and type in different directory names.

At this point, the transfer of files begins. Ami Pro's installation program does all the work for you, copying files into the appropriate places and prompting you for disk changes as it proceeds.

The last thing you will need to do is decide whether or not to install Adobe Type Manager (if you don't already have this software installed). Adobe Type Manager (ATM) keeps track of your typefaces and provides a few typefaces for downloading to laser printers. If you have at least 2MB of RAM, you should install ATM. If you

If you begin having trouble using your machine after installing a program under Windows, it may be because the program modified your AUTOEXEC.BAT and CONFIG.SYS files and saved your old files under different names. Try booting from a floppy disk without an AUTOEXEC-.BAT or a CONFIG.SYS file, and then replace the new versions with the old.

have less than 2MB (or less than 4MB and you hope to use software like Ventura Publisher for Windows), you may discover that the overhead of RAM occupied by ATM will prevent other programs from running. In that case, you'll probably want to wait until you can upgrade your computer before installing ATM.

APPENDIX B

Introduction to Windows and Word Processing

AMI PRO LOOKS THE WAY IT LOOKS AND WORKS THE way it works because it runs under Windows. If you have other Windows applications, you probably already know how to use Windows. If you are new to Windows, this appendix will provide the basic information you need to get started using Ami Pro.

ADVANTAGES OF WINDOWS

When you run Windows applications, the windows, menus, and dialog boxes work about the same in all of them. When you access Help, for example, you will note that Ami Pro Help is similar to Excel Help. Sensing that you are in familiar territory, you will not hesitate to try a new word processor or spreadsheet.

With Windows, a small amount of instruction will prepare even a computer novice to find his or her way around the program. Certain keypresses always have the same effect. For example, pressing Alt-F4 closes the current window in any Windows application.

Windows word processors offer something that few DOS word processors can: a WYSIWYG display. WYSIWYG means What You See Is What You Get. When you create a page of text on the screen and print it out, it will be a fairly accurate representation of what appears on the screen. Ami Pro makes use of this WYSIWYG capability to help you in page design, but also provides a draft mode so that you can concentrate on the text before worrying about layout.

Not only does Windows provide the interface and on-screen formatting, but it also takes over the task of printing. When you install a program under Windows, you don't have to spend time entering what kind of printer you have, as you do with DOS word processors.

WYSIWYG can be as much a curse as a blessing. Many people sit down to write, but wind up endlessly formatting and reformatting, trying to get the page to look right and forgetting about the content. To avoid this pitfall, use Ami Pro's draft mode to get the text on the page (and speedier response), and then switch to working or standard mode for formatting.

MANEUVERING YOUR MOUSE

In a Windows word processor there are two cursors: the mouse cursor, which is a pointer that usually resembles an arrow or an I-beam, and the text cursor, which marks the place in text where your typing will appear if you start using the keyboard. To position the text cursor, put the mouse cursor where you want the text cursor to appear and click the mouse button.

The mouse is an input device designed for indicating on a flat, horizontal surface the position of a pointer on a curved, vertical monitor screen. It provides an alternative to using the keyboard. Other input devices, such as the light pen, track balls, and graphics tablets, are available, but the mouse remains the most popular input device, primarily because the Windows interface itself was designed for the mouse.

Your mouse probably has two buttons (maybe three), the left mouse button—the one that naturally falls underneath your index finger when you hold the mouse in your right hand—is the button you will use most of the time. Occasionally, you will need to use the right mouse button. In most instructions (including those in this book), the left button might be referred to as just "the mouse button," while the right button is always called "the right button."

Windows recognizes three main mouse maneuvers:

Double-clicking in a text box (a box for text entry) highlights all the text in the text box. When you type, the highlighted text disappears and the new text takes its place. Double-clicking on a word in text in the Ami Pro window selects that word (clicking places the text cursor at that point and doesn't select anything).

- Clicking: To click the mouse, press the left mouse button and instantly release it. This action is used to pull down menus and select options in dialog boxes. When you are told to select a menu or dialog box item, that is just another way of saying that you should click on it.

- Double-clicking: To double-click, click the mouse button twice in rapid succession. This action is used for starting applications from icons. You can also select the default option on a menu by double-clicking on the menu name in the menu bar. In a dialog box that contains a list of file names in a list box, you can select one file from the list and accept the default options by double-clicking on the file name.

- Dragging: To drag with the mouse, place the mouse pointer on an object, press the mouse button, and hold the button down as you move the mouse. This action is used to relocate an icon, to resize a frame, or to draw in graphics mode. Dragging is also used to select text for deletion or to change its attribute, such as its font or color. When you select text by dragging over it, the normally black-on-white text will reverse, becoming white-on-black. When you drag through text, be careful with the keyboard, because pressing almost any key will cause the highlighted text to disappear.

MANAGING YOUR FILES WITH WINDOWS

⊙ Try to avoid deleting or relocating a Windows temporary file when you are shelled out to DOS.

You can use the Windows File Manager to move, copy, and delete files. If you prefer to leave Windows and use another application to manage your files, double-click on the DOS icon in the Main program group to return briefly (*shell out*) to DOS. From there, you can use the familiar DOS commands or other programs and shells you may have for file management. When you are finished, simply type EXIT at the DOS prompt to return to Windows.

Be sure to save your work before temporarily leaving Windows, because you might accidentally erase an important Windows file that will prevent your reentry to Windows. In that case, reset or reboot the computer and run Windows again. Unless you deleted a system file, you should have no trouble getting started again.

ACCESSING THE FILE MANAGER

◣ The information here applies to Windows 3.0. If you have a later version of Windows, refer to your Windows manual for details on the file-management system.

To move, copy, or delete files under Windows, you must first access the File Manager:

1. Click on the Window menu in the menu bar.

2. In the lower portion of the Window menu, click on Main to display the Main program group.

In the Main program group, you will see an icon that looks like a file cabinet. Under it will be the words *File Manager*.

3. Double-click on the File Manager icon to access the File Manager.

You will see a window with the names of the available drives along the top: A, B, C, and so on, as shown in Figure B.1.

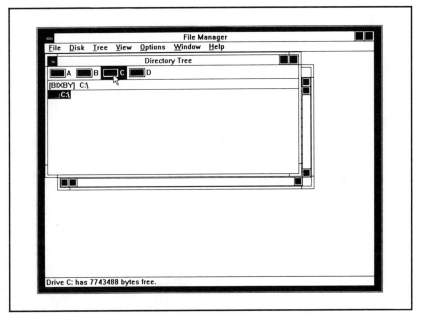

Figure B.1: Windows File Manager drives window

4. To see the files on a particular disk drive, click on that drive.

A window will open for that disk, and you will see a folder with the disk's designation beside it.

5. Double-click on the folder to see the contents of the disk, as shown in the example in Figure B.2. You could also click on the Tree menu item and select Expand All.

6. Double-click on the directory you want to examine. The file names will be displayed, as shown in Figure B.3.

With the file names displayed, you can manipulate the files, as explained in the next section.

MANIPULATING FILES

Using the File Manager, you can perform many of the same operations that you can with DOS: delete a file, copy a file, and find out

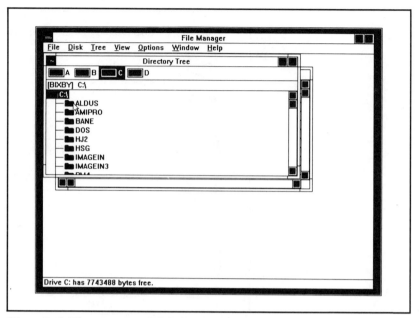

Figure B.2: The contents of disk C

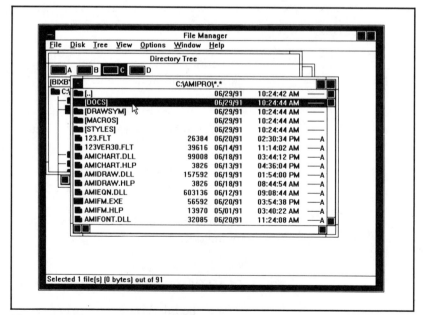

Figure B.3: The files in the AMIPRO directory

information about a file. The File Manager also provides some commands not available in DOS:

- Associate: Allows you to start up an application and load a file by clicking on the file.

- Search: Allows you to locate files on the disk or in the current directory.

- Move: Copies a file to another location, and as soon as the copy is successfully completed, it deletes the original file so there is only one copy in existence.

To perform an action, click on the name of the file you want to affect to highlight it. Then click on the File menu at the top of the screen and click on the option you want to use. You will see a dialog box requesting whatever information Windows needs to complete the action. Figure B.4 shows the dialog box that appears when you choose Copy from the File menu.

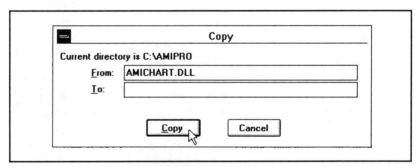

Figure B.4: Windows File Manager Copy dialog box

USING WINDOWS CONTROLS

There are several standard items in a Windows window: Minimize and Maximize boxes, scroll bars, a title/move bar, a Control menu, and a menu bar.

MINIMIZE AND MAXIMIZE BOXES

In the upper-right corner of the window are two small boxes. One has a downward-pointing arrow and the other has either arrows

A minimized window is not a dead window. Many programs can continue to operate in minimized state. For example, if you start up the clock (one of the standard Windows accessories) and minimize it, it will continue to display the correct time.

pointing up and down or an upward-pointing arrow. Clicking on the downward-pointing arrow will cause the window to be minimized, or made into an icon. Clicking on the upward- and downward-pointing arrows will cause the window to be in a state called *restored*, which means that it isn't minimized or maximized.

When a window is in its restored state, the double arrow will be replaced with an upward-pointing arrow. Click on this arrow to take the window from its restored state to a maximized state, in which the window fills the whole screen top to bottom and left to right.

In its restored or minimized state, a window can be moved. However, in its maximized state, the window is fixed in position. A window can also be sized in its restored state by placing the mouse pointer on the outside border of the window (the mouse pointer will become a double arrow) and dragging. A minimized or maximized window cannot be sized.

SCROLL BARS

A window may present only part of a document. To move around in the document, you can use the scroll bars that appear at the right and bottom edges of most windows. Generally, there will be scroll bars only when the document size exceeds the window size, but this is not true in Ami Pro; if there is a scroll bar, that doesn't necessarily mean that there is more text than can be seen.

Clicking on the space between the elevator and the arrows is approximately the same as pressing the Page Up or Page Down key in most applications.

The scroll bar consists of an elevator (also known as a thumb or slide box) situated within a long, narrow slidebar that has an arrow at either end. You can click on the arrows to move short distances, click on the slidebar between the elevator and the arrow to move longer distances (generally the width or height of the window), or you can drag the elevator to move proportionally through a document (dragging the elevator halfway down the slidebar will take you to a position halfway through the document, for example).

Some list boxes in dialog boxes also have scroll bars. Generally, the scroll bar itself will consist only of the up and down arrows. Newer list boxes may contain only the current selection or the default and have a single downward-pointing arrow at their right end. Clicking on the downward-pointing arrow will display the list of options. If the list is very long, it will have a conventional scroll bar.

TITLE/MOVE BAR

The top bar of a window is called its title or move bar. This bar serves three purposes:

You can use the Control Panel to choose from a wide palette of colors for your screen. That will make it easier to identify the active window and the parts of windows.

- As the title bar, it contains the name of the application that the window belongs to (such as Ami Pro), followed by the name of the currently open document (its file name, if it has been saved to disk previously; otherwise, [Untitled]).

- As the move bar of a window in the restored state (a window that is not maximized or minimized), it can be used to move the window to a new location. You can even use the move bar to move a window so that it is almost completely off the screen.

- When several windows are open, the title/move bar indicates which is the currently active window. Unless you have made radical changes in the setup, the title/move bar will be highlighted when that window is the currently selected window.

It's important to know where the action will occur before you issue a command. That is why there is only one selected window at a time, even though other windows may be active in the background (capturing text from a telecommunications device or recalculating a spreadsheet, for example).

Another way to tell which window is currently selected is to see which window appears to be in front of all the rest. To bring another window to the front and make it the currently selected window, you can click on that window, pull down the Control menu (described in the next section) and click on Switch To, or press Ctrl-Esc to see the Task List of available windows. You can also display the Task List by double-clicking on a part of the screen away from any window.

CONTROL MENU

The Control menu is a part of every window. It is a small box with a line through it, which appears in the upper-left corner of a window. It contains commands for controlling the window.

To access the Control menu, you can either click on it with the mouse or press Alt-spacebar. There may be additional items on the Control menu, but the seven standard items include the following:

- Restore: Returns the window to its previous condition, (maximized, minimized, or restored state) regardless of its current condition.

- Move: Allows you to reposition the window with the cursor keys. Press ⏎ when the window is where you want it.

- Size: Allows you to adjust the size of the window. Press the cursor key that corresponds to the side of the window you want to adjust (the ↑ key to adjust the top, for example). Alternatively, you can press the keys that correspond to the corner of the window you want to adjust (such as ↑ and then ← to adjust the top-left corner of the window). Then use the cursor keys to move the selected part of the window in the direction of the arrow. Press Esc to stop adjusting the window.

- Minimize: Turns the window into a small icon.

- Maximize: Makes the window fill the screen.

- Close: Closes the current window. If there is only one window open, this will also shut down the application. You can also close a window by pressing Alt-F4.

- Switch To: Opens the Task List, allowing you to select another window as the currently selected active window.

MENU BAR

All windows contain a menu bar, although some may contain only one menu name or no menus at all. The menu bar is directly beneath the title/move bar.

In Ami Pro, the menu names you will see in the menu bar are File, Edit, View, Text, Style, Page, Frame, Tools, Window, and Help. When you are using special Ami Pro functions, there will be additional names on the menu bar.

When I found that one of my applications did not appear on the Switch To list when its window was open, I complained to the manufacturer of that program. I urge you to do the same when you run across programs that are supposed to be Windows-compatible but are in some way nonstandard. Let the developers know that you want them to maintain the standards that make Windows applications easier to use.

☞ If you find yourself typing and nothing is appearing in the document, check to see whether one of the menus in the menu bar is highlighted. You may have accidentally pressed the Alt key. After you press Alt, if you press a key other than one that is underlined in the menu bar, nothing will happen.

You can access the menus by clicking on their names with the mouse or by pressing the Alt key in combination with the underlined letter. For example, when a window has a File menu, the F is underlined, indicating that pressing Alt-F will pull down that menu. When a menu is visible, you can move to another menu by pressing the → or ← key.

To select an item from a menu, either click on the option or use the ↑ or ↓ key to move the highlighting up or down in the menu. When the option you want is highlighted, press ◀┘ to select it. If you want to close the menu without making a selection, press the Esc key.

In a menu, you may see additional symbols alongside the option names, at the right edge of the menu:

- A key-combination notation, with the caret (^) representing the Ctrl key, indicates the keyboard shortcut for selecting the option without going through a menu. For example, ^S appears to the right of Save on the Ami Pro File menu, indicating that pressing Ctrl-S will automatically select this option from the keyboard.

- An ellipse (...) indicates that the menu option displays a dialog box.

- A tiny triangle (like an arrowhead) indicates that the menu item displays a submenu of choices.

☞ With a dialog box open, press the Tab key to move the highlighting from one item to another in the dialog box. When an item has several options, use the spacebar to move from one option to another. Use the ↑ and ↓ keys to access items in a list box.

An option that turns a condition on or off or selects a condition (like Bold or Italic in the Text menu) will have a check mark to its left in the menu when it is selected. Selecting this option again will turn off the condition and remove the check mark.

STARTING AND CLOSING APPLICATIONS

Generally, you will be in Windows for the purpose of running Windows applications. Some applications (Ami Pro included) create their own program group and program item when they are installed.

Ami Pro creates a program group called Lotus Apps. To access this program group, you can either click on its icon on the Windows

☑ Instead of having program groups related to manufacturers, you can create program groups with names like Word Processors and Drawing Programs and move all the applicable applications to them. If you don't have many programs, you might even put them all in a single program group, which would eliminate the step of opening the program group before you run an application.

desktop or pull down the Window menu from the menu bar of the Program Manager window and select Lotus Apps from the list of windows. If it is not listed in the Window menu, select More Windows, which should be the last item in the menu. This will display a dialog box containing a list box, which you can scroll through to find Lotus Apps.

Once the program group is open, it should contain all the Lotus applications designed to run under Windows. To start Ami Pro, double-click on its icon in the Lotus Apps program group.

When you are finished working with Ami Pro, you can leave the application by pressing Alt-F4, by pulling down the Control menu and selecting Close, or by pulling down the File menu and selecting Exit.

WHY NEWWAVE?

NewWave is an interesting product that was introduced by Hewlett-Packard, the international computer and scientific instrument manufacturer, to make up for the many shortcomings of Windows 286 and Windows 386. Putting NewWave on top of Windows 2.x made it more like Windows 3.0.

NewWave continues to offer greater file-handing power and interactivity among Windows applications than Windows alone supplies. However, it is probably not worth its high price unless you are engaged in very complex interactions among programs or a lot of your Windows activity involves macros. If you have several spreadsheet worksheets, databases, and word processor documents sharing data and if a significant proportion of your work is performed in interaction with macros, NewWave is for you.

Two of the most important differences between Windows and NewWave is that NewWave macros are editable and that connections among applications (called links) are more intelligent.

Being able to edit a macro means that you can go into the macro file and delete errors or make additions without going through the whole recording process again. Also, Windows macros are very dependent on everything on the Windows screen being in the same place each time the macro is run. If you move an important item or replace it with another item in the same location, the macro will not execute properly. A NewWave macro will find the item regardless of where it's moved.

A Windows link can be broken simply by changing the name of the file that is linked because Windows won't be able to locate the file. NewWave won't be fooled by a simple name change. You must specifically cut the link to unlink documents.

Ami Pro is completely NewWave-friendly, so you will be able to use all the NewWave advantages with it.

APPENDIX C

Standard Icons
for the
Icon Palette

See Chapter 11 of this book for details on customizing the Ami Pro icon palette.

THIS APPENDIX LISTS THE STANDARD ICONS AND functions Ami Pro provides for the icon palette. To replace an icon on the current icon palette with another standard icon, select SmartIcons from the Tools menu, click on the Customize button in the Smart-Icons dialog box, and make the change in the Customize SmartIcons dialog box.

Icon	*Function*
	Add a frame
	Add a frame using previous settings
	Import a picture
	Bring frame to front
	Send frame to back
	Scale a picture
	Toggle group/ungroup frames
	Modify frame layout
	Drawing
	Charting
	Equations
	Toggle draft/layout view
	Toggle full page/previous layout view

Icon	Function
	Toggle outline/layout view
N	Normal text
B	Bold text
I	Italic text
U	Underline text
U	Word underline text
U	Double underline text
S$	Superscript text
S$	Subscript text
aÁ	Capitalize text
Abc	Capitalize first letter of each word
	Show/hide pictures
	Show/hide ruler
	Show/hide marks
	View preferences
	Customize SmartIcons
	Floating SmartIcons
	Thesaurus
	Document compare
	Print document

Icon	*Function*
	Printer setup
	Go to
	Sort
	Find and replace
	Generate table of contents or Index
	Spell check
	Revision marking
	Insert glossary record
	Bookmarks
	Insert power fields
	Go to next power field
	Go to previous power field
	Show/hide power fields
	Update selected power fields
	Update all power fields
	Insert date
	Insert footnotes
	Insert note
	Insert index mark

Icon	*Function*
	No hyphenation
	Create a table
	Connect selected cells in a table
	Delete selected columns in a table
	Delete selected rows in a table
	Insert row in a table
	Insert column in a table
	Edit formula in a table cell
	Size columns and rows in a table
	Insert column or row
	Delete column or row
	Modify lines and shades in a table
	Modify table layout
	Create a new file
	Open a file
	Save a file
	Close a file
	File management
	Merge
	Send mail

Icon	*Function*
	Exit Ami Pro
	Cut selected text/items to Clipboard
	Copy selected text/items to Clipboard
	Paste Clipboard contents
	Delete
	Undo
	Modify page layout
	Insert a floating header/footer
	Insert a page break
	Insert a page number
	Modify a paragraph style
	Define a paragraph style
	Left align selected text
	Right align selected text
	Center selected text
	Justify selected text
	Tile all open documents
	Cascade all open documents
	Show/hide column guides

Icon	*Function*
	Show/hide margins in color
	Show/hide vertical ruler
	Show/hide notes
	Show/hide tabs and returns
	Toggle macro record start/stop
	Macro play
	Play back a quick macro
	Toggle quick macro record start/stop

INDEX

SYBEX

FREE BROCHURE!

Complete this form today, and we'll send you a full-color brochure of Sybex bestsellers.

Please supply the name of the Sybex book purchased.

_____

How would you rate it?

_____ Excellent   _____ Very Good   _____ Average   _____ Poor

Why did you select this particular book?

_____ Recommended to me by a friend

_____ Recommended to me by store personnel

_____ Saw an advertisement in _____

_____ Author's reputation

_____ Saw in Sybex catalog

_____ Required textbook

_____ Sybex reputation

_____ Read book review in _____

_____ In-store display

_____ Other _____

Where did you buy it?

_____ Bookstore

_____ Computer Store or Software Store

_____ Catalog (name: _____)

_____ Direct from Sybex

_____ Other: _____

Did you buy this book with your personal funds?

_____ Yes   _____ No

About how many computer books do you buy each year?

_____ 1-3   _____ 3-5   _____ 5-7   _____ 7-9   _____ 10+

About how many Sybex books do you own?

_____ 1-3   _____ 3-5   _____ 5-7   _____ 7-9   _____ 10+

Please indicate your level of experience with the software covered in this book:

_____ Beginner   _____ Intermediate   _____ Advanced

Which types of software packages do you use regularly?

_____ Accounting   _____ Databases   _____ Networks

_____ Amiga   _____ Desktop Publishing   _____ Operating Systems

_____ Apple/Mac   _____ File Utilities   _____ Spreadsheets

_____ CAD   _____ Money Management   _____ Word Processing

_____ Communications   _____ Languages   _____ Other _____
                                                                    (please specify)

Which of the following best describes your job title?

_____ Administrative/Secretarial   _____ President/CEO

_____ Director   _____ Manager/Supervisor

_____ Engineer/Technician   _____ Other _____
                                              (please specify)

Comments on the weaknesses/strengths of this book: _____

_____

_____

_____

_____

Name _____

Street _____

City/State/Zip _____

Phone _____

PLEASE FOLD, SEAL, AND MAIL TO SYBEX

SYBEX, INC.
Department M
2021 CHALLENGER DR.
ALAMEDA, CALIFORNIA USA
94501

SYBEX

SEAL